REJUVENATING PANCHAYATI RAJ

IDEOLOGY INDIAN STATE AND LESSONS FROM PERIPHERY

REJUVENATING PANCHAYATI RAJ

IDEOLOGY INDIAN STATE AND LESSONS FROM PERIPHERY

BHUPEN SARMAH

Omeo Kumar Das Institute of
Social Change and Development
Guwahati-781006
And
AKANSHA PUBLISHING HOUSE
NEW DELHI-110002

AKANSHA PUBLISHING HOUSE
4649-B/21, Ansari Road
Darya Ganj, New Delhi - 110 002
Email: ektabooks@yahoo.com
Ph.: 23263193/9811582579
Fax : 011-23263193

REJUVENATING PANCHAYATI RAJ :
IDEOLOGY INDIAN STATE AND LESSONS FROM PERIPHERY

First Published 2006
ISBN 81-8370-080-2

[The responsibility for the facts stated, conclusions reached etc. is entirely that of the Authors. The publisher is not responsible for them, whatsoever.]

PRINTED IN INDIA
Published by M.P Misra for Akansha Publishing House, New Delhi and Printed at Tarun Offset Press, Delhi

CONTENTS

ACKNOWLEDGMENTS

In the course of completing this study I have accumulated an enormous amount of debt, and I must take this opportunity to express my gratitude to all who have contributed to this study. I must, however, clarify that I am alone responsible for all its inadequacies, opinions and arguments.

I am grateful to the Centre for Northeast India, South and Southeast Asia Studies (CENISEAS), established as a part of the Omeo Kumar Das Institute of Social Change and Development, Guwahati in 2003 with a grant from the Ford Foundation. The present study is one of the researches financially supported by the CENISEAS. Therefore, I am also indebted to the Ford Foundation for its financial support routed through the CENISEAS.

During the course of this study I have discussed several issues with my colleagues Anuradha Dutta, Partha Ghosh, Abu Nasar Saied Ahmed, Indranee Dutta, Kalyan Das, Saswati Choudhury and Joydeep Baruah. They have not only helped me by providing many critical inputs but also constantly inspired me.

My Research Associate, Shabeena Yasmin Saikia has helped me in collection of a large amount of the required information. During my field study, a number of people have also helped me in various ways, and I must specifically mention the help I have received from Tasaduk Ariful Hussain, Executive Director, North East Social Trust, and Biren Choudhury, Ex-MLA, Goalpara. I am grateful to all who have extended support and cooperated with me during my interaction with the panchayat functionaries in different parts of Assam.

Rustam Ali has helped me in the typing works and Triveni Goswami has done the difficult work of proof reading. They deserve special thanks. Also, I must thank the library staff, Gajendra Ballav Dev choudhury, Lohit Talukdar and Ramen Sharma, and all other members of the OKDISCD family for their constant support and cooperation.

Finally, I must express my gratitude to my wife Meghali and my little daughter Meghna, without their constant support and inspiration this study would not have been possible.

1

INTRODUCTION

With the neo-liberal democratic perspective, the present development discourse in India is largely preoccupied with the notion of 'good governance'. It is considered to be one of the most crucial variables, or perceived as the prerequisite of a sustainable development trajectory. 'Good governance' has to be concretized through the process of institutionalizing democratic decentralization in decision-making involving wider participation, which warrants social justice besides equity in distribution of resources. At the operational plane, therefore, 'good governance' is seen as a mechanism for empowerment of the hitherto disadvantaged sections ensuring efficiency of and accountability and transparency in the development process. Role of the State has to be restricted only to the extent of institutionalization of the mechanism of decentralization as an aid to a free market economy. The development process to be followed is seen in terms of a State-Civil Society synergy.

In this neo liberal paradigm, emphasis has been given on panchayats essentially to provide a democratic veneer to a market driven development process. Panchayats can play a decisive role in driving 'good governance' to the grassroots. Panchayats can be instrumental in institutionalizing the process of democratic decentralization by ensuring visible political participation and other crucial ingredients of 'good governance' such as transparency and accountability at the operational plane. Considering the crucial issue, the role that has been assigned to the State in the present context, this can be considered as a paradigm shift.

Within the liberal democratic framework, interpretations of State and the political processes in post-colonial India have focused primarily on the institutions. State is seen in terms of organizational arrangement with a set of definite objectives that shape the political processes. Some of the early narratives highlighted success of the State in strengthening democratic ideology and institutions in a pluralist society, and ushering in economic development with distributive justice, which together provided a momentum to the process of transformation of a traditional apolitical society. The crucial role of the postcolonial State in the process of transforming India has been the core of the remarkably rich liberal modernist theoretical formulations of Kothari and many other contemporary scholars who subscribed to a similar perspective (see for instance, Kothari, 1970; 1988; Morris-Jones, 1971 etc.) The relatively recent theoretical formulations on autonomy of State have also focused on the functional domain of the postcolonial political institution, which is independent of class interests but in the interests of all groups (for instance, Kohli, 1987).

However, the present concern for decentralization in India has been significantly influenced by the paradigm shift. Undoubtedly, absence of democratic decentralization implies a bureaucratically determined mode of allocation and use of limited plan resources. Therefore, democratic decentralization, in its true meaning and content, provides an opportunity even to the poorer section of the rural mass including the hitherto disadvantaged sections to assert themselves politically through representation in the decision-making, and hence, in getting their share of the resources. It can therefore, significantly help the poor and the disadvantaged sections in realization of their subjectivity to sustain the process of socio-economic development. However, in the neo-liberal paradigm eulogized by the World Bank, decentralization is seen essentially as a mechanism to promote an environment conducive to free market economy. Though it endorses the process of devolution of powers and resources to the lower rung of administration, the institutions of local government are expected to work together with the nongovernmental organizations (NGOs) to create a new organizational form to improve service delivery, adding the commercial principles even to the basic amenities (The World Bank, 2002). Therefore, instead of greater accountability of the State, decentralization in the neo-liberal perspective implies withdrawal of the State from its autonomous role in the social sector to create space for both market and NGOs, which are neither accountable to nor constituted by representatives of the people.

Decentralization, both as a concept and mechanism of administration is, however, not a new addition to the development process in India. The colonial regime in the late nineteenth century introduced a system of decentralized administration by promoting certain institutions of local self-government as appendages to the centralized system (Maddick, 1970). The basic objective was to involve the 'intelligent class of public-spirited men' in management of the local affairs by mobilizing the local resources. Such institutions, as is understood, were given certain limited responsibilities, which mainly included maintenance of roads, schools, hospitals etc. Though their development role was highly constricted by the colonial ethos, superimposition of the mechanism of decentralization on the feudal social structure in rural India induced the idea of modern institution to gradually replace the traditional village panchayats.

Nevertheless, a reconstructed notion of village panchayats, or in other words, the 'self-sufficient village republic' constituted the core of Gandhian ideology to decisively influence both content and nature of the nationalist movement in India since the early twentieth century. Though the Gandhian notion of panchayat is intrinsically linked with the utopia of an 'enlightened anarchy', its ideological appeal was instrumental in converting the Indian National Congress to a mass based political movement for purna swaraj. The ideology was legitimized by reconstruction and glorification of the past with a coloured projection of the Indian villages on the one hand, and through the 'rural reconstruction programmes' initiated by Gandhi on the other.

When the nationalist movement reached a more mature stage after the Civil Disobedience Movement, the 'left intelligentsia' within the Congress started contesting the Gandhian ideology to reinforce the nation state ideology. The nationalist movement was to be led with an unambiguously defined political objective of a sovereign nation state. Besides the basic concerns for welfare, progress and economic development, the nation state ideology was constructed to address the issues of individual civil rights to ensure legal protection and full growth of citizenship within a liberal democratic perspective. The Gandhian ideology was buried when Gandhi was alive with his diminishing influence over the nationalist movement.

The Constituent Assembly began to work before independence with a liberal democratic perspective imagining a nation state with universal suffrage, democratic decision-making and modern citizenship as its key institutions. The Constitution that envisaged a modern democratic nation state in India on the premise of a centralized parliamentary system relegated the panchayats to the Directive Principles and to survive at the mercy of the provincial legislatures.

The major challenges before the postcolonial Indian State were the socio-economic as well as political aberrations caused by centuries of colonial domination. With a deep anxiety about the political turmoil and agrarian unrest, rural (community) development was considered as 'a necessary antidote to rural unrest' (Thorner, 1981). The Community Development Projects were launched in the early 1950s when some of the states started taking initiatives to reestablish panchayats with a positive response to the Directive principles of the Constitution. However, brushing off such initiatives or in some cases making the panchayats a mere appendage to the welfare programmes, the State preferred to depend heavily on the highly centralized administrative structure inherited from the colonial past. Nevertheless, the subsequent decades have witnessed several experiments with panchayats made by the State to accelerate the development process in rural India. In absence of any radical initiative to redistribute the productive resources, the State dispensations have largely benefited the rural propertied classes instead of the pauperized masses.

When a free market economy came as the panacea not only for economic development but also for the political crisis of hegemony of the nation state, the State in India has reiterated the significance of democratic decentralization through panchayats. The renewed concern for panchayats as instrumentality of democratic decentralization within a neo liberal perspective has resulted in the Seventy-third amendment of the Constitution. This renewed emphasis on panchayats with a definite space for them in the Constitution, has also been occupying substantive political and intellectual space in India since the early 1990s. Many of the scholars have euphorically perceived it as a renewed concern for the Gandhian principles. The experiences of this experimentation during more than last one decade have been recorded in a number of empirical studies. Yet, it is necessary to locate the reemphasis on panchayats in the context of its own history, beginning as an ideology of Indian nationalism to the Seventy-third amendment of the Constitution. It would provide an understanding of the process of evolution of panchayats and its role in the implementation of the development initiatives.

Considering the small size of population as well as territorial space the state occupies, Assam cannot be considered as a representative sample for any broad generalization on panchayats in India. Yet, an understanding of the system of democratic decentralization through the panchayats in the state is crucial to address several vital issues. Can the present system of decentralization through panchayats provide a solution to the burning political issues of the state? What are the experiences of the earlier similar experiments? If the system was not effective in the past, what contributed to its ineffectiveness? Is it likely to work now? If not, what are the hindering factors?

The present study begins with an attempt to understand how and why Gandhi constructed the notion of 'self-sufficient village republics' emphasizing panchayats. Then it goes to address the second question, why did the nationalist leadership in India refuse to accept the Gandhian principles when nationalism reached a more matured stage, and finally relegate the panchayats to the Directive Principles. These questions are addressed in the narratives of the political processes before independence. A substantial part of the arguments made in Chapter II and Chapter III is based on the analysis of Gandhi and the nationalist movement made by different scholars. Partha Chatterjee's contributions in this regard must be specifically mentioned (Partha Chatterjee, 1999).

An understanding of the experiments with panchayats and other rural development programmes initiated in the country after independence along with the political processes is necessary to comprehend the rationale behind the Seventy-third constitutional amendment. An attempt has been made in Chapter IV to address some of the crucial questions before a brief analysis of the historic Seventy-third amendment, which has been occupying a substantive intellectual and political space in India since the early 1990s.

With a brief analysis of the historical antecedents of the process of decentralized administration that grew in Assam prior to colonial annexation, Chapter V attempts to provide an understanding of the changes brought about in the process by the colonial regime. This has been followed by a brief analysis of the experiments with panchayats in the state till the late 1990s since independence. Focusing on some of the issues pertinent to the regional society, such as immigration and land reform, the chapter points out the probable role of panchayats in resolving the issues. Some of the observations on functioning of panchayats in Assam after the Seventy-third amendment are summarized in Chapter VI. The observations are based on interaction with several panchayat functionaries of mainly three districts, Kamrup, Golaghat and Goalpara. With this backdrop, the concluding chapter of this narration has focused on some of the pertinent issues, which derailed panchayats in the past and are still influential.

2

LOCATING THE 'SELF-SUFFICIENT VILLAGE REPUBLICS' IN GANDHI'S NATIONALIST IDEOLOGY

Many of the writings on Panchayati Raj in India referred to what Gandhi had talked about—the system of rural governance—either by uncritically accepting Gandhi's particular theoretical formulation on panchayat or by condemning the critiques of it. More often than not, such studies have attempted to glorify a 'Gandhian perspective' or to project a 'Gandhian model', which, for them is still relevant. For this, such studies isolate one of the precise and quite crucial aspects of Gandhi's theoretical concern (which is also relevant for their immediate purpose of subscribing to a goal) from the remaining part of his philosophy. However, one has to remember that a simplistic glorification or dismissal of any one of the concepts propounded by Gandhi can be dangerously misleading, because his thought is quite deceptively simple to be comprehended for making any broad theoretical generalization. Being aware of such a risk, an attempt has been made in this chapter to understand Gandhi's concern for the 'self-sufficient village republics' governed by an elected panchayat in the context of his other major concerns.

GANDHI AS A CRITIQUE OF MODERN CIVILASATION

A systematic exposition of Gandhi's political philosophy can be found in one of his initial contributions *Hind Swaraj,* the dialogue he wrote while going back from London to South Africa in November 1909. In *Hind Swaraj*, Gandhi analyzed the reasons behind India's subjugation and eloquently articulated his concept of swaraj, the concept that he formulated long before he emerged as the leader of India's struggle for freedom[1] that continued to guide his political activism in India, and perhaps more importantly, influenced heavily the subsequent history of the nationalist discourse in the subcontinent.

Hind Swaraj has widely been viewed as a critique of modern civilization as Gandhi attempted to construct the notion of swaraj in the context of a struggle between modern civilization and ancient Indian civilization constituted by British colonialism in India. Thus, Gandhi sets the agenda for the dialogue:

> "I must frankly confess that I am not so much concerned about the stability of the Empire as I am about that of the ancient civilisation of India which, in my opinion, represents the best that the world has ever seen. The British Government in India constitutes a struggle between the Modern Civilisation, which is the kingdom of Satan, and the Ancient Civilisation, which is the kingdom of God.... My countrymen impute the evils of modern civilization to the English people and, therefore, believe that the English people are bad, and not the civilization they represent. My countrymen, therefore, believe that they should adopt modern civilization and modern methods of violence to drive out the English. *Hind Swaraj* has been written in order to show that they are following suicidal policy, and that, if they would but revert to their own glorious civilization, either the English would adopt the latter and become Indianized

or find their occupation in India gone" {*Collected Works of Mahatma Gandhi*, (hereafter *CWMG*) Vol. 10, p.189}.

In Gandhi's philosophy, the essence of swaraj is, therefore, to be traced in the context of ancient civilization. However, Gandhi's task was not to glorify Indian civilization as a communal strategy of political mobilization. Gandhi's attempt was to consciously place it in sharp contrast to modern civilization. Thus, his philosophy starts as a critique of modern civilization, a 'disease' that engulfed the western societies, and made the European nations imperialist and India a subject nation. Gandhi argues:

> "The English have not taken India; we have given it to them.... They came to our country originally for purposes of trade. Recall the Company Bahadur. Who made it Bahadur? They had not the slightest intention at the time of establishing a kingdom. Who assisted the Company's officers? Who was tempted at the sight of their silver? Who bought their goods? History testifies that we did all this.... the English merchants were able to get a footing in India because we encouraged them. When our Princes fought among themselves, they sought the assistance of Company Bahadur. That corporation was versed alike in commerce and war. It was unhampered by questions of morality. Its object was to increase its commerce and to make money. It accepted our assistance, and increased the number of its warehouses.... Is it not then useless to blame the English for what we did at that time? The Hindus and the Mahomedans were at daggers drawn. This, too, gave the Company its opportunity and thus we created the circumstances that gave the Company its control over India. Hence it is truer to say that we gave India to the English than that India was lost" (*CWMG*, Vol. 10, pp. 22-23).

Interestingly, Gandhi adds a moral dimension to the economic factors while addressing the question of colonialism.

To be precise, for Gandhi, it was moral failure on the part of a section of the Indian people that culminated in subjugation of India. Gandhi then explains the reason behind the moral failure. The Indians were attracted by the outer manifestations of modern civilization and wanted to become rich all at once. Gandhi has emphatically stated, "India is being ground down, not under the English heel, but under that of modern civilization. It is groaning under the monster's terrible weight" (*CWMG,* Vol. 10, pp. 24).

In his indictment of modern civilization, Gandhi takes conscious note of all the fundamental aspects of western society, the capitalist system of production and the supporting political institutions. Gandhi attacks the very notions of modernity and progress and subverts the central claims made on behalf of those notions, viz. their correspondence with a new organization of society in which the productive capacities of human labour are multiplied several times, creating increased wealth and prosperity for all and hence increased leisure, comfort, health and happiness (Chatterjee, 1999, p. 86).

Contrary to the teachings of all religions of the world to control worldly ambition, Gandhi argues, the sole concern of modern civilization is promotion of bodily happiness. Western societies are enslaved by temptation of money and of the luxuries that money can buy. To repeat Gandhi, "Napolean is said to have described the English as a nation of shop-keepers. It is a fitting description". Gandhi argues that the English hold whatever dominions they have for the sake of their commerce. Gandhi cites the example of the Transvall. When it offered no such attraction, the English considered that it was not right for them to hold it. But when it became a paying proposition, England enjoyed suzerainty over the Transvall. "... someone asked the late President Kruger whether there was gold in the moon. He replied that it was highly unlikely because, if there were, the English would have annexed it" (*CWMG,* Vol. 10, p. 23). Gandhi argues that modern civilization takes note neither of morality nor of religion. Immorality is often taught in the name of morality. Modern civilization looks at man as a limitless consumer and thus sets out to open the floodgates of industrial production, the source of inequality, oppression and violence on a scale hitherto unknown in human history.

Gandhi thus argues, machinery, the chief symbol of modern civilization, has desolated Europe, and started affecting India by inflicting poverty and helplessness on the people at large on the one hand and leading to moral degradation of the rich on the other. The moneyed men in India support British rule and their interest is bound up with its stability. To quote Gandhi:

> "When I read Dutt's *Economic History of India,* I wept; and as I think of it again my heart sickens. It is machinery that has impoverished India. It is difficult to measure the harm that Manchester has done to us. It is due to Manchester that Indian handicraft has all but disappeared" (*CWMG,* Vol. 10, p.57).

Therefore, Gandhi goes to the extreme to argue that it were better for Indian people to send money to Manchester and use flimsy Manchester cloth than to multiply mills in India. By using Manchester cloth, India would only waste money; but industrialization in India would gradually destroy the moral being of the Indians. Therefore, Gandhi is not in favour of industrialization in India at the cost of moral degradation of its people, and he believed that the Indians who had amassed wealth out of factories were not likely to be better than other rich men. It would be a folly to assume that an Indian Rockefeller would be better than the American Rockefeller.

Gandhi's conscious and strong disapproval of what he calls 'modern civilization' in essence is a fundamental critique of the entire edifice of bourgeois society including the political process and institutions. The parliament in England, which is considered to be the 'Mother of Parliaments', has been condemned by Gandhi as a 'sterile woman and a prostitute.' It is sterile because the parliament has never done any good thing of its own accord. Similarly, Gandhi compares the parliament with a prostitute, because it is under the control of the ministers who often change their allegiance. For Gandhi, the parliament being the sovereign political institution should not need the spur of petitions or any other external pressure, and should work smoothly with tangible results. However, the members of such an institution are hypocritical and selfish, and since fear is their guiding motive, what is done today may be undone tomorrow. As a result, 'it is not possible to recall a single instance in which finality can be predicted for its work.' Therefore, for Gandhi, 'Parliament is simply a costly toy of the nation.' True to the ethos of bourgeois democracy, the political leaders have neither real honesty nor a living conscience. Gandhi also unequivocally criticizes the process of election and the influence of media on it:

> "To the English voters their newspaper is their Bible. They take their cue from their newspapers which are often dishonest. The same fact is differently interpreted by different newspapers, according to the party in whose interests they are edited. One newspaper would consider a great Englishman to be a paragon of honesty, another would consider him dishonest"(*CWMG,* Vol. 10, p.18).

Under such circumstances, Gandhi argues, the voters change their views frequently. Their views swing like the pendulum of a clock and are never steadfast. 'The people would follow a powerful orator or a man who gives them parties, reception etc. As are the people, so their Parliament' (*CWMG*, Vol. 10, p18). Therefore, Gandhi unequivocally rejects the bourgeois political institutions.

Then, the question obviously is, what is the alternative reinforced by Gandhi's political philosophy, or in other words, what is true civilization. In Gandhi's political philosophy, civilization is that mode of conduct, which points out to the people the path of their duty, where performance of duty and observance of morality are convertible terms. The notion of duty has consciously been converged to morality to reinforce the fundamental principle of ancient Indian civilization with a secular overtone in an environment of ever increasing influence of capitalism. Happiness is considered as a state of mind independent of the material conditions of life. The mind being a restless bird always strives for more and more and thus remains unsatisfied with any amount of material gains. Therefore, the true civilization is the one which sets a limit to the passionate mind and dissuades people from life-corroding competition for worldly luxuries and pleasure.

SWARAJ IN GANDHI'S IMAGINATION

While conceptualizing swaraj and contemplating the means to achieve it, Gandhi took cognizance of the socio-religious as well as political discourses that started gaining momentum in different parts of India since the early nineteenth century. With varying ideological and religious convictions, the socio-religious reform movements such as the Brahmo Samaj (1828), the Prarthana Samaj (1869), the Sarvajanik Samaj (1870) the Arya Samaj (1875) sprang up in different regions[2] and sought to revitalize Hinduism. Leading these movements, a section of the religious nationalist leaders started articulating their vision for an independent India, and as a means to heightening patriotic fervor, they glorified Hinduism.[3] Along with this, the Indian National Congress which came into being in 1885, became the frontline nationalist movement towards the end of the first decade of the last century. Nevertheless, the notion of swaraj remained undefined. For the moderate wing of the nationalist movement, independence meant autonomous status for India within the British Empire, and they sought to achieve it through constitutional means. The extremist wing, however, identified independence as replacing colonial rule with Indian rule, brought about by any means, if necessary by use of terror and rebellion. The notion of swaraj, therefore, involved nothing more than expulsion of the British from India.

Gandhi, thus noted, "you and I and all Indians are impatient to obtain Swaraj, but we are certainly not decided as to what it is. To drive the English out of India is a thought heard from many mouths, but it does not seem that many have properly considered why it should be"(*CWMG*, Vol. 10, p.14). Gandhi, however, categorically refused the ideology of swaraj, which limits itself just to drive out the English from India by any means, as advanced by the contemporary nationalist discourse in the subcontinent. For him, such a narrow ideological notion of swaraj would mean, "English rule without the Englishman" and euphemistically, it is a strive for the "tiger's nature but not the tiger."

Based on his explanation of colonialism Gandhi attempted to reconstruct the notion of swaraj on a much wider ideological plane. The notion of swaraj as formulated by Gandhi, is essentially national independence (freedom from alien rule) to ensure political freedom of the individual (freedom from oppression by other individual, group or state), economic freedom of the individual (freedom from poverty) and, self-rule. For Gandhi, national independence without an enduring capacity for self-rule on the part of the individual would inevitably lead to rule of the strong – the economically and politically strong – over the economically and politically weak. Therefore, self-rule is the fundamental aspect of national independence or swaraj in Gandhi's political philosophy.

Gandhi clearly articulates the concept of swaraj in the *Draft Declaration for January 26*, which he wrote on behalf of the Indian National Congress[4] on January 10, 1930 with the primary objective to 'educate the people as to its why and wherefore' of independence (*CWMG*, Vol.71, p.116). The Declaration starts with providing a philosophical base for India's independence.

> "We believe that it is the inalienable right of the Indian people, as of any other people, to have freedom and to enjoy the fruits of their toil and have the necessities of life, so that they may have full opportunities of growth. We believe also that if any government deprives a people of these rights and oppresses them, the people have a further right to alter it or abolish it."

In this Declaration, therefore, Gandhi constructs the notion of swaraj with the perspective of rights, and first of all, he points to the individual right to the fruits of toil and necessities of life, and then talks about collective right to alter or abolish an oppressive political system. The Declaration then provides a justification for the Indians' collective right to independence by pointing out precisely the political, economic, cultural and spiritual damages caused by the colonial rule in India. The Declaration emphatically stated that 'we hold it to be a crime against men and God to submit any longer to a rule that has caused this fourfold disaster to our country.' Finally, to end with inhuman colonial rule, Gandhi emphasizes on the means of non-violence to achieve purna swaraj.

The historic Resolution on Fundamental Rights and Economic Changes[5] passed by the 1931 session of the Indian National Congress reveals Gandhi's deep concern for political freedom of the individual.[6] The basic objective of the resolution was to enable the masses to understand what is swaraj. This resolution includes twenty basic rights along with a set of nine fundamental rights to the individual. And, according to this resolution, political freedom must include real economic freedom of the starving millions.

It is, however, worth considering the distinction Gandhi makes between independence and swaraj. The word 'swaraj' is positive, a sacred word, a Vedic word, and the root meaning of which is self-rule and self-restraint or 'disciplined rule from within', not freedom from all restraint which 'independence' often means. 'Independence', on the other hand, is negative, free from the limitations sets by self-rule or not conditioned by 'disciplined rules from within', and therefore, it may mean 'licence to do as you like' (*CWMG*, Vol.45, pp. 263-4).

Gandhi further articulates the notion of swaraj, beyond the perspective of right, in the text entitled *Constructive Programme: Its Meaning and Place,* which he wrote in 1941 (CWMG, Vol.75, pp.146-66). For Gandhi, purna swaraj or complete independence, which is never exclusive, is essentially to ensure independence of every unit of the nation without distinction of race, colour or creed. However, reinforcing the moral aspect, he argues, complete independence will be complete only to the extent of our approach in practice to truth and non-violence. Therefore, Gandhi strongly argues in favour of reconstruction of a moral society to ensure perfect equality, economic or otherwise, without which independence is inconceivable. The 'Constructive Programme' therefore, provides a brief outline of the primary tasks before the nation as prerequisite for purna swaraj. The major tasks are, communal unity, removal of caste system and untouchability, promotion of village industry, village sanitation, adult education, emancipation of women, health and hygiene, improvement of the lot of students, peasants industrial workers and tribal.

Nevertheless, as it has already been pointed out, the central theme of Gandhi's economic freedom is freedom from poverty, and the criteria he sets are, access to the basic needs of life of the individual, the ability to enjoy the fruits of one's toil and the opportunities for growth of the individual. In *Hind Swaraj*, while describing handloom and spinning wheel as the panacea for the growing pauperism of India, Gandhi took it as 'understood that anything that helped India to get rid of the grinding poverty of her masses would in the same process also establish swaraj' (*CWMG*, Vol.39, pp. 389).

In order to achieve economic freedom, when the question of reorganization of the society comes, it is not surprising that Gandhi uncompromisingly takes his position in opposition to the notion of economic freedom propounded by the laissez-faire theorists or the concept of *homo economicus*.

> "I am always reminded of one thing which the well-known economist Adam Smith has said in his famous treatise The Wealth of Nations. In it he has described some economic laws as universal and absolute. Then he has described certain situations, which may be an obstacle to the operation of these laws. These disturbing factors are the human nature, the temperament or altruism inherent in it. Now, the economics of khadi is just the opposite of it. Benevolence, which is inherent in human nature, is the very foundation of the economics of khadi. What Adam Smith has described as pure economic activity based merely on the calculations of profit and loss is a selfish attitude and it is an obstacle to the development of khadi; and it is the function of a champion of khadi to counteract this tendency" (*CWMG*, Vol.59, pp. 205-6).

The fundamental question that Gandhi had to address in this context was how to regulate or discipline the rich and the owners of productive assets, or in other words, how to resolve the conflict between capital and labour. Proffered solution ranged from liquidation of private ownership to its self-regulation, allowing the state to exercise its control in the process, if necessary. The basic principles of economic freedom can be traced in the doctrine of trusteeship, which is essentially an ethical, ontological and epistemological corollary of the 'science of nonviolence' propounded by Gandhi. The doctrine of trusteeship is based on Gandhi's notion of trust between individuals rooted in trustworthiness of man. For him, the most practical and dignified way of going on in the world is to take people at their word when there is no positive reason to the contrary.

The doctrine of trusteeship in Gandhi's own words is the master key to non-violent independence. But, like most of his other notions, it also has not been systematically expounded by Gandhi at one place. Nevertheless, Gandhi's notion of trusteeship has been summarized by some of his closest colleagues and got approved by Gandhi with few changes in it in 1942 (Pyarelal, 1958). The final draft is as follows:

1. Trusteeship provides a means of transforming the present capitalist order of society into an egalitarian one. It gives no quarter to capitalism, but gives the present owning class a chance of reforming itself. It is based on the faith that human nature is never beyond redemption.
2. It does not recognize any right to private ownership of property except so far as it may be permitted by society for its own welfare.
3. It does not exclude legislative regulation of the ownership and use of wealth.
4. Thus, under state-regulated trusteeship, an individual will not be free to hold or use his wealth for selfish satisfaction or in disregard of the interest of society.
5. Just as it proposed to fix a decent minimum living wage, even so a limit should be fixed for the maximum income that could be allowed to any person in society. The difference between such minimum and maximum incomes should be reasonable and equitable and variable from time to time so much so that tendency would be towards obliteration of the difference.

6. Under the Gandhian economic order the character of production will be determined by social necessity and not by personal whim or greed.

The doctrine of trusteeship presupposes absence of absolute right to private property or wealth of an individual. For Gandhi, everything belongs to God and is from God. Therefore, it is for his people as a whole, not for a particular individual. When an individual has more than his proportionate portion he becomes a trustee of that portion for God's people. Gandhi argues:

> "Supposing I have come by a fair amount of wealth either by way of legacy, or by means of trade and industry – I must know that all that wealth does not belong to me; what belongs to me is the right to an honourable livelihood, no better than that enjoyed by millions of others. The rest of my wealth belongs to the community and must be used for the welfare of the community. I enunciated this theory when the socialist theory was placed before the country in respect to the possessions held by zamindars and ruling chiefs. They would do away with these privileged classes. I want them to outgrow their greed and sense of possession, and to come down in spite of their wealth to the level of those who earn their bread by labour.... If the theory is true, it is immaterial whether many live up to it or only one man lives up to it. The question is of conviction. If you accept the principle of Ahimsa, you have to strive to live up to it, no matter whether you succeed or fail"(Sethi, 1986, p. 204).

To Gandhi, economic equality means leveling down of the few rich in whose hands is concentrated the bulk of the nation's wealth on the one hand, and a leveling up of the semi-starved naked millions on the other, and he firmly holds that a non-violent system of government is clearly an impossibility so long as the wide gulf between the rich and hungry millions persists (*CWMG*, Vol.75, pp.146-166).

Therefore, through the theory of trusteeship, Gandhi seeks to resolve the conflict between capital and labour to ensure economic freedom of the millions on the one hand and a non-violent system of government on the other.

As an alternative to the capitalist system of production, Gandhi in the given historical context of India conceptualizes certain economic arrangements independent of large-scale industrialization. The exchange relations and the process of production determined by large-scale industrialization, as Gandhi argues, would inevitably lead to unemployment and poverty in the villages.

> "Industrialization on a mass scale will necessarily lead to passive or active exploitation of the villages as the problems of competition and marketing come in. Therefore we have to concentrate on the village being self-contained, manufacturing mainly for use"(*CWMG*, Vol.63, p.241).

In the context of Indian society characterized by a large agrarian economy with abundance of a huge unemployed labour force, Gandhi provides strict economic argument against large-scale industrialization. "I have no partiality", he argues, "for return to the primitive methods of grinding and husking for the sake of them. I suggest the return, because there is no other way of giving employment to the millions of villagers who are living in idleness" (*CWMG*, Vol.63, pp.77-78). Nevertheless, Gandhi does not deny economic logic of industrialization in a situation of scarcity of labour:

> "Mechanization is good when the hands are too few for the work intended to be accomplished. It is an evil when there are more hands than required for the work, as in the case of India.... The problem with us is not how to find leisure for the teeming millions inhabiting our villages. The problem is how to utilize their idle hours, which are equal to the working days of six months in

> the year. Strange as it may appear, every mill generally is a menace to the villagers.... I am quite safe in saying that every mill-hand does the work of at least ten labourers doing the same work in their villages.... Thus spinning and weaving mills have deprived the villagers of a substantial means of livelihood. It is no answer in reply to that they turn out cheaper, better cloth, if they do so at all. For, if they have displaced thousands of workers, the cheapest mill cloth is dearer than the dearest khadi woven in the villages" (*CWMG,* Vol. 59, p.356).

Gandhi, therefore, famously argued that what India needed was not mass production but production by the masses. Gandhi was not opposed to machinery *per se,* but what he essentially opposed was the craze for it regardless of the interest of the overwhelming majority. "If we are able to judge when to use a machine and when to avoid it and if while using it we do so with understanding", he agrees, "quite a few of our difficulties will be solved" (*CWMG*, Vol. 87, p.249). Machine power can make a valuable contribution towards economic progress, but those who have control over the machinery hardly pay any attention to the interests of the common people. Gandhi, therefore, believes that machinery is a grand, yet awful invention. It is possible to visualize a stage at which the machines invented by man may finally engulf a civilization. If man controls the machines, then they will not; but should man lose his control over the machines and allow them to control him, then they certainly will engulf civilization and everything (*CWMG*, Vol.48, p.353).

Therefore, Gandhi reiterated two fundamental threats to freedom caused by a civilization driven by machinery and market oriented large-scale production. The first is imperialistic aggression for expansion of market, and the second is inhuman exploitation of the overwhelming majority in the domestic market by those who enjoy control over large-scale industries. He has also clearly pointed out the relationship between industrial economy and imperialism, and therefore, he argues that "we cannot industrialize ourselves, unless we make up our minds to enslave humanity" (*CWMG*, Vol. 58, p.400).

In order to ensure independence for the "dumb millions" of India, Gandhi endeavours to work out an alternative to capitalism. His continuous emphasis on spinning wheel and production of *khadi* made through hand spinning and hand weaving is best seen in the light of his basic concern for an alternative to industrial capitalism:

> "When as a nation we adopt the spinning wheel, we not only solve the question of unemployment but we declare that we have no intention of exploiting any nation, and we also end the exploitation of the poor by the rich.... When I say I want independence for the millions, I mean to say not only that the millions may have something to eat and to cover themselves with, but that they will be free from the exploitation of people here and outside. We can never industrialize India, unless, of course, we reduce our population from 350 millions to 35 millions or hit upon market wider than our own and dependent on us. It is time we realize that, where there is unlimited human power, complicated machinery on a large scale has no place" (*CWMG*, Vol.58, p.400).

Another integral component of Gandhian notion of swaraj is self-rule, which is to be achieved by an individual through an internal process finally to attain spiritual freedom. Self-rule is indispensable for social existence of man, and it distinguishes human beings from brutes. For Gandhi, 'the essential difference between man and brute is that the former can respond to the call of spirit in him and raise superior to the passions that he owns in common with the brute' (*CWMG*, Vol. 58, p.248). The internal process of achieving self rule involves removal of all internal obstacles to freedom, which is not something that 'may be either taken from us by anybody or which can be given us by anybody' (*CWMG*, Vol.20, p.133). The Gandhian notion of swaraj, therefore, is to be seen as a process in which self-rule plays a crucial role by providing a linkage between the internal world of spiritual freedom and the external world of political and economic freedom. To quote Gandhi:

> "It is Swaraj when we learn to rule ourselves. It is, therefore, in the palm of our hands. Do not consider this Swaraj to be like a dream. There is no idea of sitting still. The Swaraj that I wish to picture is such that, after we have once realized it, we shall endeavour to the end of our lifetime to persuade others to do likewise. But such Swaraj has to be experienced, by each one for himself. One drowning man will never save another. Slaves ourselves, it would be a mere pretension to think of freeing others" (*CWMG*, Vol.10, p.39).

Through the experiences of his own life, Gandhi emphasized on the linkage between spiritual freedom and his political activism. In the introduction to his biography, he stated that the goal of his life was to attain spiritual freedom, and he strived to attain it through all his continuous political activities. 'All that I do by way of speaking and writing, and all my ventures in the political field, are determined to this same end' (*CWMG,* Vol. 39, p.3). In the concluding chapter, he reiterated, an individual who aspires after spiritual freedom and self-rule cannot afford to keep out of any field of life. And, he stated that his devotion to truth has drawn him into the field of politics (*CWMG*, Vol.39, p.401).

With a strong conviction that self rule or spiritual freedom is inseparably linked with political and economic freedom, Gandhi submitted that swaraj is an all satisfying goal for all time, and he wanted India to be free from the fourfold disaster (political, economic, cultural and spiritual) caused by the colonial rule.

RAMARAJYA: THE STATE OF ENLIGHTENED ANARCHY

Gandhism unequivocally rejects the bourgeois state and its entire politico-legal edifice, including the institution of representative democracy, as the whole political machinery abrogates moral responsibility and widens the gap between the rulers and the people at large. Vested interest of those who rule and suppose to represent the society leads to the dissociation of political values from social morality and ethical values. In such a political process the rich and the politically powerful section enjoys enormous opportunities to manipulate the political machinery for fulfillment of their own self interests, and therefore, the State in the guise of neutrality perpetuates socio-economic inequalities. Citing the example of colonial State in India, Gandhi argues:

> "The caste system, as it exists at present, is entirely the bane of Hindu life. Its rigour is unmitigated by the British rule. On the contrary it gains force because of the so-called neutrality necessarily observed by the ruling power for the sake of itself" (*CWMG*, Vol.59,p.45).

With the notion of swaraj as 'an all satisfying goal for all time', Gandhism provides an alternative to the bourgeois state by redefining political power in relation to the national life.

> "The power to control national life through national representatives is called political power. Representatives will become unnecessary if the national life becomes so perfect as to be self-controlled. It will then be a state of enlightened anarchy in which each person will become his own ruler. He will conduct himself in such a way that his behaviour will not hamper the well being of his neighbours. In an ideal State there will be no political institution and therefore no political power. That is why Thoreau has said in his classic statement that the government is the best which governs the least" (*CWMG,* Vol.68, p. 265).

The Gandhian ideal state, therefore, provides no space for political institutions to control the national life, as it presupposes a moral national life constituted by the politically, economically, culturally and spiritually free individuals. The utopia that Gandhi propounds is *Ramarajya*, a patriarchy in which both the rulers and his subjects are inclined towards self-sacrifice, both exercise restraint and self-control while enjoying worldly pleasures, and the relation between the two is as good 'as that between a father and a son' (*CWMG*, Vol.35, p.489). For Gandhi, a government founded on public opinion which is 'not artificially created' is *Ramarajya*, and it implies an era of truth or swaraj or the 'people's raj' (democracy) (*CWMG*, Vol. 45, p.328).

Gandhi emphatically stated that independence of his dream means *Ramarjya*, i.e. the 'kingdom of God on Earth', and in concrete terms he reiterates, independence should be political, economic and moral:

> 'Political' necessarily means the removal of the control of the British army in every shape and form.
>
> 'Economic' means entire freedom from British capitalists and capital, as also their Indian counterparts. In other words, the humblest must feel equal to the tallest. This can take place only by capital or capitalists sharing their skill and capital with the lowliest and the least.
>
> 'Moral' means freedom from armed defence forces. My conception of Ramarajya excludes replacement of the British army by a national army of occupation. A country that is governed by even its national army can never be morally free and, therefore, its so-called weakest member can never rise to his full moral height (*CWMG*, Vol.84, p.80).

Gandhism posits the utopia of *Ramrajya* as the ideology for reconstruction of national life based on moral principles, and therefore, the basic question before Gandhi is not whether statelessness can ever be achieved.

> "Would there be State power in an ideal society or would such a society be Stateless? I think the question is futile. If we continue to work towards the building of such a society, to some extent it is bound to be realized and to that extent people will benefit by it. Euclid has defined a straight line as having no breadth, but no one has yet succeeded in drawing such a line and no one ever will. Still we can progress in geometry only by postulating such a line. This is true of every ideal"(*CWMG*, Vol.85, p.267).

Gandhi admits that stateless society does not exist anywhere in the world. Nevertheless, his conviction is that if such a society is possible, it can be established first in India as the nation through its struggle for freedom has made attempts towards bringing about such a society. The only way is for those who believe in it to set the example.

THE VILLAGE REPUBLICS

An intrinsic component of the utopia of *Ramarjya* is the 'Gandhian Programme' for reconstruction of the rural society encompassing every dimension of the village life with an emphasis on sanitation and basic education. The mechanism is decentralization of both authority and economy. The smallest social unit in this crucial process of decentralization is the village, which should be made self-sufficient not only in terms of economy but also in the matters of governance as well as defence. Gandhi thus points out:

> "Independence must begin at the bottom. Thus, every village will be republic or *panchayat* having full powers. It follows, therefore, that every village has to be self-sustained and capable of managing its affairs even to the extent of defending itself against the whole world. It will be trained and prepared to perish in the attempt to defend itself against any onslaught from without" (*CWMG*, Vol.85, p.32).

Ultimately, in this scheme of decentralization, the individual who is self-sufficient and 'knows what he or she wants', and more importantly, 'knows that no one should want anything that others cannot have with equal labour' is the unit of the village republic. Thus Gandhi visualizes 'a highly cultured society', which must naturally be based on truth and non-violence.

In the Gandhian notion of decentralization, the nation is organized in the form of ever-widening circles – a group of villages, the *taluka*, the district, the province and so on, the unit of each circle would strive for self-sufficiency without depending on the larger unit or dominating over the smaller one (*CWMG*, Vol.85, pp.459-460). As Gandhi describes it:

> "In this structure composed of innumerable villages, there will be ever-widening, never-ascending circles. Life will not be a pyramid with the apex sustained by the bottom. But it will be an oceanic circle whose centre will be the individual always ready to perish for the village, the latter ready to perish for the circle of villages, till at last the whole becomes one life.... The outermost circumference will not wield power to crush the inner circle but will give strength to all within and derive its own strength from it" (*CWMG*, Vol.85, p.33).

However, Gandhi's primary concern is the idea of village swaraj, a 'complete republic' independent of its neighbours for its own vital needs. The government of such a village republic is to be conducted by the panchayat of five persons who possess a minimum prescribed qualification and annually elected by the adult villagers, both male and female. Since non-violence with its technique of *satyagraha* and non-cooperation will be an inherent part of the village community, there will be no system of punishment in the accepted sense. Nevertheless, the panchayat will enjoy the required legislative, judicial and executive authority.

Gandhi believes that any village can become such a republic free from interference from the government whose sole effective connection with the villages is the exaction of revenue. The Gandhian village republic enjoys 'perfect democracy' based upon individual freedom. The individual is the architect of the village government, and the law of non-violence rules the individual and his government. 'He and his village are able to defy the might of a world. For the law governing every villager is that he will suffer death in the defense of his and his village's honour' (*CWMG*, Vol. 76, p. 309).

With the help of this ideal village republic, Gandhi provides a picture of 'an India continually progressing along the lines best suited to her genius'. And, he believes that if every one of the seven lakhs villages becomes a well-living republic, there will be no illiteracy, no one will remain idle for want of work, every one will have nourishing food, well-ventilated dwellings and sufficient *khadi* for covering the body (*CWMG*, Vol.67, p.211).

While drawing the picture of such self-sufficient village republics, Gandhi has not seen any possibility of complete disappearance of the cities. Every village producing and manufacturing everything for its own use would also imply generation of some surplus by the villages for the cities. This small surplus should go out of the villages to the cities for automatic stoppage of all exploitation and prosperity of the villages without having to exploit the outer world, (*CWMG*, Vol.80, p.244) 700,000 villages of India will dominate 'the centre with its few towns required in the interests of the villages' (*CWMG*, Vol.80, p.353). Here Gandhi agrees with Henry James Summer Maine[7] who said that ancient India was a conglomeration of village republics. The towns were then subservient to the villages. They were emporia for the surplus village products and beautiful manufactures. However, this is only the skeleton of Gandhi's picture to serve as a pattern for independent India, which will also be free from the faults of the ancient Indian village system (*CWMG*, Vol.85, p.79).

The whole idea of self-sufficient village republic is definitely a utopia, but Gandhi argues, if the Euclid's point, though incapable of being drawn by human agency, has an imperishable value, his picture has its own for mankind to live. India should live for this true picture, though never realizable in its completeness. 'We must have a proper picture of what we want, before we can have something approaching it', Gandhi argues. 'If there ever is to be a republic of every village in India, then I claim verity for my picture in which the last is equal to the first or, in other words, no one is to be the first and none the last' (*CWMG*, Vol. 85, p. 33).

A BRIEF CRITICAL APPRAISAL

Gandhi began with a moral critique of modern civilization or the system of social production, which encouraged in the western societies an endless desire for production, and an ethos of ruthless competition. Being enslaved by temptation of money and the luxuries that money can buy, the western societies sought colonial possessions for expansion of market and economic exploitation. In Gandhi's understanding, therefore, modern civilization, which was necessarily the outcome of industrial revolution in Europe, led to socio-economic division, oppression and violence on a scale hitherto unknown in human history. The bourgeoisie society and its political structure that served the interests of the propertied classes had entirely dislodged moral social responsibility. The State became an instrument of economic exploitation of the overwhelming majority as it provided disproportionate opportunities to the propertied classes. Modern civilization, which was characterized as a disease, naturally affected India. A section of the Indian society for its own vested interests sought help of the British. Consequently, India became a British colony inflicting poverty and helplessness on the people at large and moral degradation of the rich. Thus, Gandhi attempted to construct the notion of a true civilization, which would set the limit to the passionate mind and dissuade people from ever increasing competition for worldly luxuries and pleasure that money could buy. Unambiguously, Gandhi took this position as early as in *Hind Swaraj*, and it not only influenced his political activism but also the entire course of India's struggle for freedom led by the Indian National Congress.

Gandhi's notion of swaraj was built upon his understanding of modern civilization and colonialism on a much wider ideological plane than his contemporary nationalist discourses, which viewed swaraj as merely political independence. Besides political independence, Gandhian notion of swaraj encompassed economic freedom and self-rule or spiritual freedom. Therefore, Gandhi emphatically stated that it would be a crime against men and god to submit any longer to a rule that had caused political, economic, cultural and spiritual damage to the Indian society.

Gandhi's unequivocal disapproval of what he called 'modern civilization' in fact was a fundamental critique of bourgeois society to idealize a moral, non-competitive just and peaceful pre-capitalist society with its proclaimed universal applicability. For that, Gandhi went beyond the theme of his contemporary nationalist discourses in India, and sought to provide a moral justification of his project of achieving true swaraj by dismissing all historical objections to the means to achieve it. Therefore, as early as in *Hind Swaraj*, Gandhi imagined such an Indian society which was to be achieved not by the strength of arms but by the force of soul, and emphatically stated that 'to believe that what has not occurred in history will not occur at all is to argue disbelief in the dignity of man'. History to him, is built upon the records not of the working of the force of the soul, and therefore, does not record the 'Truth', which is universal, moral, unchanging and transcendental. Truth has no history of its own.

With such a notion of 'true swaraj', Gandhism addressed

the problematic of Indian nationalism and became the political ideology of a nationalist movement inevitably waged within the politico-legal structure of a colonial state. More importantly, in the given historical context, Gandhism had to ensure continuation of support of the nascent Indian bourgeoisie and the big landlords to the nationalist movement, which accepted the idea of an 'enlightened anarchy' as an alternative to a centralized State.

Gandhi found a practical solution in *satyagraha*, the most celebrated Gandhian form of mass political action. While beginning his political activism in India, Gandhi explained *satyagraha* as a means to make the people free from the unjust rule of a government by defying the unjust rule and accepting the punishments that go with it. Therefore, it does not mean passive resistance, but implies intense political activity by large masses of people and their legitimate, moral and truthful form of resistance to unjust rule. A *satyagrahi* does not fear for his body nor does he wish for the destruction of his antagonist. The *satyagrahi* does not vent anger on his antagonist but has only compassion for him. And, Gandhi firmly believed that the people of India are perfectly fit to adopt this means to fight against colonialism (*CWMG*, Vol.13, pp.520-526).

As a necessary complement to *satyagraha*, Gandhi evolved another quite celebrated concept, that is *ahimsa* to be applied politically, as it also implied 'intense political activity' by the masses. Nevertheless, as a political concept, *ahimsa* is essentially concerned more with modalities of resistance, organizational principles and rules of conduct than the political activity of resistance itself. *Ahimsa* for Gandhi was a creed, but he preferred to place it before the Congress as a political weapon to be employed for the solution of political problems (*CWMG*, Vol.75 p.220). Therefore, with the notion of *satyagraha* complimented by *ahmisa*, Gandhism addressed itself to the problematic of nationalism and attempted to provide the ideological basis for Indian nationalism in the given historical context.

And yet, Gandhism as a nationalist ideology had perforce to bridge not only the most sanctified socio-religious cleavages in a highly complex social system, but also the clearly demarcated economic division in a predominantly feudal economy. The challenge before Gandhism was to integrate the people of India as a whole with the political nation for attaining independence depending solely on 'soul-force'. The political strategy was *satyagraha* based on non-violence embedded in truth.

Essentially therefore, Gandhism reconstructs the notion of swaraj beyond the perspective of rights and political independence. Gandhi imagines a moral society with *purna swaraj* encompassing perfect equality, economic or otherwise, as the goal of the nation, and adds to the nationalist agenda the constructive programme and trusteeship. With his strenuous efforts to obliterate the 'sin' of existing caste system, and more particularly the 'deadly sin' of untouchability in Indian society, Gandhi provides an idealized scheme of society based on *varna*, which to him is a non-hierarchical occupational category.

Gandhism constructs the utopian notion of trusteeship primarily to resolve the conflict between capital and labour through non-violent means. Inevitably, Gandhi has to reckon with the growing influence of socialist ideology on the nationalist discourse in India on the one hand and reconcile the interests of the propertied classes with the political movement on the other. Therefore, Gandhi suggested:

> "Let us not be obsessed with catchwords and slogans imported from the West. Have we not our own distinct Eastern traditions? Are we not capable of finding our own solution to the question of capital and labour? .... Let us study our Eastern institutions in the spirit of scientific inquiry and we shall evolve a true socialism

> and a true communism than the world has yet dreamed of. It is surely wrong to presume that western socialism or communism is the last word on the question of mass poverty" (*CWMG*, Vol.58, p.219).

Within the framework of his 'Eastern model of communism' based on the ethos of non-violence or *ahimsa*, Gandhi urged the privileged classes to outgrow their greed and sense of possession, and come down, in spite of their wealth, to the level of those who earn their bread by labour. The *zamindars* must regard themselves as trustees holding their wealth for the good of their wards. Gandhi is also convinced that:

> "There is no other choice than between voluntary surrender on the part of the capitalist of superfluities and consequent acquisition of the real happiness of all on the one hand, and on the other the impending chaos into which, if the capitalist does not wake up betimes, awakened but ignorant, famishing millions will plunge the country and which not even the armed force that a powerful Government can bring into play can avert" (*CWMG*, Vol.42, pp.239-240).

However, to Gandhi, class war is not only avoidable but also inevitable if the nation has understood the message of non-violence. Gandhi is also quite clear that if a strictly honest and unchallengeable referendum of the million Indians were to be taken, they would definitely reject the wholesale expropriation of the propertied classes, (*CWMG*, Vol.58, p. 247) but at the same time, he does not want the nationalist movement to take a definite stand for the rights of the masses irrespective of the interests of the capitalists and the landlords. Instead, Gandhi asserts that the immediate need is to transform the existing relationship between them and the masses into something 'healthier' and 'purer' (*CWMG*, Vol.58, p.219).

The doctrine of trusteeship aimed not at destruction of

the capitalist but of capitalism by appealing to the subjective consciousness of human agents. Gandhi's conviction is that the capitalist not devoid of morality and nationalist consciousness would regard himself as a trustee for those on whom he depends for the making, retention and increase of his capital. The privileged classes are not averse to progressively sharing their riches with the masses, if their confidence is won and put them at their ease.

At the same time, Gandhi's nationalist ideology provides an alternative to capitalism. As early as in *Hind Swaraj*, Gandhi made the plea for return to a simple self-sufficient traditional village life, and idealized a pre-capitalist form of social production. The argument was that, the millions living in the seven hundred thousand villages of India would not retain the freedom they have enjoyed from time immemorial if they do not control the production of the prime necessities of life. 'Anything that helped India to get rid of the grinding poverty of the masses would in the same process also establish swaraj'. The machinery method is not an answer before the millions of unemployed people. Gandhi concretized the alternative in the form of *khadi* and projected it as the most powerful means for attaining swaraj. The primary objective is not merely material welfare but spiritual welfare of the people. While attempting to conceptualize an economic rearrangement embedded in *khadi*, the determining factor is benevolence, which is inherent in human nature. Therefore, *khadi* is not a pure economic proposition to be based merely on the calculations of profit and loss. And hence, the tactics normally adopted in a profiteering business have no place in *khadi* (*CWMG*, Vol. 59, pp.205-208). With a strong moral presupposition, Gandhi has emphasized on economic necessities of *khadi* in the context of an overwhelmingly agrarian society, and idealized it as the most powerful means for attaining swaraj. Thus, *khadi* became the symbol of the struggle for freedom.

The utopianism that shaped Gandhi's political philosophy finally culminates in the concept of 'state of enlightened anarchy', the alternative to bourgeois state. Gandhi concretized it in the form of '*Ramrajya*' to fulfill the aspiration for purna swaraj. The utopian patriarchy, which implies an era of truth, does not provide space for any political institution to control the national life.

However, when the political struggle for freedom almost reached its climax and the nationalist leadership saw that political freedom was not too far, Gandhism had to address itself certain practical questions without compromising with its basic principles i.e. truth and non-violence. At this crucial juncture, Gandhi had to quite consciously bridge the gap between the ideal construction and the institution of power that would soon be under control of the nationalist leadership. The basic questions before Gandhi were what should be the responsibilities of the Congress leadership while running the State, and more importantly, whether the nationalist leadership should stay away from the parliamentary politics to continue with the struggle beyond political freedom. Gandhi's conviction was that the true *satyagrahi* should stay away, because parliamentary government could at best bring only political freedom, which is not true swaraj.

At this crucial historical juncture Gandhism re-emphasized on the unaccomplished task of reconstruction of the moral national life as the nationalist agenda, and urged the political leadership not to relinquish the moral principles. Gandhism, therefore, more forcefully projected the utopia of *Ramarajya* than ever before. One had to accept the practical existence of the State, and therefore, to Gandhi, the question – would there be State power in an ideal society or would such a society be stateless – was a futile question. But at the same time, he believed that India could set the example of establishing an ideal society, i.e. *Ramarajya*.

The concept of 'self-sufficient village republic' primarily drawn from the ancient Indian village system was the core of Gandhian 'rural reconstruction programme', and Gandhi conceived this idea at the early phase of the nationalist movement. However, inevitably Gandhi made a more serious attempt to construct the notion of an ideal village republic as an intrinsic component of the utopia of *Ramarajya* towards the latter part of the political movement for true swaraj. Increasingly, emphasis was on the mechanism of decentralization of both political powers and economy. In the utopian notion of decentralization of political and administrative powers, the village should become a republic for itself, exercising all legislative, judicial and executive powers, governed by an elected body of five members called panchayat. And perhaps more importantly, it must be capable of managing all its affairs even to the extent of defending itself against the whole world, when necessary. In terms of economy, such a village republic should be capable of producing everything to fulfill the basic needs of the villagers, and such a village economy must be non-exploitative and also free from exploitation by other. With the suggested political and economic self-reliance, Gandhi believed, seven hundred thousand villages of India would dominate the centre.

The notion of 'self-sufficient village republic' governed by a panchayat was constructed by Gandhi essentially as the means to reach the 'state of enlightened anarchy' or *Ramarajya*. Gandhi projected such a 'picture', which to him had an imperishable value for the mankind to live, and as he believed, India should live for this 'true picture' though never realizable in its completeness.

NOTES

1. Gandhi emerged as the leader of the Indian National Congress after his success in Champaran in 1917 and it was in Champaran that he came to be known as 'Mahatma'. J.B.Kripalani, *Gandhi: His Life and Thought,* Publication Division, New Delhi,1970.
2. The reformist movement that spearheaded the Indian Renaissance in the 19th century had been initiated by the Brahmo Samaj in 1828 by Raja Ram Mohan Roy. Having its nucleus in Bengal, it became an all India sect by the end of 1860s under the leadership of Keshav Ch. Sen. In Maharashtra, it came to be known as Prarthana Samaj, and gradually it became popular in the southern provinces. In Bombay, a social revivalist movement took shape under the banner of Arya Samaj founded in 1875 by Swami Dayanand Saraswati with its head quarters in Lahore. It took deep roots particularly in northern India. Another noteworthy revivalist movement came up through the Ramakrishna Mission founded in Bengal in 1896/97 by Swami Vivekananda with its branches all over India.
3. In this context one can point out the influence of the religious nationalist leaders such as Dayanand Saraswati, Bal Gangadhar Tilak, Madan Mohan Malavya, Swami Vivekanand and Lajpat Rai.
4. This Declaration was written when Gandhi firmly resumed leadership of the Indian National Congress after a lapse of nearly eight years and accepted *purna* swaraj or complete independence as the country's goal. *CWMG*,Vol.42, pp.384-5.
5. This Resolution was presumably drafted by Gandhi, *CWMG*, Vol.45, p.370.
6. Early in his political life, Gandhi realized that life worthy of human being is not possible without political freedom and the basic rights. He recalls, "My public life began in 1893 in South Africa in troubled weather. My first contact with the British authority was not a happy character. I discovered that as a man and as Indian I had no rights as a man because I was an Indian." *CWMG*, Vol. 23, p.115.
7. Gandhi referred to Sir Henry James Summer Maine, the author of *Village Communities in the East and West.*

3

NATION STATE IDEOLOGY, CONSTITUENT ASSEMBLY AND PANCHAYAT

The narratives on Panchayati Raj necessarily refer to the debates in the Constituent Assembly on the question of space for panchayat in the Constitution of India. On the basis of what Ambedkar had said while placing the Draft Constitution before the Constituent Assembly, he had often been projected or understood as a strong opponent of the Gandhian notion of decentralization, mainly responsible for drafting the constitution denying the panchayat its due space. Such interpretations, however, often overlook or ignore one of the crucial aspects - the ideology, with which the nationalist movement was approaching independence and the Constituent Assembly was framing the constitution. This chapter makes an attempt to understand the ideology that was consciously constructed in the later part of the nationalist movement in India imagining a nation state, and then it goes to analyze the debates in the Constituent Assembly on the question of providing space for panchayat in the nation state.

RECONSTRUCTION OF IDEOLOGY: CONCERN FOR A MODERN SOVEREIGN NATION STATE

In the backdrop of post World War I politico-economic

scenario of India marked by inhuman political repression, inexorable and continuous exploitation, which together made India a derelict nation, and at the same time, when the political movement was almost directionless, in Nehru's opinion, Gandhi appeared 'like a powerful current of fresh air' that enabled people to take deep breaths; 'like a beam of light' that pierced the darkness and removed the scales from the eyes of the Indians; 'like a whirlwind' that upset many things, but most of all the working of people's minds. To Nehru, Gandhi 'did not descend from the top; he seemed to emerge from the millions of India, speaking their language and increasingly drawing attention to them and their appalling condition. Get off the backs of these peasants and workers, he told us, all you who live by their exploitation; get rid of the system that produces this poverty and misery. Political freedom took a new shape then and acquired a new content'. And to Nehru, in such a crucial historical juncture, the essence of Gandhi's teaching was fearlessness and truth, and action allied to these, always keeping the welfare of the masses in view. Nehru contextualized Gandhi's teaching .... the dominant impulse in India under British rule was that of fear – pervasive, oppressing, strangling fear; fear of the army, the police, the widespread secrete service; fear of official class; fear of laws meant to suppress and of prison; fear of the landlord's agent; fear of the money lenders; fear of unemployment and starvation, which were always on the threshold. It was against this all-pervading fear that Gandhi's quite and determined voice was raised: Be not afraid' (Nehru, 2004, pp. 392-3).

Therefore, with a strong intervention of Gandhi in the political movement 'that black pall of fear was lifted from the peoples shoulders.... to an amzing degree. As fear is close companion to falsehood, so truth follows fearlessness.... A sea change was visible as the need for falsehood and furtive behaviour lessened' (Nehru, 2004, p. 393). This was the phase of psychological revolution 'almost as if some expert in psycho-analytical methods had probed deep into the patient's past, found out the origins of his complexes, exposed them to his view, and thus rid him of that burden' (Nehru, 2004, p. 393). Gandhi's entry into the political movement also immediately brought about a complete change in its social composition. 'Now the peasants rolled in and, in its new grab, it began to assume the look of a vast agrarian organization with a strong sprinkling of the middle classes' (Nehru, 2004, p.395).

Gandhi's action involved challenging and resisting foreign rule on the one hand, and fighting the social evils on the other. Apart from the fundamental objective of the Congress, that is freedom, political movement with the Gandhian ideology of non-violence and truth also addressed the question of minority, depressed classes and untouchability. Therefore, Gandhi 'effected a vast psychological revolution not only among those who followed his lead but also among those who could not make up their minds what to think and what to do' (Nehru, 2004, p.399).

Gandhi's political activism that made the Congress a broad based struggle for freedom involving the mass of peasantry and the working people mainly through the rural reconstruction programme and relentless persuasion of his utopia had received almost uncritical support from most of the nationalist leaders till the early 1930s. However, the utopianism that constituted the core of the Gandhian philosophy was contested within the political movement by its 'left intelligentsia' led by Nehru, particularly after the collapse of the Civil Disobedience Movement in the early 1930s, when the political movement for freedom reached a mature stage. Raising the crucial issue of class character of the freedom movement, Nehru dismissed the Gandhian notion of economic freedom for the masses and the means he propagated to achieve it. 'Congress cannot escape having to answer the question now or later for the freedom of which class or classes in India are we especially striving for? Do we place the masses, the peasantry and workers first, or some small class at the head of list? In my own mind it is clear that if an indigenous government took the place of a foreign government and kept the vested interests intact, this would not even be the shadow of freedom' (Frankel, 2005, p.53).

For the 'left intelligentsia' within the Congress, the fundamental objective of the nationalist movement was to establish a sovereign nation state, and to achieve that political objective, the crucial task before them was to re-orient the ideology of nationalism. Gandhian reform programmes attempted to associate social and economic questions with nationalism. All such initiatives were necessary for political mobilization, but, efforts to achieve a just society, both socially and economically, within the colonial set up would mean wastage of energy. Therefore, nationalism in its mature stage demanded more concrete social and economic content in it. Mass movement for a sovereign nation state must proceed with social and economic reform agenda, but the political objective had to be unambiguously defined. Therefore, Gandhi's utopianism was to be countered by an ideology of a sovereign nation state explicitly recognizing its existence as an autonomous political institution with its interventionist and regulatory role to ensure economic progress with social justice, and also legitimizing coercion. Such a concern is clearly witnessed by the writings and speeches of the chief political architect of modern India, that is, Jawaharlal Nehru.

Gandhi's repeated assertion that 'look after the means and the end will take care of itself', to a pragmatic and modern nationalist leader such as Nehru, revealed neither a political or scientific nor even ethical attitude. But, it was a narrowly moralist attitude, with which Gandhi was 'passionately desirous of going in a certain direction', wholly at variance with the 'modern ideas and conditions'. Therefore, when the nationalist movement reached a mature stage, the Gandhian thought appeared to be 'utterly wrong and harmful doctrine, and impossible of achievement' (Nehru, 2004, pp.526-528). The basic premise of Gandhian philosophy that progress and civilization consist not in the multiplication of wants, of higher standard of living, but deliberate and voluntary restriction of wants, which promotes real happiness and contentment, was not acceptable to Nehru, because this premise necessarily justifies the notion of self sufficient village essentially associated with primitivism.

'Scientific' attitude towards politics, to Nehru, involves understanding of history taking cognizance of the political processes determined by class interests in a given society, economic enquiry as to what is most desirable or beneficial for the people, and therefore, recognition of the necessities of change with clarity of the envisaged objectives. With such a 'scientific' attitude, Nehru wanted to proceed to address the social, political or economic problems considering primacy of the sphere of economy. 'If there is nothing that history shows it is this: that economic interests shape the political views of groups and classes. Neither reason nor moral considerations override those interests' (Nehru, 2004, p.562).

With such an understanding, after the withdrawal of the Civil Disobedience Movement by Gandhi in 1933, the modern nationalist leader painfully admitted that a vast distance separated him from Gandhi, and the allegiance that had bound him to Gandhi for many years had snapped. The differences that gradually grew between Gandhi and Nehru were essentially the differences of views regarding definiteness and clarity of the basic objective of the nationalist movement. Nehru in the past tried to subordinate the differences, as far as he could, to what he conceived to be the larger loyalty—the cause of nationalist movement. 'Inspite of the closest association with him for many years', wrote Nehru, 'I am not clear in my own mind about his objective. I doubt if he is clear himself' (Nehru, 2004, p.524).

What made Nehru a modern nationalist leader of the twentieth century was his way of understanding the Indian society in the colonial context and the perspective that he had of a sovereign democratic nation state, which determined the strategy and the ideological contents of the nationalist movement. Gandhi's one of the objections to mechanization that it would lead to a problem of finding meaningful utilization of the surplus labour, Nehru agreed, was applicable to all societies suffering from unemployment under the colonial economic set up where the workforce remained idle as it was not profitable for the employers to engage it entirely. But, after overthrowing the colonial system, there would not be any problem of unemployment. The post-colonial reconstruction programme for development and progress to be undertaken by a sovereign State would demand a massive workforce for development of the required infrastructure, for the spread of sanitation, medical facilities, industry, electricity, social and cultural services, education, and the provision of the scores of necessary articles that the people lack. 'All our millions can work hard for the next fifty years' (Nehru, 2004, p.543). The objection to industrialization would, therefore, necessarily lead to restriction of progress and development including expansion of railways and communication infrastructure that would be against the fundamental interests of the nation including its defence. 'If we want to have the means of defence we must not only have the basic industries but a highly developed industrial system. No country today is really independent or capable of resisting aggression unless it is industrially developed' (Nehru, 2004, p.544).

The doctrine of trusteeship propounded by Gandhi to ensure economic freedom to the downtrodden and oppressed section of the society by resolving the contradiction between capital and labour, in Nehru's view, was essentially to maintain the *status quo* of class exploitation. Despite his keen intellect and passion for economic freedom of the poor, paradoxically, Gandhi supported a system, which was decaying and responsible for creating misery for the people at large. Gandhi 'blesses all the relics of the old order which stands as obstacles in the way of advance – the feudal state, the big zamindaris and taluqadaris, the present capitalist system. Is it reasonable to believe in the theory of trusteeship – to give unchecked power and wealth to an individual and to expect him to use it entirely for the public good?' (Nehru, 2004, p.545). Such a benevolent 'superman' can only be imagined, but, 'there are only frail human beings who cannot help thinking that their own personal good or the advancement of their own ideas is identical with the public good. The snobbery of birth, position, and economic power is perpetuated, and consequences in many ways are disastrous' (Nehru, 2004, p.546).

The basic concern of Nehru was, therefore, the process of change, to clearly envisage the objective by recognizing the social, economic and political necessities. The emphasis that Gandhian philosophy laid on changing the people's heart instead of the economic relations of domination and exploitation was the true religious attitude to the life and problems, and 'it has nothing to do with politics or economics or sociology' (Nehru, 2004, p.553). It was responsibility of the leaders and thinkers to envisage and state the objective to convert the people to their way of thinking and to develop the necessary ideology (Nehru, 2004, p.546).

Therefore, the ideology that Nehru attempted to reconstruct at the given historical juncture of the nationalist movement was the ideology of a sovereign nation state projecting the apparatus of rule as the vehicle of socio-economic progress. Essentially it reinforced a structure of government in the form of parliamentary democracy to make the State a neutral political entity above the interest of class domination, and to resolve the inherent contradiction between democracy that laid stress on the power of the many, and capitalism, which gave real power to the few.

The blueprint of such a State, however, demanded legitimacy of coercion and violence. The notion of non-violence embedded in human thought as individual religious affairs, which had never been applied as a method of resolving large social problems and changing conditions, was brought by Gandhi to the realm of nationalism. As it was in the harmony with Indian thought, people accepted it, and consequently, it changed millions of people in the country by giving them character, strength and self-reliance. These contributed immensely to the growth of nationalism in 1920s. However, to Nehru, the non-violent method would not carry the struggle to its final goal:

> "We looked at the non-violent method fifteen years ago because it promised to take us to our goal in the most desirable and effective way. The goal was then apart from non-violence; it was not a mere appendage or outcome of it. No one could have said then that freedom or independence must only be aimed at if they are attainable by non-violent means. But now our goal itself is judged in terms of non-violence and rejected if it does not seem to fit in with it. The idea of non-violence is thus becoming an inflexible dogma, which may not be challenged. As such it is losing its spiritual appeal to the intellect, and taking its place in the pigeon-holes of faith and religion. It is even becoming a sheet-anchor for vested interests, who exploit it to maintain the *status quo*" (Nehru, 2004, p.566).

In the name of non-violence, it was neither desirable nor acceptable to the nationalist movement to submit to the unjust colonial regime based on violence. Change of the hitherto existing social order through spiritual conversion of the individual was not the answer based on any historical or scientific analysis of the social realities. Any attempt to convert a privileged class to give up its unjust privileges would definitely fail. Therefore, some amount of coercion would be required on the part of a modern State to bring about a just social order through proper planning. Without violence and force of the modern State apparatus, the privileged classes would refuse to give up the privileges given to them by the colonial regime. Non-violent method to achieve the desired goal would imply an attempt to camouflage the class contradictions, and therefore, suppression of the truth to legitimize special privileges of the exploiting classes. Therefore, to ensure India a modern social system based on planned economy as well as to make it capable of protecting itself, the modern state must be allowed to apply some amount of violence and coercion. 'Violence itself, though bad, cannot be considered intrinsically immoral. There are shades and grades of it and often it may be preferable to something that is worse' (Nehru, 2004, p.557).

Besides the basic concerns for welfare, progress and development, Nehru also attempted to provide a liberal democratic premise on which individual civil rights would be established to ensure legal protection and full growth of citizenship. For instance, while addressing the question of communalism, which deeply influenced Indian nationalism, Nehru's simple answer was legal guarantee of equal rights of citizenship to all irrespective of religious or other socio-cultural differences of the communities. The prerequisite, however, was elimination of the oppressive, exploiting and divisive colonial regime. Nehru in mid 1930s, therefore, essentially attempted to reconstruct an ideology of a nation state of India embracing the entire people, to give every one equal right of citizenship, irrespective of sex, religion, caste, class or language.

While reiterating his ideological position throughout his writings and speeches in 1930s, Nehru also quite often referred to socialism, which to him symbolized a 'new civilization' and could be a better alternative to parliamentary democracy before the nation. Seemingly, he was convinced that socialism could provide answer to the world's as well as India's problems, and socialism was not to be perceived in vague humanitarian way but in the scientific, economic sense. 'I work for India's independence because the nationalist in me cannot tolerate alien domination;.... I should like the Congress to become a socialist organization and to join hands with other forces in the world who are working for the new civilization' (Nehru, 1936).

However, Nehru was also equally conscious about the class composition and character of the Congress, which would not go thus far. The Congress leadership, in Nehru's understanding, was a middle class leadership. 'Being too much tied up with property and the goods of this world, it is fearful of losing them, and it is easier to bring pressure on it and to exhaust its stamina' (Nehru, 1936). Yet, the Congress was a nationalist organization, and it thought and worked on the nationalist plane. 'Much as I think for the advancement of socialism in this country', said the pragmatic nationalist leader, 'I have no desire to force the issue in the Congress and thereby create difficulties in the way of our struggle for independence. I shall cooperate gladly and will all the strength in me with all those who work for independence even though they do not agree with the socialist solution' (Nehru, 1936). Nehru, therefore, preferred to push his socialist agenda to the back seat to be taken up by an independent nation state. At the same time, however, he frequently made the slogan of scientific socialism, even at the cost of annoying some of his close colleagues in the course of the nationalist movement. It was essentially to keep intact the support base of the mass of peasantry to the nationalist movement.

PROVINCIAL GOVERNMENT AND PLANNING

With the reconstructed ideology, the Congress took a definite position to gear up the struggle for a democratic state by utilizing whatever limited opportunities could be effectively utilized through the legislatures. Though the immediate objective of the anti-imperialist struggle was not socialism, it was expected that the attempts to reconstruct India after independence through a planned economy would inevitably lead to socialism. The struggle for a democratic State, notwithstanding, the Government of India Act of 1935 was characterized as a 'charter of bondage' and the Congress started preparing itself to go for the elections under the provisions of that Act. Although the basic purpose of going to the legislatures was not to pursue the path of constitutionalism or a barren reformism, the Congress wanted to avail the opportunities with a dual purpose – to carry on the struggle for independence and also to carry through the legislatures' constructive measures of reform.

The Congress leaders such as Nehru made all possible efforts to reach the masses with the reconstructed ideology of nationalism before the elections.[1] And owing to their rigorous efforts, the Congress was successful in the elections in 1937 to win a clear majority in five out of eleven provinces and emerged as the single largest party in another four provinces while it had a minority position in the remaining two provinces.[2]However, until it received a vague assurance from the colonial regime that there would be no interference from the Governor or Viceroy, the Congress was hesitant to accept the responsibility of provincial governments. Ultimately in July 1937, the Congress decided to form provincial governments in eight out of eleven provinces, to work within the framework of provincial autonomy, however limited and restricted, to get the maximum political benefit out of it. Being dominated by rural representatives, the provincial governments under the Congress leadership had to address some of the fundamental issues such as land reform, rural development, education, local-self government etc., but inevitably they failed to achieve anything worth considering.

The initial experiment with provincial autonomy within the colonial structure came to an end in 1939 without having much economic significance, but more importantly, the initiatives that the Congress took through the provincial governments within the short period made the nationalist movement confident about its capabilities of running a State. At the same time, the failure of the provincial governments reinforced the ideology of a sovereign nation state. Without political independence, it would be futile to make any attempt for progress and development, because the major obstacle before progress and development in India was the political and economic structure imposed by colonialism. This reconstructed ideology of nation state continued to guide the political movement for independence till it achieved the final goal.

Soon after the formation of the Provincial governments, the Congress Working Committee at its meeting in Wardha in August 1937 adopted a resolution recommending to the Congress ministers 'the appointment of a committee of experts to consider urgent and vital problems, the solution of which is necessary to any scheme of national reconstruction and social planning. Such solution will require extensive surveys and the collection of data, as well as a clearly defined social objective. Many of these problems cannot be dealt with effectively on a provincial basis, and the interests of adjoining provinces are interlinked.... The Working Committee advises therefore that, to begin with, an inter-provisional committee of experts be appointed to consider the general nature of the problems to be faced, and to suggest how, and in what order, those should be tackled' (Nehru, 2004, p.411). In the context of formation of the Congress ministries in six (later eight) provinces under the new constitutional arrangements, this resolution was significant as it witnessed the importance attached by the Congress Working Committee to state planning as an instrument of resolving the basic issues before the Congress ministries in the provinces. The 'left intelligentsia' within the Congress also sought to resolve the nagging ideological questions regarding industrialization raised especially by the Gandhians, and decide the responsibilities of the Provincial ministries in regulating the growth of a modern industrial sector in the country within the framework of an 'all India industrial plan.' In his presidential address at the Haripura Congress in February 1938, Subhas Chandra Bose emphasized on the formation of a Planning Commission to advice a comprehensive scheme for socializing the entire agricultural and industrial system in the sphere of both production and appropriation. Accordingly, in October 1938 he organized a conference of the Ministers of Industries of the Provincial governments and announced the formation of a National Planning Committee (NPC) comprising fifteen members including Jawaharlal Nehru as the chairman. The Committee included four leading financiers and industrialists, five scientists, three economists, and three leading political leaders including Nehru. The Committee also included the representatives of the provincial governments and other Indian states, which were willing to collaborate, and it enjoyed cooperation from the non-Congress provincial governments (Bengal, Punjab and Sind) and some of the major states (Hyderabad, Mysore, Baroda, Travancore, Bhopal); and began its work in December that year.

The Congress at this stage of the nationalist movement was absolutely clear that the planning for introducing fundamental changes in the social and economic structure through the provincial governments would be futile under the colonial regime. Nevertheless, the Congress initiated the process as an integral component of the state policy not much for the present but for the future, which was not a distant one, and meanwhile indicating to provincial governments and states the lines on which they should proceed and develop their resources (Nehru, 2004, p.436). The basic objective of constituting the NPC including the experts in different fields and political leaders with different ideologies was, however, to project industrialization as the answer to the questions of poverty and unemployment, national defence and economic regeneration without ignoring the importance of the agricultural sector and social services.

The NPC could not continue with the exercise of planning for more than a year and a half due to the outbreak of the war and resignation of the Congress ministries in the provinces nor could it bring about any significant change in the economy of the provinces under the colonial regime. But, it had been instrumental in resolving the ideological discourse within the Congress—between Gandhi and his followers and the Congress left intelligentsia—on the question of industrialization. It was firmly established that industrialization would be the prerequisite for socio-economic development and national reconstruction. The NPC proved Gandhi's ideological position politically as well as economically unsuitable for progress and development of an independent nation. And at the same time, it had made the economic critique of colonialism creating and perpetuating socio-economic backwardness of India central to the nationalist discourse.

CONSTITUENT ASSEMBLY AND PANCHAYAT

The demand for a constituent assembly elected on the basis of adult franchise became an important part of the nationalist movement in 1934.[3] With the nation state ideology, the Congress in all its subsequent congresses till the Shimla Conference in 1945 reiterated that India would accept a constitution only if it is framed 'without any interference by a foreign authority.' Finally in December 1946, a constituent assembly which 'derived from the people.... all the powers and authority' became a reality, and with the partition and independence, it came under exclusive domination of the Congress. Including all the prominent personalities who led the Congress at least for a decade and a half, more than eighty per cent of the members of the Constituent Assembly belonged to the Congress.[4] In addition, on recommendation of the Congress Working Committee, the Provincial Congress Committees also elected to the Constituent Assembly some persons, who were formally not part of the Congress but had exceptional ability, so that their talents in administration, law and experiences in national affairs would be available to the Assembly. This category of members included among others A.K. Ayyar, N.G. Ayyanger, Dr. Ambedkar, [5] K. Santhanam, Sachchidananda Sinha and K.M. Munsshi. Although indirectly elected, and therefore, not responsible to the mass of Indians, the Constituent Assembly was representative of India and its internal decision-making processes were democratic (Austin, 1966).

Nevertheless, witnessing almost complete ideological domination of the Congress, in 1949, fourteen out of the eighteen members of the Congress Working Committee were active in the Constituent Assembly. Among them, the most notable were the four Congress chiefs, Jawaharlal Nehru, Vallabhbhai Patel, Maulana Azad, and Rajendra Prasad, who also held important positions in the Union Government besides the party. Nehru was the Prime Minister, Patel was the Deputy Prime Minister, and Azad was the Minister of Education. Prasad was Congress President in 1948, and the Minister of Food and Agriculture, until he gave up his portfolio because it conflicted with his duties as President of the Constituent Assembly. The Constituent Assembly worked through several committees, of which, eight were major committees – Rules, Steering, Advisory, Drafting, Union Subjects, Union Constitution, Provincial Constitution, and States – with a total membership of about three dozen. Except for the Drafting Committee, either Nehru, Patel, or Prasad chaired each of these committees. And in many cases, all of them were present. These four top Congress leaders with seven other members of the Constituent Assembly constituted an inner circle in the Assembly's committee system, demonstrating an interlocking of the Congress, the Union Government and the Constituent Assembly. A brief account of the members of this inner circle is shown in Annexure – 1.

The circumstances in which India gained independence and the Constituent Assembly initiated the process of framing the constitution for a nation state were, however, extremely complex as well as ambivalent, both globally and nationally. The years preceding India's independence, since the breakout of the World War II in 1939 experienced unprecedented turmoil, traumas of Nazism and Fascism and communist expansion in the West. In the national scenario, India experienced the worst form of human carnages based on religious bigotry and sheer inhumanity, which resulted in the country's vivisection. And therefore, it was a time when both India and the world as a whole, were trying to come out of the trauma and preparing for a better future with new ideas as the political processes unfolded. This included the triumph of liberal democracies and the Keynesian model in the form of the Welfare State. Almost as powerful as the appeal of democracy and democratic institutions were two other ideological pedigrees, one of 'development' and the role of the state in taking it forward through a pursuit of modernization and social uplift based on liberation from antecedent inequities, and the other of secularism suited to a multi-religious and highly plural social order, which had gone through a frightening experience just prior to independence (Kothari, 1998).

Imagining a modern nation state with liberal democracy, universal suffrage, democratic decision making and modern citizenship as its key institutions, (Austin,1999) the Constitution Assembly began its work, drawing the spirit from the Objectives Resolution moved by Nehru and adopted by its first session in December 1946. The resolution declared that there should be 'secured to all the people.... justice, social, economic and political; equality of all status, of opportunity, and before the laws; freedom of thought, expression, belief, faith, worship, vocation, association and action, subject to law and public morality'. The resolution also called for adequate safeguards for minorities, depressed and 'backward' classes, and underdeveloped and tribal areas (Constituent Assembly Debates [hereafter CAD], Vol.1, no.5, p.59). With such an ethos, the Constituent Assembly assigned itself the task, in Nehru's words, 'to free India through a new constitution to feed the starving people and clothe the naked masses and to give every Indian fullest opportunity to develop himself according to his capacity' (CAD, Vol. II p. 316). Through the Constitution, Radhakrishnan wanted to aim at 'revolutionary changes' through peaceful methods, and hence he wished to design the Constitution 'to bring about a fundamental alteration in the structure of Indian society' (CAD, Vol.II, p.269). Prasad assured the nation that the Constituent Assembly would 'endeavour to end poverty and squalor and its companions, hunger and disease; to abolish distinction and exploitation and to ensure decent condition of living' (CAD, Vol. V, p.2).

The principal issue before the Constituent Assembly, therefore, was to determine the form of the political institutions in the nation state, which could inevitably ensure fundamental changes in the structure of Indian society without excluding its economy. The basic questions intrinsic to this issue were regarding the constitutional pattern and political tradition to be followed while framing the Constitution of a newly emerged democratic nation state to fulfill all the aspirations of the people after the prolonged struggle for independence.

The choices before the Constituent assembly were, however, not many. Given the class composition and ideology of the Congress as indicated earlier, the socialist constitutionalism as demonstrated by the U.S.S.R would be an unacceptable proposition. And, to follow the Euro-American constitutional tradition would in all probability, mean continuing in the direction, India had taken during the colonial period (Austin, 1966). As an alternative to both socialist and capitalist frameworks, and to make the Constitution of India effective for a fundamental social change, one of the options before the Constituent Assembly was to depend on the strong heritage of the nation and its indigenous institutions. This would, however, most likely result in establishment of a highly decentralized system of governance based on panchayats as envisaged by Gandhi.

However, the notion of the self-sufficient village republic governed by a panchayat, constructed by Gandhi essentially as the means to reach the 'state of enlightened anarchy' or *Ramarajya,* or in other words, the utopian patriarchy, was undoubtedly contrary to the ethos of the Constituent Assembly, which envisaged a modern democratic nation state of India. Yet, some of Gandhi's followers attempted to systematize his views on the government by commending to the Constituent Assembly, the suggestions Gandhi made to revise the Congress Constitution in January 1948. The suggestions that Gandhi presented on the day of his assassination, would disband the Congress.

> "Though split into two, India having attained political independence through means devised by the Indian National Congress, the Congress in its present shape and form i.e. as a propaganda vehicle and parliamentary machine, has outlived its use.... For these and other similar reasons, the A.I.C.C. resolves to disband the existing Congress organization and flower into a Lok Sevak Sangh...."(CWMG Vol.90 pp.526-527).

For the suggested Lok Sevak Sangh, in Gandhi's plan, every panchayat of five adult men or women would form a unit, and two such contiguous panchayats would form a working party under a leader elected from among themselves. When there would be one hundred such panchayats, the fifty first-grade leaders would elect from among themselves a second-grade leader. The second-grade leaders shall serve jointly for the whole of India and severally for their respective areas. The second-grade leaders may elect, if they feel necessary, a chief, who would regulate and command all the groups.

Such suggestions made by Gandhi were not acceptable to the Congress Working Committee as it was felt that the Congress could neither forego its political responsibilities nor become so highly decentralized. However, the new constitution of the Congress for the first time established 'Primary Congress Panchayats in a village or group of villages' as the basic organizational unit of the party without much decentralization of power. The central high command of the party maintained its complete control over the party.

Rebutting the argument that the Congress should be dissolved, the Congress made its position clear in a party circular that, '... if India's destiny is to be fulfilled and it is to take its proper place in the comity of nations, then its unity is essential, and there is no other organization more fitted for this difficult task than the Congress....'(Austin, 1966). To Assembly members, the consequential question clearly was: If the nation needed a centrally controlled mass party, did it not also need a centralized constitution?

Borrowing freely and modifying when considered necessary the provisions of British and American constitutions and the Government of India Act, 1935, the Constituent Assembly decided to frame the Constitution of India to provide a strong foundation for a centralized parliamentary system without taking cognizance of the indigenous institutions of local self-government. This was explicit from the very beginning, and more so in the course of the debate in the Assembly. This tendency was, however, backed strongly by the Congress Working Committee through the Expert Committee on Constituent Assembly set up in 1946 with Nehru as its Chairman. The Expert Committee, which was constituted by the Congress Working Committee with the purpose of preparing materials for the Assembly, rejected the Gandhian notion of decentralization, and recommended a loose federation for India (Austin, 1966). In the first session of the Constituent Assembly, which began in December 1946, Nehru moved the Objectives Resolution. The Resolution which was apparently drafted by Nehru himself was discussed by the Expert Committee and approved by the Congress Working Committee and it proclaimed India as an 'Independent Sovereign Republic'. According to this resolution:

> "... the territories that now comprise British India, the territories that now form the Indian States, and such other parts of India as are outside British India and the States as well as such other territories as are willing to be continued into the Independent Sovereign India, shall be a Union of them all; and.... shall possess and retain the status of autonomous Units, together with residuary powers, and exercise all powers and functions of government and administration, save and except such powers and functions as are vested in or assigned to the Union, or as are inherent or implied in the Union or resulting there from...." (CAD, Vol. I, p.59).

The Objectives Resolution neither talked about panchayat nor pointed out any mechanism of decentralization below the level of a state. Taking part in the debates on the resolution, the members of the Constituent Assembly emphasized on democracy, socialism etc., but remained conspicuously silent on the omission of panchayat or any other suitable mechanism of democratic decentralization below the level of a state.

In its fourth and fifth sessions in July and August 1947, the Constituent Assembly debated extensively on the two crucial reports of the Union and Provincial Constitution

Committees. These two important committees were constituted by the Constituent Assembly to discuss the principles on which the Constitution of India should be based on, and to prepare model Constitutions, one for the Union and the other for the provinces. The reports of both the committees neither referred to the indigenous institutions of local self-government nor contained anything, which was essentially Gandhian. The issue of decentralization was discussed in the context of Euro-American constitutionalism, essentially over the issue of unitary versus federal government. Taking part in the debates, the members of the Constitutional assembly too, except for a few, never raised the issue of panchayat or the Gandhian principles of decentralization. Only Narayan Singh, a Gandhian from Bihar, expressed his desire that 'the primary units of government should be established in villages. The greatest measure of power should vest, in village republics and then in provinces and then in the Centre'. Singh added, 'unfortunately we have not as yet got village republics' (CAD, Vol.V, p.88). However, this mild Gandhian voice was completely ignored by the Assembly.

After extensive debates on the basic principles of the Constitution of India formulated by the committees, the Constituent Assembly approved them and handed over to its Drafting Committee appointed on 29August, 1947 and to the Constitutional Adviser. Accordingly, the Drafting Committee prepared the Draft Constitution, which contained 315 Articles and eight Schedules, but categorically denied any space for panchayats or 'village republics'. The Draft Constitution was before the public for eight months enabling the members of the Constituent Assembly as well as the people at large to contemplate on the provisions contained in it and express reaction. The President of the Constituent Assembly, Prasad noted the omission of panchayat in the Draft Constitution, and on 10 May 1948 wrote to the Constitutional Adviser,

B.N. Rau that he liked the idea 'of making the Constitution begin with the village and go up to the Centre'; the village 'has been and will ever continue to be our unit in this country'. Prasad believed that the necessary articles could be redrafted, whilst leaving the provincial and central government structure more or less as they were. This 'will put the whole thing in the right perspective,' Prasad wrote, and he added, 'I strongly advocate the idea of utilizing the adult franchise only for the village panchayat and making the village panchayats the electoral college for electing representatives to the provinces and the Centre' (Austin, 1966). However, Rau rejected the suggestions made by Prasad. Many other members of the Constituent Assembly also submitted amendments to the Draft Constitution favouring panchayats as a form of local-self government, instrument of strengthening democracy and village uplift. M.A. Ayyangar and N.C. Ranga wanted that 'The state shall establish self-governing panchayats for every village or a group of villages with adequate powers and funds to give training to rural people in democracy and to pave the way for effective decentralization of political and economic power' (Austin, 1966). These amendments were, however, neither in favour of a Gandhian Constitution nor against the centralized parliamentary system as formulated in the Draft Constitution. Essentially, the amendments were proposed to ensure a mechanism of decentralization below the level of the provincial government.

The Draft Constitution was introduced in the Assembly session on 4 November, 1948 where Ambedkar pointed out the basic criticisms against the Draft Constitution, one of which was that, no part of it represented the ancient polity of India, and instead of incorporating Western theories, the new Constitution should have been raised and built upon village and district panchayats. Justifying the position of the Drafting Committee, Ambedkar stated 'I hold that these village republics have been the ruination of India. I am therefore, surprised that those who condemn Provincialism and Communalism should come forward as champions of the village. What is the village but a sink of localism, a den of ignorance, narrow-mindedness and communalism? I am glad that the Draft Constitution has discarded the village and adopted the individual as its unit' (CAD,Vol. VII, p.39).

The statement made by Ambedkar had obviously generated deep-seated resentment and evoked severe criticism. Criticizing Ambedkar, many of the members emphasized on incorporation of panchayat in the Constitution. Damodar Swarup Seth believed that 'it was because of the villages and because of their might that India became free' and the Constitution of independent India should be based on local self-government (CAD, Vol. VII, p.212). For the omission of panchayat in the Draft Constitution, H.V. Kamath argued, 'the fault lies with the composition of the Drafting Committee, among the members of which no one, with the sole exception of Sriyut Munshi, has taken any active part in the struggle for our country's freedom. None of them is therefore capable of entering into the spirit of our struggle, the spirit that animated us; they cannot comprehend with their hearts .... the turmoiled birth of our nation after years of travail and tribulation'(CAD, Vol.VII, p.219). Pointing out the importance of the village panchayat, Arun Chandra Guha argued 'We have been in the Congress for years. We have been taught to think of the village panchayats as the future basis of administrative machinery. The Gandhian and the Congress outlook has been that the future constitution of India would be a pyramidal structure and its basis would be the village panchayats'. He added, 'I admit we require a strong Centre; but that does not mean that its limbs should be weak... if we can build the whole structure on the village panchayats, on the willing co-operation of the people, then I feel the Centre would automatically become strong' (CAD,

Vol.VII, p.256). Similarly, mainly on the ideological ground, and also acknowledging the contribution of the villages to India's independence, T. Prakasam (CAD,Vol.VII, pp.258-259), Shibban Lal Saksena (CAD,Vol.VII, p.285), Gokulbhai Daulatram Bhatt (CAD, Vol. VII, p.316), and Mahavir Tyagi (CAD, Vol. VII, p.362), strongly argued for incorporation of village panchayat in the constitution.

M.A. Ayyangar too, favoured the establishment and development of panchayat, and he argued, 'let to myself, I would like very much that this Constitution must be based upon autonomous village republics'. 'Democracy is not worth anything' he believed, 'if once in blue moon individuals are brought together for one common purpose, merely electing X, Y and Z to this Assembly or that Assembly and thereafter disperse' (CAD,Vol. VII, p.352). However, Ayyangar also pointed out that colonialism had totally destroyed decentralized economy and village republics that India had in the past, and therefore, the task before the nation would be to reconstruct such institutions to make democratic processes effective. Therefore, he did not support the opinion that the Constitution should immediately be based on village republics, instead he felt, that ought to be the objective before the nation. The panchayats were yet to be brought into existence. In the given context, he believed, 'we cannot have a better Constitution than the one that has been placed before us on the model of some Western Constitutions. Therefore, I would advise, that in the directives, a clause must be added, which would insist upon the various Governments that may come into existence in future, to establish Village Panchayats, give them political autonomy and also economic independence in their own way to manage their own affairs. Later on, a time will come when on the basis of these republics or autonomous panchayats a future Constitution may be built' (CAD, Vol.VII, pp.352-353).

Referring to the efforts made by the Mysore Government for more than three decades preceding independence to revive the village panchayats, and also in the light of his own experiences, N. Madhava Rau too argued in favour of the establishment and development of panchayats to uplift the villages. And, he found that there was nothing in the Draft Constitution, which could prevent provincial governments from developing the village panchayat system 'as vigorously and as rapidly as they are capable of doing' (CAD, Vol.VII, p.386).

The long debate over the issue of creating the required space for the panchayat in the Draft Constitution, often accompanied by emotional and romantic characterization of the village scenario, besides many realistic administrative considerations, had come to an end when K. Santhanam staged the amendment:

That after article 31, the following new article be added:

"31-A. The State shall take steps to organize village panchayats and endow them with such powers and authority as may be necessary to enable them to function as units of self-government" (CAD, Vol. VII, p. 520).

Justifying his position, Santhanam provided reason for his outright opposition to the similar amendments moved by many other members of the Constituent Assembly to make village panchayats a part of the Draft Constitution, because they had also attached conditions like self-sufficiency and other matters. In his view, such conditions were not desirable to be put into the directives. On the question of powers and functions of the panchayat, he believed that it was not desirable to specify any hard and fast direction in the Constitution, and this question should be left to the provincial legislatures. 'That the entire structure of self-government, of independence in this country should be based on organized village community life is the common factor of all the amendments tabled and that factor has been made the principle basis of this amendment' (CAD, Vol.VII, p.520). Ambedkar, the Chairman of the Drafting Committee immediately accepted the amendment and many other members, who strongly advocated for panchayat, enthusiastically welcomed it. Consequently, the panchayats were relegated to the Directive Principles to survive at the mercy of the provincial legislatures, and the Gandhian principles of decentralization and indirect election died a natural death.

SUMMING UP

The 'left intelligentsia' within the Congress accepted Gandhi's unparalleled contribution to the nationalist movement in its early phase making the Congress a broad political platform providing political space for different segments of the Indian society irrespective of their class position. Drawing its political legitimacy from all sections of the people, the Congress under the leadership of Gandhi, with all his utopian constructions and imagination of independence, emerged as the most effective nationalist movement for swaraj. However, the 'left intelligentsia' started questioning the utopianism that constituted the core of Gandhian philosophy as well as the political strategy of class alliance for swaraj, when the nationalist movement reached its more mature stage in the 1930s, and demanded a more realistic political objective to approach independence. In that crucial historical juncture, essentially, the task before the 'left intelligentsia' under the leadership of Nehru was to redefine the primary objective of nationalism. It necessitated reconstruction of the nationalist ideology to legitimize a sovereign nation state rejecting the Gandhian utopia of 'enlightened anarchy'. Most of the Gandhian notions were contested with alternative ideological formulations and imagination of a nation state. Gandhian thought, thus appeared to be 'utterly wrong and harmful doctrine' and 'impossible of achievement' before the much more 'realistic scientific and modern' ideological formulations. All these were to politically legitimize the imagination of a nation state as a neutral autonomous political entity, which could be the most effective engine of socio-economic development and post-colonial reconstruction.

To provide a solid political base and consolidation of the reconstructed ideology of Indian nationalism, the Congress leadership, despite steep opposition from Gandhi, decided to enter the provincial legislatures in 1937, a mechanism that was devised by the Government of India Act of 1935, and once characterized by the Congress as a 'charter of bondage'. Although the purpose was not to follow the path of constitutionalism or barren reformism, the Congress leadership after forming the provincial legislatures contemplated national planning, essentially to resolve the nagging ideological questions regarding industrialization raised by Gandhi. The National Planning Committee (NPC), with Nehru as its chairman, came into being in 1938, though the Congress was absolutely clear that plans for introducing fundamental changes in the social and economic structure of India through the provincial legislatures would be futile under the colonial regime. But, through the NPC, as it was expected, the Congress under the leadership of Nehru was particularly successful in projecting industrialization as the answer to most of the fundamental problems that the independent nation state would confront. The experiences of both provincial legislatures and planning helped the national leadership to consolidate and politically legitimize the nation state ideology.

With the consolidated ideology of a nation state, the Congress leadership that led the nationalist movement in the difficult years during and after the World War II, the period in which the whole world prepared for a transition with the hope of a better future, consistently demanded for a constituent assembly to frame the Constitution of independent India 'without any interference by foreign authority'. Finally, the Constituent Assembly came into being, and it apparently 'derived from the people ...... all the powers and authority' to frame the Constitution. And, it started functioning under exclusive domination, both numerical and ideological, of the Congress Working Committee. Most of the members of the Assembly who led the Congress at the national and regional level, and also the other influential members who were elected under Congress nomination, were obviously the people who strongly believed in the nation state ideology. Therefore, the collective ethos of the Constituent Assembly was to provide a strong foundation for a centralized parliamentary system following the Euro-American constitutional traditions without taking cognizance of the indigenous institutions of local-self government. The Draft Constitution that was placed before the Constituent Assembly by Ambedkar, the Chairman of the Drafting Committee, therefore, totally ignored the institution of panchayat, despite several suggestions from the members to incorporate it in the Draft Constitution.

In the subsequent debates, the arguments, which came strongly in favour of the panchayats had, however, did not reflect any sense of rejection of the basic principles of the Draft Constitution in support of the Gandhian notion of decentralization. All the pro-panchayat members in the assembly accepted the basic premise of a centralized parliamentary system, but what they had emphasized upon was to make panchayat a part of the system to ensure decentralization below the level of the provincial governments. Essentially, they projected panchayat as the means to ensure decentralized administration primarily to uplift the villages, both socially and economically, and to train the rural mass the essence of democracy. The Gandhian philosophy was not at all contemplated, and therefore, almost all the members of the Constitutional Assembly could wholeheartedly welcome the official amendment of the Congress moved by Santhanam, on the basis of which the institution of panchayat was relegated by the Constitution to the Directive Principles and to survive at the mercy of the provincial legislatures.

NOTES:

1. During about four months of election campaigns, Nehru traveled about fifty thousand miles all over the country including remote rural areas, and addressed a dozen of meetings a day. On his rough estimate, about ten million persons actually attended the meetings he addressed and probably several million more were brought into some kind of touch during his journeying by road. Jawaharlal Nehru, *An Auto Biography*, Penguin Books, New Delhi, 2004, p. 625
2. Congress won clear majority in Madras, United provinces, Central Provinces, Bihar and Orissa; it emerged as the single largest party in Bombay, Bengal, Assam and the North Western Frontier Province; and had minority position in Sind and Punjab.
3. Gandhi in 1922 made an indirect but definite reference to a Constituent Assembly while he wrote, ' Swaraj will not be a free gift of the British Parliament. It will be a declaration of India's full self- expression, expressed through an Act of Parliament. But it will be merely a courteous ratification of the declared wish of the people of India. The ratification will be a treaty to which Britain will be a party. The British Parliament, when the statement comes, will ratify the wishes of the people of India as expressed through the freely chosen representatives'. This demand of Gandhi was affirmed, from time to time, by various public bodies and political leaders, but in May 1934, the Swaraj party made an explicit demand for a Constituent assembly by passing a resolution claiming for India 'the right of self-determination, and the only method of applying that principle is to convene a Constituent assembly, representative of all sections of the Indian people, to frame an acceptable Constitution'. The policy embodied in this resolution was approved by the All India Congress Committee, in May 1934. *Constituent Assembly Debates,* Vol.I, pp. 5-6

4. The Constituent Assembly that emerged in 1946 had six past or present Congress Presidents, and fourteen Provincial Congress Committee Presidents.
5. Ambedkar was originally elected to the Assembly as a member of the Scheduled Castes Federation, but he lost his seat with the partition of Bengal. The Bombay Congress re-elected him at the request of the Congress high command. G. Austin, *The Indian Constitution: Cornerstone of a Nation*, Oxford University Press, New Delhi, 1966.

4

EXPERIMENTS WITH PANCHAYATI RAJ AFTER INDEPENDENCE

During the five decades that followed independence, the Indian State has grappled with poverty, hunger and malnutrition in the rural areas caused primarily by the precarious semi-feudal relations in the agrarian sector. Several experiments have been made to eradicate poverty, to generate self-esteem in rural life, and also to ensure participation of the people in the welfare projects. The driving force, however, has always been the centralized bureaucratic structure, which bypassed the institutions of panchayats initially established by the state legislatures following the Directive Principle of the Indian Constitution, and which were subsequently modified in accordance with the recommendations of different expert committees. The overall rural scenario, however, has remained unchanged. The renewed concern of the State for strengthening the process of democratic decentralization has been offered by the Seventy-third amendment, which provided space for the panchayats in the Constitution that was denied at the time of its promulgation. This chapter attempts to review the process that led to the widely concerned constitutional amendment.

POLITICO-ECONOMIC BACKDROP

With independence, India inherited from the colonial regime, a social structure marked by lop-sided and unbalanced position of agriculture in the national economy, mass ruination of artisans, over-pressure on land, increasing diminution in the size of holdings and fragmentation of land leading to the alarming increase of uneconomic holdings. The other features of such a socio-economic scenario comprised of low yields, rise of massive indebtedness of the peasant population, extending grip of money lenders, traders, landlords and substantial farmers over poor peasantry, steady passing of land from cultivators to creditors with the resultant growth of absentee landlordism and rise in the number of landless labourers (Joshi, 1969). For almost five decades prior to independence, agriculture was more or less stagnant with an ever-increasing burden of population on it. At the time of independence, nearly 73 per cent of the total population in the country had to depend on agriculture for livelihood. During the same period, population in the country increased by almost 38 per cent, production of food grains remained stationary resulting in food grains deficit of 10 million tons. Nearly 30 per cent of the total population in the country suffered from chronic mal-nutrition and under nutrition (Joshi, 1969).

Looking at the pattern of landownership, an acute land scarcity coexisted with profound inequalities. The land-man ratio in rural India was .92 acre, and about 22 per cent of rural households were landless. Another 25 per cent owned less than one acre. Slightly above this mass of the landless or near-landless stood those who owned between 1 to 2.5 acres, and their numbers constituted about 14 per cent of the rural households. Over 60 per cent of rural India, thus, was landless or owned holdings below 2.5 acres. Taken together, they owned less than 8 per cent of the total cultivable land. In contrast, those owning holdings of more than 10 acres constituted 13 per cent of the total rural households and accounted for 64 per cent of the area. Of these, 5 per cent (of the total) owned 20 acres or more, comprising 41 per cent of the total area. Less than 1 per cent of the rural households had holdings over 50 acres (Varshney, 1995).

The agrarian scenario that emerged in colonial India was essentially the outcome of the colonial rule and its attempts to reorganize the agrarian structure by introducing different types of land tenure systems, which on the one hand promoted semi-feudal land relations, and retarded the agrarian economy on the other. The social and political implications of the colonial agrarian policies manifested themselves in wide spread peasant discontent and organized movements of the peasantry, which significantly influenced the nationalist movement in the country. The U.P. Zamindari Abolition Committee Report (1948) succinctly sums up the agrarian scenario of the country on the eve of independence:

> "Our agrarian system has collapsed. It has become a drag on the development of productive forces in the country.... Landlordism today has reached the state when it cannot be tolerated any longer.... The age-long simmering discontent bursting into acts of open defiance and sometimes of violence in our province and other parts of India has reached a critical state. Whether forbearance and self-restraint we find in the countryside among the tenants is due to the hope that those who are running the State will undo the wrong done to them. Once that hope has gone, the tenant will be driven to desperation. The discontent may develop into revolt and our social security may be threatened by the outbreak of violence.... One can only hope that the entire landed gentry is not blind to the writing on the walls" (Joshi, 1969 p.448).

Though this report did not refer to the series of peasant uprisings throughout the colonial period, including the Tebhaga Movement and the Telengana Movement experienced by the country just before independence, it strongly indicated the possibility of recurrence of such phenomena in the absence of radical agrarian reforms to be initiated by the post colonial State.

Learning from the past, and also reinforcing the essence of a 'social revolution' that occupied a prominent place in the agenda of post-colonial Indian State, the Congress Economic Programme Committee (1947-48) suggested certain major changes in the agrarian structure. The Committee suggested that land should be held for use (as opposed to profit) and as a source of employment. Further, limit should be fixed for the maximum size of holding, and the surplus land over such a maximum should be acquired and placed at the disposal of the village cooperative. This approach was reinforced and further elaborated in the Report of the Congress Agrarian Reforms Committee appointed in December 1947, by the Congress President to examine and make recommendations about agrarian reforms. The Committee submitted a quite radical policy document and its recommendations approximated to a large extent to the objective of 'land to the tiller' and abolition of non-cultivating interests from land (Joshi, 1969).

All such recommendations also reflected the promise that was made by the Congress in its Election Manifesto of 1945, which assured agrarian reforms in the country by removing intermediaries between the peasants and the state. However, the rights of the intermediaries, said the manifesto, be acquired by payment of 'equitable compensation'. Subsequently, many of the state legislatures initiated the process of agrarian reforms. For instance, both Uttar Pradesh and Madhya Pradesh contemplated agrarian reforms through zamindari abolition as early as in 1946. By the end of 1948, different states such as Bihar, Madras and Assam had either introduced or passed Zamindari Abolition Bills or land tenure legislations while Bombay passed land tenure legislation in 1949.

At the same time, the Constituent Assembly was debating on various issues related to fundamental rights of the citizens of independent India to foster the 'social revolution' by making all citizens equally free from coercion or restriction by the State or by the society. Thus, the fundamental rights were not only to include the basic political rights such as equality before the law and freedom of religion, speech, expression, assembly, association, and movement, but also the freedom of property. Along with all other political rights, the zamindars or the landlords must enjoy right to property, the Constitution had nothing to do with their past, the way they acquired their property. Therefore, the Interim Report on Fundamental Rights tabled for discussion in the Constituent Assembly by Patel included in it the clause, which stated:

> "No property, movable or immovable, of any person or corporation including any interest in any commercial or industrial undertaking, shall be taken or acquired for public use unless the law provides for the payment of compensation for the property taken or acquired and specified the principles on which and the manner in which the compensation is to be determined." (CAD, Vol. III, p.511)

The Assembly welcomed the clause to make the right to property a fundamental right, and only a few members opposed the provision of compensation to the zamindars because, it would protect the interests of the microscopic minority of the propertied class and deny right of social justice to the masses. Concluding the debate, Patel stated:

> "This clause here will not become the law tomorrow or the day after; it will take at least a year more, and before that, most of the Zamindaris will be liquidated. Even under the present Acts or laws in the different provinces legislation is being brought in to liquidate Zamindaris either by paying just compensation or adequate compensation or whatever the legislatures

> there think fit. Therefore, it is wrong to think that this clause is intended really for them". (CAD, Vol. III, p. 522)

When the question of right to property once again appeared before the Constituent Assembly during the debate on the Draft Constitution, the Assembly with little debate adopted the right 'to acquire, hold and dispose of property'. However, with the fundamental right to possess property, the debate in the Assembly veered back to the question of justifiable compensation to the zamindars and landlords in case of acquisition of their land and the manner in which the compensation should be paid. Discussing pros and cons of justifiable compensation, the Assembly finally resolved the long debate by making the provision in the Constitution that no property could be acquired for a public purpose unless government paid compensation. The Constitution also guaranteed the right of individuals to challenge such compensation awards in the courts as inadequate or in violation of the right to equal protection of the law (Austin, 2001).

Therefore, in the initial phase of the 'social revolution' with the stated egalitarian goals, when different state legislatures were attempting agrarian reforms especially through abolition of zamindaris and other intermediaries between the state and the tenants, the Constitution made provisions for justifiable compensation to the zamindars and landlords. However, the agrarian reform programmes adopted by different state legislatures ostensibly inspired by egalitarianism also had failed to alter the agrarian structure of India. As Daniel Thorner observed, the small minority of oligarchs could get around these laws in which, in any event, the loopholes were so large as to give them ample maneuvering ground. By passing themselves off, whether legally or illegally, as tillers and cultivators, the village oligarchs continued to run India's rural life (Thorner, 1969).

At the same time, in the years between 1947 and 1950, India had experienced a series of ad hoc economic policies, which were designed to promote private investment. In a situation of overall scarcity, the government decided to remove sugarcane and food grains from control in December 1947, and cotton and cloths were decontrolled in the following month. The rise in prices and profit taking that followed was spectacular. During the period between December 1947 and July 1948, the wholesale price index for food grains rose by almost 58 per cent, and prices of all other consumer goods increased by about one third. Control on cloths and cotton, and also food grains were re-imposed, but in the two years between November 1947 and November 1949, the general price index had increased substantially. The Industrial Policy Resolution declared by the government in April 1948 was clearly in favour of private investment. The Resolution attempted to establish public sector monopoly only over the manufacture of arms and ammunition, atomic energy, and the railways, while it favoured private investment in all other enterprises. The Resolution also assured the business community that no existing enterprises would be nationalized, and new ventures were to be exempted from all possibility of public acquisition for a period of ten years (Frankel, 2005).

Nevertheless, the State had to legitimize its role as the mediator in ameliorating the exploitative rural social order, protector of the marginalized and oppressed communities, an engine of growth and development, and as an autonomous political institution with preponderant powers to design and enforce the policies aimed at postcolonial reconstruction. Although the panchayat was relegated to the Directive Principles of the Constitution, in the euphoria of planned development it was expected that the state legislatures would show earnestness in reviving the institutions of Panchayati Raj. The First Five Year Plan, therefore, emphasized on panchayat as an institution, which would be responsible for collective welfare of the village community including many other activities such as framing programmes for production, obtaining and managing governmental grants for building roads, tanks etc., introducing improvements in agricultural methods, and assisting in the implementation of legislation for economic and social reform. Similarly, the Village Panchayat Committee of the Congress in 1954 expected that the panchayats would provide a sound basis for the establishment of healthy, democratic tradition in the country, and they should 'not only serve as units of local self-Government but also as effective institutions for securing social justice and fostering corporate life, leading to conditions of fuller employment laid down in the Constitution'. Thus the Committee recommended that the 'State should provide scope for the Village Panchayats to perform in the village society, functions such as credit, marketing, supplies, etc. The function of the Panchayats should include municipal, social, economic and judicial activities etc' (Mehta, 1969).

At the same time, with the same objective of reconstruction of the agrarian economy and rural structure, the Government of India inaugurated the Community Development Programme on October 2, 1952. The First Five-Year Plan had described the Community Development Programme as the method through which the Five-Year Plan sought to initiate a process of transformation of the social and economic life of the villages. It therefore, aimed at inculcating in the villagers new desires, new incentives, new techniques, and a new confidence so that the vast reservoir of human resources might be used for the growing economic development of the country.

The Community Development Programme started with 55 Community Projects, each project comprising around 300 villages. A project area was divided into three development Blocks of hundred villages. Each Block was further divided into about 20 groups, each containing five villages, and each group of villages was served by a Gram Sevak. By the end of the First Five-Year Plan, the programme was extended to 603 National Extension Service Blocks, and 553 Community Development Blocks covering a total of 1,57,000 villages inhabited by 88.8 million people, and therefore, nearly one out of three villages in India was brought within the orbit of this programme before the beginning of the Second Five-Year Plan, which proposed to bring every village in India under the programme.

To implement the wide range of activities[1] under the programme, an elaborate administrative structure was created (Community Project Administration) under the Planning Commission. The bureaucratic administrative structure with its well-demarcated hierarchy was composed of the central administration, the state administration, the district administration, and the project administration. The highly bureaucratic administrative apparatus was, however, dominated either by the officers of the British trained Indian Civil Service (ICS) who could retain their privileged position after independence by virtue of seniority, or by the immediate successor Indian Administrative Service (IAS), who retained the structure and style of its colonial forerunners, perpetuating a national administrative system that in numbers and outlook was more suitable to carry out the narrow colonial functions of law and order than the broad responsibility of economic development (Frankel, 2005).

The Community Development Programmes have been evaluated by a good number of scholars as well as policy planners, and the experiences have been summarized. Based on most of such evaluations, Desai observes that the philosophy underlying the programme, (read as development ideology of the State) in the context of the Indian agrarian society, implicitly accepted the following major sociological assumptions: (i) the individuals, sections, groups and strata forming the Village Community have a large number of common interests, sufficiently strong to bind them together; (ii) the interests of the various groups and classes within the village are both sufficiently alike and common to create general enthusiasm as well as a feeling of development for all; (iii) the interests of the different sections of the community are not irreconcilably conflicting; (iv) the State is a super-class, impartial, non-partisan association and that the major policies of the Government are of such a nature that they do not further sharpen the inequalities between the existing social groups; (v) people's initiatives and enthusiasm and active participation are possible in the extent village communities because they have common interests (Desai, 1969).

Most of the evaluation studies, however, pointed out that the Community development programme had essentially benefited the propertied class, and therefore further sharpened the class division in the rural social structure. As Dube pointed out:

> "Although the ideal of the Community Development Projects was to work for the many-sided development of the entire community.... it is clear that significant and best organized activities were confined to the field of agricultural extension and consequently the group of agriculturists benefited the most from them. A closer analysis of the agricultural extension work itself reveals that nearly 70 per cent of the benefits went to the elite group and to the more affluent and influential agriculturists. The gains to the poorer agriculturists were considerably smaller.... For the economic development of this group, as well as for that of the artisans and agricultural labourers, no programmes were initiated by the Project" (Desai, 1969, p. 618).

Similar observations were made by many of the evaluation studies, and Dube clearly pointed out that the

Community Development Programme helped the government to maintain a *status quo* in the internal power relations within the village communities and indirectly to support the domination of the landowning groups. Desai concludes:

> "This reliance on the upper stratum of the village population by the Government has sociological significance which cannot be underestimated.... It implies not merely a hold over the economic resources in that area by small upper class, but also a hold over the political, social and cultural life of the community. It further means that in agrarian area, as a result of the functioning of the community development programmes, a stratum becomes strengthened economically and politically, and utilizes various institutions for its own end. It also means that in agrarian area, the Community Development Projects are creating an institutional and associational matrix wherein the Government buttresses the economically dominant classes, and in their turn, the economically dominant classes strengthen the power of the present rulers of the State. This development has dangerous significance for the all-round development of the rural society and also for the unprivileged strata of the agrarian area, which constitute the bulk of the rural people. It is very unfortunate that the implication of this development tendency in terms of class polarization in agrarian area, and the role of the state as an agency of the upper stratum is not fully appreciated." (Desai, 1969, p. 619)

Pointing out the major shortcomings of the Community Development Programmes, the Study Team on the working of Community Projects and National Extension Service under the auspices of the Committee on Plan Project (came to be known as Balwantrai Mehta Committee) constituted in 1957, made a set of recommendations for strengthening of the Panchayati Raj. One of the major shortcomings of the Community Development Projects and National Extension

Service, as the committee noted, had been the failure of the programmes to generate enthusiasm and involve people in the process of implementation. The Committee observed that each development block had an advisory committee composed of the official and non-official representatives who did not have roots amongst the people on the one hand, and such block level advisory committee neither enjoyed adequate power nor had defined responsibilities on the other. Planning and execution was done by the block staff, the people who were in their own bureaucratic style of function, concerned mainly with timely utilization of fund rather than ethos of the programme. The Committee, in order to generate enthusiasm by ensuring peoples participation in planning and execution recommended that all development programmes under the Block areas should be brought under the institutions composed of elected representatives of people, and the Block staff and other officials should be placed at the disposal of those institutions. Along with this, as the Committee recommended, provisions of necessary funds and sources of revenue should be made for these local institutions to enable them to discharge their responsibilities.

TO MAKE THE BEGINNING: FIRST GENERATION PANCHAYATS

Instead of making panchayats a mere appendage to the development endeavours, the Balwantrai Mehta Committee strongly recommended a Panchayati Raj with a three-tier structure consisteing of directly elected panchayats at the village level, Panchayat Samiti at the Block, and Zila Parishad at the district level to plan and effectively implement the development programmes. The Pachayat Samiti would have a tenure of five years, and its major functions would be development of agriculture, promotion of local industries, improvement of cattle, public health, administration of primary schools etc. Since almost the entire rural development works would come under the purview of the Panchayat Samiti, the Committee also suggested its major resources, which would include, a share of the land revenue collected within the block, tax on professions, surcharge of duty on transfer of immovable property, net proceeds of tools and leases, proceeds from fairs and markets etc. Further, the Panchayat Samiti would be responsible to scrutinize and approve the budgets of the Village Panchayats, as the Committee recommended.

Essentially to ensure coordination of the Panchayat Samitis, the Balvantray Mehta Committee envisaged the Zila Parishad consisting of the Presidents of the Panchayat Samitis, members of the State Legislatures and of the Parliament representing the area, and the district level officers. The chairman of the Zila Parishad would be the Collector, and the Parishad would have the power to examine and approve the budgets of the Panchayat Samitis. It would also generally supervise the activities of the Panchayat Samitis, but it would not be invested with any executive function. Therefore, although the Committee recommended a three-tier Panchayati Raj, in the given context of the development ethos, the Committee had emphasized more on the Panchayat Samitis. Nevertheless, the recommendations of the Committee, which were strongly in favour of democratic decentralization were accepted by the Government of India and consequently, it accelerated the pace of constituting Panchayati Raj Institutions (PRIs) throughout the country.

In response to the Directive Principles of the Constitution (Article 40), different state legislatures initiated the process of 'democratic decentralization', however vague or erroneous it might be, by establishing village panchayats. But, these initiatives were overshadowed by the bureaucratic process of rural development sponsored the State immediately after independence. Witnessing a positive trend, the number of Village Panchayats increased from 83,098 in 1950-51 to

123,670 at the end of March 1956, and then to 164,358 at the end of March 1958 (Mehta, 1969 p. 581).

On January 12, 1958 the National Development Council endorsed the recommendations of the Balvantray Mehta Committee, and Rajasthan was the first state to inaugurate Panchayati Raj on October 2, 1959. By the mid-1960s, Panchayati Raj had reached all parts of the country. More than 217,300 Village Panchayats were established, which covered over 96 per cent of the inhabited villages, and 92 per cent of the rural population of India (Mathew, 2000, p. 6).

The initiatives taken by the states to establish PRIs following recommendations of the Balvantray Mehta Committee generated enormous hope and expectations of the common people. The architects of modern India consciously promoted the initial optimism. Inaugurating Panchayati Raj in Rajasthan, Nehru hailed the system as 'the most revolutionary and historical step in the context of new India'. As Nehru emphasized, democracy at the top would not be a success unless it was built from below. S.K. Dey, Minister for Community Development in Nehru's cabinet elevated the whole idea to a philosophical level and viewed it as an instrument, which linked the individuals with the universe. In the sphere of national democracy he visualized an organic relationship between the gram sabha and the Lok Sabha (Matthew, 2000, p.6).

Nevertheless, the Panchayati Raj that emerged till the mid-1960s, which could be considered as the first generation of PRIs, had failed to reach the people at large. Contrary to the ethos of democratic decentralization, the first generation PRIs mainly promoted a category of corrupt rural leadership comprising especially the landowning class, which could consolidate its position by using the loopholes of the land reform legislations and accruing the benefits of Community Development Programmes and other such development measures taken by the State immediately after independence.

The traditional pattern of domination by the zamindars was replaced by domination of a new landowning class, which emerged as the most powerful and potent force in every sphere of rural life in India. Through the first generation of PRIs, therefore, the Congress successfully organized a group of supporters who could economically, socially and politically influence rural India, (Mehta, 1969) the process, which was essentially a component of the 'Congress System' as it was called by Rajni Kothari (Kothari, 1964; 1988).

Yet, the rural scenario could have been changed to a great extent by holding elections to the PRIs at regular intervals. 'If regular elections were held', as observed by George Mathew, 'permutations and combinations could change, traditional rivalries could disappear and issue-oriented groupings would have emerged. In this process, simple mechanical solidarity gives way to more organic solidarity where individual freedom of opinion and group decisions emerges. It is precisely this process that had been arrested for years by the state governments, by either postponing elections frequently or not holding them at all'. As he points out, 'there was a deliberate plan by the bureaucracy, local vested interests and their elected representatives in the state legislatures and in Parliament to cripple and eventually discard panchayati raj, because its ascendancy was feared' (Mathew, 2000, p. 7).

Alongside the process of consolidation of its support base comprising the rural propertied classes with local influence for political expediency in an electoral democracy, the Congress in power had to forge a political process for mobilizing support for state policy. The large segments of the society should accept a benevolent form of the State, and its role as an independent political actor committed to social transformation. Nehru inaugurated Panchayati Raj in 1959, but the government of India in 1960 launched the Intensive Agricultural District Programme (IADP) bypassing both, the Community Development Programmes and the Panchayati

Raj. Similarly, several other programmes, such as Small Farmers Development Agency (SFDA), Drought Prone Areas Programme (DPAP), and Intensive Tribal Development Programme (ITDP) etc. were also launched beyond the purview of Panchayati Raj. The stated objective of all such programmes was to do away with the maladies of development caused by the strategy of agricultural growth and development embodied in the Green Revolution, which led to regional imbalances and income disparities among the rural population.

In the mid-1960s, the Ministry of Community Development was relegated to the status of a department under the Ministry of Food and Agriculture, and in 1971, the very title, 'Community Development' was dropped and replaced by 'Rural Development'. "This was not just a cosmetic change. It marked the end of both the 'Community' and 'panchayats' as agents of change and agencies of development" as L.C. Jain observes (Jain et.al. 1985, p.44).

The Nehruvian model of development was based on a unique coalition of diverse economic interests, which the Congress represented in the decades after independence. Capitalist development was sought to promote without launching any serious attack on the pre-capitalist property relations in the agrarian structure. The bourgeoisie-landlord coalition that was built on one-party dominance with certain amount of internal flexibility provided political stability for a long period. Nonetheless, it failed to alter the rural power structure on the one hand and to enlist the social support of the rural masses on the other. At the same time, failure on the part of the Congress to politically integrate the people at large with the economic process of development by strengthening the institutions of democratic decentralization in the true sense essentially encouraged a centralized bureaucratic regime that was lacking any sound philosophy of economic as well as social justice. Therefore, the so-called welfare measures and the technological package of rural development designed to apparently benefit the poor had perpetuated inequalities and created a structure of myriad vested interests. As Kothari observes, corruption, centralization and arrogance of central authority, erosion of the party and the rise of a ruling class consisting of rich peasants, feudal lords, an all-pervasive civil service, a sprawling public sector, and a business class presiding over an urban-industrial-mafia power nexus, a lot of these a result of state policies and Nehru's own imported vision about the 'temples of new India', all began before his reign came to an end (Kothari, 1998, pp.28-29).

The 'economic modernization' project launched by Nehru during the 20 years after independence provided an impressive industrial base to the economy. However, its failure to expand the social base of development resulted in raising popular discontent in different parts of the country since the mid-1960s. The mass discontent, which had been triggered off by several development issues such as rising prices, increasing income disparities, food scarcity, and uneven economic development, was mobilized around ideological, linguistic, regional, ethnic and also communal cleavages leading to a series of protest movements in different parts of the country. The linguistic discourse in Madras on the immediate issue of promulgation of Hindi as the official language of the Union, in January 1965, was essentially linked with job opportunities. Despite coercive measures, the government could not restore normalcy until the Centre agreed to continue the use of English along with Hindi as the language of government administration. Uneven economic development coupled with ethno-political aspirations rejuvenated secessionism in the hill areas of Assam. That was partially defused by creation of the separate states of Nagaland in 1963 and Meghalaya in 1967, though the Mizos continued with their struggle for independence. While the

Communist Party of India (CPI) and Communist Party of India (Marxist) [CPI (M)], despite the initial set back caused by the split in 1964, had been successful in mobilizing the working class and peasantry particularly in West Bengal and Kerala with socialist ideology; the Jan Sangh sought to capitalize the social discontent revitalizing the ideology of Hindu communalism.

The regional, ethnic, ideological and communal discourses that reappeared in the political scene of post-colonial India with considerably strong support base, alongside posing a serious threat to the Congress monopoly in the country, contested the development paradigm on the one hand and questioned autonomy of the State on the other. That had been reflected by the striking losses of the Congress in the 1967 elections bringing an end to one-party domination. In the emerging political order, the Congress with its shrinking support base occupied the political center along with the growing challenges to its hegemonic position from the Communists on the left and a conservative and communal alignment of political forces on the right (Frankel 2005). Failure of the Congress to resolve its internal conflicts, which finally resulted in the split of the party in 1969, had more forcefully forged the crisis of political stability in the country. The State apparatus controlled by the bourgeoisie-landlord coalition headed by Indira Gandhi, instead of making a sincere attempt to democratically resolve the politico-economic crisis that emerged in the mid-1960s and aggravated subsequently, resorted to an unprecedented coercive mechanism. Emergency was imposed on June 25, 1975 and had throttled all the democratic institutions, which were developed during the period after independence.

Indira Gandhi's defeat in the 1977 parliamentary elections brought for the first time the non-Congress government at the center headed by the Janata Party, an umbrella organization of different political ideologies. During its short period in power (collapsed in 1980), the Janata government, though never attempted to provide any radical alternative to the Congress regime, sought to address the basic issues of decentralized development focusing on micro-level planning and Panchayati Raj. The report submitted in 1978 by the Working Group on Block Level Planning headed by Dantwala made some crucial observations and recommended certain institutional change. Expressing its reservation about Panchayati Raj, the Working Group observed:

> "Our (second) reservation about the role of the panchayati raj institutions in the formulation of micro-level plans arises from a widely shared view that the worker sections of the rural community do not feel that their interests will be fully protected under the panchayati raj institutions. A stronger version of the feeling is that the leadership of the panchayati raj institutions acts as a 'gate-keeper' and prevents the flow of benefits for the weaker sections of the rural community. This is hardly surprising in the given context of the inegalitarian structure of the rural economy. Unless and until adequate safeguards are provided against the likelihood of the dominance of the panchayati raj institutions by the vested interests, giving them a decisive voice in the preparation of micro-level or grassroots plans, one of its major objectives, namely, removal of poverty, exploitation and unemployment will not have much chance of being realized" (Bhattacharya, 1978).

With such reservation about the existing PRIs, the Working Group emphasized on certain institutional arrangements for safeguarding interests of the rural poor. Considering Block as a unit of planning, it recommended preparation of basic records of land right for effective implementation of the land reform programmes, emphasized on reviving and strengthening the non-farm economy, and the necessity to develop enterprises such as animal husbandry, forestry, horticulture, fisheries, craft and cottage industries etc. The Working Group also emphasized on making available institutional credit for all such economic activities proposing the concept of 'lead branch' and the post of a credit planning officer for coordinating the activities at the block level. The Working Group, therefore, was not willing to provide any space for Panchayati Raj in its strategy of development through micro-level planning.

At the same time, however, another quite crucial report came to the government submitted by the Ashok Mehta Committee on Panchayati Raj Institutions, which was set up in 1977 to enquire into the working of the PRIs and to suggest measures to strengthen them in order to facilitate a process of decentralized planning and development in the country. The Ashok Mehta Committee observed that being dominated by economically and socially privileged sections of the society, the PRIs under the hitherto existing administrative system facilitated emergence of the oligarchic forces yielding no benefits to the weaker sections. Nevertheless, the Committee believed:

> "Panchayati Raj like democracy at the national and state level is both an end and a means. As an end it is an inevitable extension of democracy as a means it would continue to be responsible for discharging obligations entrusted to it by the national and state governments in spheres not transferred to its exclusive jurisdiction. Altogether both as an end and means Panchayati Raj should contribute to the philosophy as well as practice of a rich, rewarding life in rural India" (Datta, 1998).

With such an approach and along with certain practical considerations, the Committee recommended a two-tier system of Panchayati Raj to replace the moribund three-tier system of PRIs. It envisaged district as the first point of decentralization below the state level, because, first of all, it could assure the availability of technical expertise to a high order required for development projects. Secondly, district was traditionally a unit of administration to which all were acclimatized and a key unit for overall strategies, resource allocation and declination of the different types of project. Thirdly, it was a level where higher-level leadership could emerge. Therefore, the Committee contemplated sort of a district government, [2] the Zila Parishad, below the state as an effective mechanism of democratic decentralization and responsible for preparation of district level plan. And further below, the Committee envisaged the Mandal Panchayat constituted by a group of villages to ensure a balance between technological as well as administrative requirements and meaningful participation of the people at the grassroots in development management. Considering PRIs as political rather than mere development agencies, the Ashok Mehta Committee favoured open participation of the political parties with their symbols in the elections to PRIs. Besides a policy of positive discrimination in favour of women and Scheduled Castes and Scheduled Tribes, the Committee recommended to endow the PRIs with taxation power, and emphasized on their regular elections. Examining the question of according constitutional sanction, the Committee made the first official recommendation for including Panchayati Raj in the Constitution.

PANCHAYATS AS POLITICAL INSTITUTION: THEORY AND PRACTICE

The Ashok Mehta Committee had prepared the ground for the emergence of the second generation of Panchayati Raj in India. The West Bengal government began the process in 1978 to revive the PRIs in the state broadly in accordance with the recommendations of the Ashok Mehta Committee, and some other states such as Karnataka and Andhra Pradesh also initiated a similar process either by revising their existing panchayat Acts or by passing new Acts, in theory, accepting the recommendations made by the Ashok Mehta Committee. Consequent upon such initiatives, the second generation of PRIs emerged with a change in their character from development organizations at the local level into political institutions. Particularly in the case of West Bengal, Panchayati Raj was designed to become a microcosm of the state itself, making the elected representatives more crucial than the bureaucracy in shaping the rural life. Nevertheless, most of the other states, including those ruled by the Janata Party, preferred to remain more or less indifferent in practice showing allegiance to the bureaucracy-driven development process.

When recommendations of the Working Group headed by Dantwala and the Ashok Mehta Committee were at loggerheads on the issue of institutions for rural development, the government at the Centre headed by the Janata Party preferred to follow broadly the former. The mechanism of rural development that was designed basically with a techno-bureaucratic approach by the Centre and followed by most of the states, therefore, again intended to bypass the Panchayati Raj in the process of development planning and execution. The Sixth Five-Year Plan emphasized on integrated rural development as an instrument of intervention for eradication of poverty, aiming at different target groups comprising small and marginal farmers, agricultural labourers, and rural artisans. The on going special programmes such as SFDA, DPAP etc., which were broadly area development programmes, were to be continued in particular areas with the objectives of employment generation and increased production. Thus, the Integrated Rural Development Programme (IRDP) was envisaged as the panacea for rural poverty contemplating comprehensive Block level plans for production, employment generation, development of infrastructure and social services. The Block plan would be tied up vertically with the district plan and the state plan. Taking into consideration of the requirements of the Block plans, the necessary district level supportive infrastructure would be provided through the district plan, which would also resolve the problem of coordination between different departments, institutions and organizations. For administration of this new dispensation, the District Rural Development Agencies (DRDAs) were constituted. The administrative coast of each DRDA was to be met by way of setting apart a share of the allocation for each anti-poverty programme sponsored by the Centre. As an integral part of the state bureaucracy, each DRDA is still headed by a Project Director who should preferably be a senior scale IAS officer or a senior officer of the State Service, eligible of appointment to the All India Services. Effectively, the DRDAs became the channel for flowing of the entire central fund for the anti-poverty programmes sponsored by the Centre. Adopting such a techno-bureaucratic approach with overwhelming dependency on the DRDAs, the State had clearly proved its intention to completely bypass the elected PRIs in the process of rural development planning.

Yet, following the recommendations of the Ashok Mehta Committee, some of the states took initiatives to develop the second generation of PRIs as political institutions. Notable among them were West Bengal and Karnataka where many policy functions were devolved to the PRIs. But, except for West Bengal, the second generation PRIs had a pre-mature death in most of the states largely due to lack of political will reinforced by failure of the state governments to hold regular elections (Raghavalu and Narayana, 1991). The success of West Bengal to develop the PRIs as political institution has been a landmark in the history of Panchayati Raj, and it has drawn much attention of both academic and political circle. Although it might be repetitive, a brief discussion on the basic features of the second generation PRIs in the state would not be out of context.

The CPI (M) led Left Front after coming to the power in 1977 in West Bengal, initiated the policy of rural development based on agrarian reforms to be carried forward by the PRIs as political institutions. [3] The integration of rural development programmes with the agenda of agrarian reform of the Left Front and its political will to promote PRIs as self-conscious political institutions capable of addressing the class questions in the backward semi-feudal agrarian structure (Sengupta, 1981; Bose, 1993) to a considerably large extent, helped the Left Front to establish and maintain the quite stable political order in West Bengal. In sharp contrast to the policies of its predecessors, and also other states of India, the Left Front in 1980s particularly emphasized on redistribution programme, which had been less dramatic and more institutionalized. Besides actively involving the peasant organizations, the main mechanisms of the land reform policy were the PRIs.

The policy of rural development based on agrarian reforms, and the crucial role that he PRIs as political institutions had played led to certain basic changes in the rural power structure and co-relations of political forces. In contrast to a few exceptions, (Acharya, 1993; Bandyopadhyay, 1993; Mallick, 1993; Rogaly et al. 1999 etc.) quite a good number of studies have pointed out the achievements made by the Left Front Government in West Bengal by revitalizing the PRIs in the state. (Bergmann, 1984; Bandyopadhyaya, 1988; Kohli, 1987; Lieten, 1992; 1996; 2003; John Harriss, 1993; Sengupta, Gazdar, 1996 etc.) In case of other rural development programmes too, for instance the IRDP (however erroneous policy it might be), many of the inter-state comparisons pointed out the benefits that the rural poor section in West Bengal could gain mainly due to the decisive role of the PRIs (Dreze, 1990; Swaminathan, 1990).

The structure of the second generation of PRIs that emerged in West Bengal was not much different from the other states. Nor did West Bengal add any distinctive innovations to the policy recommendations of the Ashok Mehta Committee. Remarkably, however, the factor that made the PRIs in West Bengal more effective and different from those of other states was that the elections to the PRIs were overtly party-political and had been held at great regularity. This particular aspect, though recommended by the Ashok Mehta Committee, was largely ignored by most of other states. With the active role in agrarian reforms, the PRIs in the state became instrumental in diminishing economic as well as political domination of the landed elites on the one hand and opening the door for wider participation of the subaltern classes in the political process on the other. The PRIs in West Bengal, therefore, emerged as the epicentres of political power in the rural areas, and obviously became important arenas of political activities not only for the Left Front in power but also for all other political contenders. Besides the response of the political parties, electoral accountability of the newly emerged panchayat leaders contributed immensely to the overall functioning of the PRIs.

PROVIDING SPACE FOR PANCHAYATS IN THE CONSTITUTION: THE SEVENTY-THIRD AMENDMENT

An analysis of the third generation of PRIs would remain incomplete, if it is done isolating the Seventy-third amendment to the Constitution from the major politico-economic shifts that the State had witnessed in 1980s. A brief analysis in retrospect would help to address a fundamental question. What were the politico-economic necessities of the State to provide space for the PRIs in the Constitution after more than four decades of its adoption? A comprehensive analysis of the political process would also provide a backdrop to the understanding of the basic characteristics of the third generation PRIs.

The Panchayati Raj that was contemplated during the Janata government could not make any headway in most of the states, it proved to be an effective instrument of development in West Bengal. Consequent upon collapse of the Janata government mainly due to internal conflicts and defections, the Congress under exclusive domination of Indira Gandhi (Congress-I) came back to the power in January 1980 with a comfortable majority in the Parliament. Indira Gandhi, as the Prime Minister and also the unequivocal leader of the party, emphasized on continuation of dominance of the Congress high command consisting of the people close to her in the party affairs. To run the government, she preferred centralization of powers in the hands of the central executive with key bureaucrats. On the economic front, with a mark difference from the development strategy followed since independence, Indira Gandhi emphasized on promotion of a private sector in industry free from the tight government control, and import liberalization with export promotion. The efforts continued till her assassination in October 1984.

The eighth general elections were held in December 1984 in the shadow of Indira Gandhi's assassination. With an unprecedented electoral victory, Rajiv Gandhi emerged as a new leader in Congress. Rajiv Gandhi as the Prime Minister, who had no political past, neither attempted to alter the highly centralized control system of the Congress nor made any efforts to redefine the economic agenda. He reiterated the policy of import liberalization with a great reliance on the private sector.

The continuous Congress rule in the country, however, was once again disrupted in 1989. The National Front led by the new political formation, the Janata Dal, came to the power with outside support from the Bharatiya Janata Party (BJP) on the one hand and the Left parties on the other. However, the National Front could not remain in power for long because of its internal as well as external crisis. Internally, the broad political formation failed to maintain political stability reconciling the political interests of its major constituents. And, externally, the major challenge came from the BJP. The Front-BJP relationship that was based on the opportunistic political understanding of defeating the Congress – I soon got snapped when the Hindu communal forces sought to re-assert themselves and could see the possibility of capturing power. The so-called Sangh Parivar consisting of the BJP, the RSS and the Vishwa Hindu Parishad launched a massive campaign on the issue of Ram Janam Bhumi. Amidst that political turmoil, the National Front government headed by V.P. Singh announced that the government would implement the Mandal commission recommendations, made several years earlier, for reservation of seats in the government jobs for the Other Backward Classes. This announcement also led to violent protests in most of the cities launched by the upper caste students and youths. Failure of the National Front government to resolve the political issues led to its defeat in a confidence vote in November 1990.

In a situation of political turmoil, Chandra Shekhar became Prime Minister of a minority government with support from the Congress – I. However, consequent upon his resignation in March 1991, the ninth Lok Sabha was dissolved and the country had to go for the next general elections in May 1991. But, halfway through the general elections Rajiv Gandhi was assassinated. Though the Congress –I could not win a majority, it became the single largest party, and once again, a Congress–I government was formed with P.V. Narasimha Rao as Prime Minister.

The basic nature of political turmoil and its associated pessimism since the period of Emergency were, however, different from the political crisis that erupted after the death of Nehru. The political crisis that began in the mid-1960s distinctly led to the decline of the Congress, the party that was in power uninterruptedly since independence, and not the institutional structure of the Indian State. The period since 1975 has, however, been marked by unprecedented political disorder, which has eventually led to a crisis in the institutional structure of the state. Despite all the populist slogan of the crisis-laden ruling group, the Emergency, could not improve the economic performance of the State. Instead, it revealed the vulnerability of bourgeois democracy, a system that could be gratuitously replaced by authoritarianism.

The crisis of hegemony of the Indian State did not come to an end with the victory of the Janata Party. The total failure of the Janata regime in its mandate can be broadly attributed to lack of political maturity to forge an alternative to the Congress regime. Instead of addressing the basic principle questions, the Janata Party during its short period in power preferred to focus more on personal vendetta. Its acceptance to the terms set by the political fear of an out of power Indira Gandhi coupled with its own internal conflicts led the Janata regime to its failure in restoring policies, values, and principles of a bourgeois democratic government.

After coming back to power, Indira Gandhi emphasized mainly the dislodging of opposition consolidations, both at the center and the states as part of her political strategy. Witnessing further decline of the democratic principles and values, her strategy ranged from promotion of dissension in the ranks of the oppositions to undemocratic intervention of the central government to destabilize the non-Congress government in the states without considering the political implications. The dissensions that were promoted within the Akali Dal helped the extremist elements in Punjab, while the undemocratic interventions in the non-Congress governments in the states led to extremely bitter federal relations. Decline of the hegemonic role of the State further aggravated the regional political scenario. Besides on going insurgency in the pockets of North East India, the regional opposition to Indira Gandhi's regime triggered off a spate of secessionism in Assam and Punjab. With its secessionist ideology, the United Liberation Front of Assam began gaining popularity amidst the political turmoil created by the Assam Movement, which was being led by the All Assam Students' Union on the issue of foreigners. Similarly, the extremist fringe of the Akali Dal in Punjab became increasingly assertive with the demand for a sovereign state of Khalistan. Such phenomena, which contested political legitimacy of the Indian State, clearly revealed that Indira Gandhi's leadership, despite all rhetoric, resulted in gradual decline of political ideology of the bourgeois-land lord coalition. The two regional movements that erupted during the last years of Indira Gandhi's regime also witnessed political resentment against regional disparity and distributive inequality ushered by unrestricted capitalist development.

Nevertheless, instead of adopting any policy backed by serious historical thinking to address the issues of regional disparity and distributive justice, Indira Gandhi's regime sought to rationalize a more pragmatic economic programme. The pragmatism led to adoption of the measures to provide momentum for privatization of industry and other economic enterprises at the cost of public investment. This was accompanied by launching of open attacks on the public sector on the grounds of its inefficiency without taking any measure to prevent the public sector from the interference and wasteful exploitation of the bureaucracy and political leaders.

Indira Gandhi's successor regime headed by Rajiv Gandhi attempted to restore political stability through a series of accords signed with the political leadership of the regional discourses wherever negotiations were feasible. For a political settlement in Punjab, an accord was signed with the Akali Dal leaders. Elections to the Punjab state assembly were held in September 1985, and Akali Dal won an absolute majority. To resolve the crisis in Assam, an accord was signed with the

All Assam Students' Union. In the subsequent elections to the state assembly, Asom Gana Parishad formed by the ex-student leaders, won a clear victory to form the government. Rajiv Gandhi signed another accord with Laldenga, the extremist Mizo leader in 1986. The accord provided full statehood to Mizoram, and Laldenga became the Chief Minister. Although, the mechanism of the accords undoubtedly helped a section of the regional political elite, nonetheless, the problem of insurgency remained unresolved in most of the North East states including Assam, and in Punjab.

Without giving much serious economic thought to the regional political discourses, Rajiv Gandhi's regime endorsed the economic liberalization programme initiated by Indira Gandhi, and decided to carry it forward more vigorously. Consequently, the economic role of the State had substantially been reduced to push the country to the trajectory of market-driven capitalism, alongside opening the floodgates for foreign capital. Both because of internal and external factors, the neo-liberal agenda that became more crucial since the early 1990s, demanded a drastic change in the relationship between the State and the economy. The change essentially involved greater reliance on market mechanisms, which necessitated the policies of deregulation and considerable reduction of government controls, import liberalization, greater autonomy of private investment, lessening importance of the public sector, and opening the economy to international trade and direct foreign investment in different sectors. Thus, the role of the State had been reduced merely to facilitate and regulate the market, and economic liberalization was projected as the panacea for all the maladies.

Although the Ashok Mehta Committee made the first official recommendation for including Panchayati Raj in the Constitution, the successive political regimes headed by Indira

Gandhi and Rajiv Gandhi, remained silent on the issue till the late 1980s. Meanwhile, several other committees set up for different purposes emphasized on importance of Panchayati Raj and recommended its inclusion in the Constitution. The Planning Commission appointed a working group in 1983 known as Hanumantha Rao Committee to suggest measures for making decentralized planning at district level more effective. The Committee recommended that PRIs should provide the framework for the popular participation as well as organize development programmes. Therefore, the Committee recommended that the PRIs should be associated with the formulation of district planning. Similarly, the Committee on Administrative arrangement for Rural Development, set up under the chairmanship of G.V.K. Rao in 1985 also recommended that PRIs at the district and lower levels be given greater powers in relation to planning, implementation and monitoring of rural development plans.

In 1986, another important committee of the Department of Rural Development, known as L.M. Singhvi Committee, recommended constitutional status for Panchayati Raj Criticizing the existing approach to panchayats primarily as convenient tools of administering rural development programmes, the Committee conceptualized PRIs as basic units of self-government and emphasized on Gram Sabha as the embodiment of direct democracy. The Committee recommended that the PRIs be organized as a part of the process of democratic decentralization for building up institutional edifice.

Amidst political instability that contested the hegemonic role of the Indian State, and when the neo-liberal agenda reached a more mature stage with a significant change in the relationship between the State and the economy, consequently resulting in diminishing public investment, the political regime under the leadership of Rajiv Gandhi contemplated drastic reform in the Panchayati Raj creating space for it in the Constitution. Broadly following the recommendations of the L.M. Singhvi Committee, the Constitution (64th Amendment) Bill was introduced in the Parliament on 15 May, 1989. Along with other reforms, this bill also sought the mandatory setting up of PRIs in all states with fixed tenure, holding of elections at regular intervals, greater devolution of powers and functions, reservation of seats for SC/ST and women. The bill, however, could not be passed in the Rajya Sabha although it got a two-third majority in the Lok Sabha.

The major criticism against the bill was based on the question of Centre-State relations. First, the Bill took Panchayati Raj out of the State List and put it in the Concurrent List of the Constitution. That would allow the Centre to interfere in the legislative arena of the state government. Secondly, the bill made the provision of elections to the PRIs under supervision of the Chief Election Commissioner instead of the state government. Third, the Bill made provision of financial devolution to the PRIs through finance commission bypassing the state government. Fourth, the bill provided the governor with the powers to dismiss the panchayats. That would, as it was feared, enhance control of the Centre over the panchayats. The bill, therefore, was perceived by its political critiques as a retrograde step to weaken the foundation of the federal structure, a surreptitious attempt to gorge direct link between the Centre and the PRIs, which would probably lead to an authoritarian regime once again.

In response to the wide spread criticism, the National Front government appointed a committee headed by S.R. Bommai to prepare an alternative legislation. The Committee released its report in July 1989. Accordingly, the National Front government introduced the 74th Amendment Bill, combining both panchayats and municipalities, in September 1990. However, the bill could not be discussed during the short tenure of the National Front government.

The Congress government headed by Narasimha Rao introduced the 72nd (Panchayats) and 73rd (Nagarpalikas) constitutional amendment bills in September 1991, and both Lok Sabha and Rajya Sabha passed them in December 1992. By the time the Parliament passed the bills, their sequence changed to 73rd and 74th respectively. After their ratification by majority of the state assemblies, the president gave his assent in April 1993, and consequently, they came into force as the Constitution (Seventy-third Amendment) Act 1992 in April 1993 and Constitution (Seventy-fourth Amendment) Act 1992 in June 1993. The Seventy-third Constitutional Amendment, therefore, laid the foundation of the third generation of PRIs in the country.

The overarching aim of the Seventy-third amendment, which is one of the longest and most detailed amendments made to the Constitution ever since its promulgation, is to 'endow the Panchayats with such powers and authority as may be necessary to enable them to function as institutions of self-government' (Article 243G). With this aim, the amendment sought to alter position of the PRIs making the following constitutional provisions:

1. Formation of Gram Sabha at the village consisting of persons registered in the electoral roles of the village besides mandating the states to constitute panchayats at the village, intermediate and district level. Therefore, by bringing back the three-tier system of PRIs, the Constitution recognized the institution of Gram Sabha as an integral part of Panchayati Raj.
2. All the seats in a Panchayat are to be filled by persons chosen by direct election from the territorial constituencies in the panchayats.
3. The term of a panchayat has been fixed at five years and 'no longer', and the period has to the counted from the date of its first meeting. The elections to the panchayats have to be completed before the expiry of the mandated

term. In case of dissolution of the panchayat, elections have to be completed within six months from the date of dissolution and the elected representatives are to hold office for the remaining period for which the dissolved panchayat would have continued.

4. Reservation of one-third of the seats for women, and similar provision for reservation of seats for Scheduled Castes and Scheduled Tribes in proportion to their population.
5. Mandating the Governor of a state to set up a Finance Commission within one year from the commencement of the Seventy-third amendment, and thereafter at the expiration of every five-year term to review the financial position of the panchayats and to make recommendation to the Governor.
6. Mandating the Governor of a state to set up an Election Commission for the purpose of superintendence, direction and control of the preparation of electoral rolls for, and the conduct of all elections to panchayats.
7. The Eleventh Schedule has been added to the Constitution enlisting the 'matters' that may be entrusted to the panchayats for preparation of plans and implementation of schemes for economic development and social justice.

The Seventy-third amendment, though has not drastically altered the institutional set up of rural governance, has endorsed afresh the role that the PRIs can play in promoting economic development and social justice in rural India. This has generated immense hope and optimism in both political and academic circles. The initial optimism was best reflected in the words of Jain. The Seventy-third amendment, as he believed 'has opened a window to a million possibilities'. The mandatory five-year elections to village panchayats would lend rare dynamism to the political process including enlargement of the base for drawing and nursing political leadership with grassroots experience. Given the mandatory representation in panchayats to women and scheduled castes, a tremendous and unprecedented social force would be unleashed to fight their won battle for justice and equality. In the economic sphere, there would emerge possibility of a radical redressal of past weaknesses. The village panchayats, being elected democratically, would be accountable to the local population almost on a day to day basis, and therefore, would have much greater stake in local development. They would be under pressure to be more equitable and provide chances of protest and resistance to injustices by the weak with a better prospect of success. The panchayat leadership would be motivated and better placed to raise local resources for economic and social development without depending entirely on the central or the state support. The pace and pressure for development would undergo a dynamic change given the periodical elections to the panchayats where each candidate and party would be competing with the other for showing better and more satisfactory results. (Jain, 1995).

However, for some scholars, the Seventy-third amendment to the Constitution mandated a third level of governance in the country at a time when fiscal corrections called for a retreat in the role of government rather than an expansion. The assumption was that delivery of certain public goods and services that remained among the core responsibilities of the government, whether of maintenance variety or development variety, would be more responsive to local conditions and preferences at local levels of governance, and thereby more effective (Rajaraman, Bohra, Renganathan, 1996; Vyasulu, 2004). And, for some others, the Seventy-third amendment was only an expression of intention rather than a mandate to the states to transfer the functions and schemes relating to the subjects given in the schedule (Eleventh Schedule) accompanied by funds and staff (Srivastava, 2002).

Nevertheless, after the Seventy-third amendment, the states have met their legal obligations, often mechanically. Conformity legislation has been passed, but the preambles to many of such legislations passed by the states have declared that the purpose behind creating panchayats is to improve rural administration and ensure peoples participation in the development programmes, and only a few states have described panchayats in their legislations as institution of self-government. However, other formal steps required under the law are taken by the state legislations. Reservations for women and the depressed communities have been implemented, election and finance commissions are being set up, and elections to the PRIs have been held in all the states, though some of the states have taken much time to overcome the inertia. But, mere compliance with the constitutional formalities does not mean that the PRIs have emerged as the effective instrument capable of ensuring economic development and social justice in rural India. Besides many other socio-economic and political issues, (Ghosh, Kumar, 2003) the Seventy-third amendment itself has certain serious lacunae, which have crippled the third generation PRIs since their birth.

The Seventy-third amendment (Article 243G) reiterated the responsibilities and powers given to the state legislatures under Entry 5 of the List II (State List) of the Seventh Schedule of the Constitution.[4] As discussed earlier, most of the states enacted legislations or amended the existing ones for the establishment of the panchayats and to give it responsibilities, powers and functions following the recommendations made by different expert committees. What makes the Seventy-third amendment a distinctive one, besides constitutional recognition to the panchayats, is its emphasis on economic development and social justice and addition of the Eleventh Schedule to the Constitution. Along with this, the responsibility has been entrusted with the state legislatures to endow the panchayats with powers and authority necessary to enable them to function as 'institution of self-government'. However, what constitutes 'self-government' has not been mentioned anywhere in the Constitution so as to clearly demarcate the powers, functions and responsibilities of the PRIs from that of the state government and its line departments. Lack of such conceptual clarity on the part of the Constitution has led to remarkably ineffective devolution of functions, functionaries as well as finances, and prevalence of a kind of dyrarchy at the grass roots level, which not only prevents growth of the panchayats as institutions of self-governance, but also detrimental to good governance.

According to the Article 243G, the legislature of a state 'may contain provisions for the devolution of powers and responsibilities' upon panchayats at the appropriate level, with respect to the preparation of plans for economic development and social justice and the implementation of schemes for economic development and social justice 'as may be entrusted to them' including those in relation to the 'matters' listed in the Eleventh Schedule. It is therefore, clear that there is no constitutional mandate that the states will transfer the entire responsibilities of planning and implementation of the schemes to the PRIs relating to the 'matter' (not specifically the subjects) included in the Eleventh Schedule (Srivastava, 2002).

More than twelve years have passed since Part IX of the Constitution was gazetted with the president's consent on April 12, 1993, but the results at the grass roots have fallen far short of expectations. Barring a few exceptions, almost nowhere in the country has a sincere and serious attempt been made to ensure in practice that panchayats function as 'institution of self-government' (Aiyar, 2002). Attempt has been made mechanically to devolve functions to the panchayats in most of the states. However, very few states have linked the formal devolution of functions to the means for actualizing such devolution through the devolution of finance and functionaries (Aiyar, 2002). Lack of clear division of functions between the state government and the PRIs has obviously created problems for devolution of finances and functionaries in most of the states. The reports of the State Finance Commissions constituted under Article 243 I of the Constitution clearly revealed that financial devolutions have been suggested broadly on the basis of mechanical devolution of the functions to the PRIs. In some cases the reports recommended only a percentage or amount from the state's resources for transfer to the PRIs without any assessment of their actual needs or the resources generated by them (Srivastava, 2002).

To follow the direction given by the Constitution to enable the panchayats to function as institutions of self-governance, Mani Shankar Aiyar believes that 'the central government must channel all funds for central and centrally-sponsored schemes falling within the ambit of the Eleventh Schedule direct to the panchayats at the appropriate level'. (Aiyar, 2002). Therefore, as he argues, the DRDA 'has become obsolescent and needs to be ended, especially as the DRDA is inimical to the fundamental objective of Part IX which is the establishment of institutions of self-government' (Aiyar, 2002). Similarly, the Planning Commission has also been in favour of a greater devolution of powers and finances to the PRIs. But at the same time, the ministry of rural development has been insisting on the continued operation of the DRDAs that bypass the PRIs.

THE RENEWED CONCERN

Witnessing a renewed concern of the Indian State and also its anxiety about the institutions of rural self-governance, a new Ministry of Panchayati Raj has been brought into being in May 2004. And, in view of the anomalies especially in the process of devolution of powers to the PRIs by the state legislatures, the Prime Minister convened a meeting of the Chief Ministers in the following month. The meeting decided that henceforth all poverty eradication and rural development programmes in the country would be governed through the PRIs. Following the decision of the meeting, the newly created Ministry of Panchayati Raj convened seven round table conferences during July to December 2004 in different parts of the country involving all the states and Union territories. The series of round table conferences addressed a wide range of issues and adopted several resolutions in order to strengthen the PRIs by setting a sort of uniform code of conduct for all the states and Union Territories.

Addressing the vital questions of effective devolution comprising functions, functionaries and finances, and also the issues related to empowerment of the Gram Sabhas, the first Round Table Conference[5] resolved to secure effective devolution of the functions [6]through a transparent form of activity mapping in respect to each tier of panchayat. The conference also resolved to devolve such subjects to the panchayats at an appropriate level, which would enable a more effective delivery of public services and better quality of life for citizens. Further, in order to integrate the DRDAs with District Panchayat, the conference resolved to make the DRDA officials responsible to the District Panchayat just as the state level executive is responsible to the legislature.

Emphasizing the importance of Gram Sabhas in the democratic decision-making at the grassroots, the conference resolved to enable Gram Sabha to function as a watchdog on the panchayats by mandating its association in all major aspects of decision-making, especially those decisions, which relate to need assessment before public expenditure is undertaken for development and poverty eradication. Henceforth, all plans of the panchayats would require approval of the Gram Sabha, and the accounts of the Gram Panchayat would be subject to social audit by Gram Sabha.

The second Round Table Conference[7] addressed the issues related to planning and implementation, and it emphasized on the question of parallel bodies, which emerged in some states, of course with state patronage, more conspicuously than the PRIs. The conference adopted a resolution mandating the states to constitute District Planning Committee (DPC) before March 31, 2004. The conference also mandated each tier of panchayats to prepare prospective Five-Year Plan and Annual Plans for their respective jurisdiction. The DPC should consolidate the plans prepared by the panchayats and the municipalities that come under its jurisdiction, rather than preparation of a district plan of its own accord or its own volition.

Addressing the question of the parallel body, the conference mandated the states to devolve functions, functionaries, and finances as required by the Constitution (Article 243G) only to the panchayats, and not to any parallel body. However, this does not debar the states from setting up parallel bodies. For reasons of institutional constraints, if parallel bodies have been set up or are to be set up by the states, these must be mingled into an organic, symbiotic relationship with the PRIs at the appropriate level so that PRIs are fully involved with the work of the parallel bodies.

The third Round Table Conference [8] emphasized on implementation of the provisions of the Panchayats (Extension to the Scheduled Areas) Act, 1996, besides addressing certain questions related to reservation for women. It directed the Centre and the states to consult the tribal communities and their elected representatives in evolving criteria for the constitution of Gram Panchayat and Gram Sabha in Schedule V areas.

Following the constitutional provision of reservation of seats for women in the PRIs, some of the states have gone beyond the minimum requirement of 33.33 per cent. In Karnataka, 45 per cent of the elected members to the PRIs are women. In Uttar Pradesh, 54 per cent of the Zila Panchayat Presidents are women. Similarly, in Tamil Nadu, 36 per cent of the chairpersons of Gram Panchayats are women. However, this may not indicate empowerment of women in true sense. The conference agreed that reservation of seats for women is necessary, but it alone cannot lead to empowerment in true sense. Therefore, this must be reinforced by a number of other measures such as making provision of Women Component Plans in the budgets of the PRIs; adequate training and capacity building; encouragement for political parties to put up women candidates; separate quorum for women's participation in Gram Sabhas etc.

The fourth Round Table Conference [9] urged upon the union government to implement the provisions of the Constitution relating to the Seventy-third amendment in the Union Territories. Further, it noted that the necessity to consider uncertainties, ambiguities and inconsistencies in the body of jurisprudence that has evolved since the passage of the panchayat legislations by the parliament and the states. To that end, the conference recommended that the Ministry of Panchayati Raj in consultation with different institutions and expert bodies should review and categorize the available decisions of the courts with a view to preparing a list of jurisprudential points which might be referred, on the one hand, to the authorities concerned in the union government, and, subject to the completion of the procedural formalities, to the Law Commission and the Law Commissions which have been set up in some states, as appropriate on the other.

Most of the states have made arrangements to make public annual reports on panchayats in their respective state. The fifth round table conference [10] decided to make such state reports comparable across states. It was agreed that the annual state reports on panchayats should reflect assessment with respect to each of the dimensions of Panchayati Raj on which consensus has been reached in the successive round table conferences.

Since the Indian voter is one and indivisible, the principle of parity between parliamentary and assembly elections on the one hand, and panchayat elections on the other, must be maintained. While all matters relating to panchayat elections have been vested by the Constitution in state legislatures, there is a need to work towards commonality, if not uniformity, in election procedures and provisions. To this end, as the sixth round table conference [11] believed, it would be desirable to vest all responsibilities, including preparation of electoral rolls, delimitation of constituencies, reservations and qualifications of candidates, conduct of elections, and functioning as the first stage of adjudication in election disputes, associated with the election process to the State Election Commissions rather than splitting these up. With a view to evolving a common electoral roll for all levels of elections, the conference recommended consultation between the Chief Election Commissioner and the State Election Commissioners to resolve the practical problems that might arise in the preparation, maintenance and updating of electoral rolls for elections to be held at different times for different levels of governments.

Recognizing the PRIs as the third tier of government, the conference also emphasized on the necessity to upgrade the work of the Director of Local Fund Audit (DLFA) and other similar bodies to the level required by constitutional imperatives, and to this end, the conference recommended that DLFA and other similar bodies work in concert with the Comptroller and Auditor General of India.

The last Round Table Conference[12] addressed several issues related to the fields of information and communication technology (ICT), and capacity building and training for the functionaries associated with panchayats. The conference recognized ICT as a vital input of capacity for panchayats to perform their functions better. Integrating ICTs to capacity building, the conference mandated the states to undertake a time bound exercise of process re-engineering in consonance with the activity mapping, for transfer of functions to the PRIs. The basic objective is to ensure an effective mechanism of information dissemination to the panchayat representatives and the people at large. The conference also emphasized on the basic questions related to the training, its perspective and contents, for the elected representatives and other officials at different levels of panchayats. It has been reemphasized that training and communication should not be viewed as a single onetime intervention but should be a continuous, ongoing process leading to an enhancement of a sense of self-esteem and confidence of the PRIs.

SUMMING UP

The socio-economic as well as political aberrations caused by the centuries of colonial domination constituted the major challenge before the Indian State soon after independence. The first political task before the Congress, which led the nationalist movement to the desired goal, was to legitimize the State as an autonomous political institution with its welfare and development ideology, which reinforced the modern nation state in its pristine purity. While its development interventions were primarily directed towards promotion of a modern capitalist industrial sector, the welfare initiatives apparently sought to address the issues related to inequalities generated by semi feudal agrarian relations. Secondly, the Congress with its monopoly over the State apparatus and the policies directed towards promotion of capitalism, also had to consolidate its rural support base comprising of the agrarian propertied classes, to strengthen the position of the party in an electoral democracy. A legislative battle was launched against landlordism apparently with egalitarian objectives, but the Constitution recognized the right to property as a fundamental right, and made provisions indirectly protecting the interests of the zamindars and landlords. Besides that, the agrarian reform programmes initiated by different states ostensibly inspired by egalitarianism also had failed to alter the agrarian structure because of the inbuilt loopholes. As a result, the oligarchs continued to run India's rural life.

Without bringing about any appreciable change in the structure of domination in the agrarian society, the Indian State designed the strategy of rural development again with the ideology of egalitarianism. The Community Development Projects were launched in the early 1950s when some of the states, with a positive response to the Directive Principles of the Constitution, took the initiative to establish panchayats. However, brushing off the incipient panchayats or in some cases making them a mere appendage of the welfare initiatives, the Indian State created an elaborate centralized administrative structure to implement the Community Development projects. The State dispensation again benefited the rural propertied classes instead of the pauperized masses and helped the State to maintain the *status quo* in the internal power relations within the village community and indirectly to support domination of the landowning groups. A remedy was sought through an expert committee after the lapse of five years. The Balvantray Mehta Committee recommended the replacement of the bureaucracy driven 'welfare' strategy by a strong system of Panchayati Raj elected by and accountable to the people, and capable of addressing the real issues of rural development.

Many of the states enthusiastically initiated the process to establish the first generation panchayats following the recommendations made by the Balvantray Mehta Committee in theory. The panchayats that came into being in the 1960s were, however, hijacked by a category of corrupt rural leadership comprising the landowning class, which could consolidate its position by passing off the land reform legislations, whether legally or illegally, and also accruing the benefits of the 'welfare' measures of the State. The rural scenario could have been changed, had there been a sincere commitment of the Indian State to accelerate a process of democratic decentralization by encouraging the ethos of self-government. The bourgeoisie-landlord state, with the Nehruvian model of development, continued with its old bureaucracy driven strategy of rural development with a shift of emphasis from community development to agricultural promotion, which culminated in the maladies of green revolution.

The bourgeois-landlord coalition that was built on one-party dominance provided political stability, but it failed to enlist the support of the rural mass. Consequently, the 'Congress system' started declining after the death of Nehru, the architect of modern Indian State, providing political space for various alternative articulations of mass discontent triggered off by the basic development issues. The regional, ethnic, ideological as well as communal discourses that reappeared in the political arena not only contested the Congress monopoly over Indian polity and the development paradigm, but also questioned the autonomy of the State. Amidst the crisis of political stability, the Indira Gandhi regime instead of making a sincere attempt to democratically resolve the crisis resorted to an unprecedented coercive mechanism. That led to a political defeat of the Congress in 1977 for the first time in the history of independent India.

The new and ideologically heterogeneous political formation that replaced the Indira Gandhi regime attempted to revive the democratic institutions and welfare ethos afresh by constituting a couple of expert committees to set the development perspective. Ashok Mehta Committee was one of them, and it reasserted the importance of panchayats. However, due to its political immaturity coupled with internal conflicts, the Janata regime failed in its mandate. Neither could it successfully rejuvenate the bourgeois democratic institutions nor could it re-assert hegemony of the state while the memory of Emergency continued to influence the political process. The success of the Left Front in West Bengal in developing the panchayats as political institutions to address the development issues integrating agrarian reforms and rural development programmes in a class perspective within the parameters set by the bourgeois democracy, nevertheless proves that the institutions of self-government have the potential to bring about a desired pattern of change in the rural socio-economic arena.

Failure of the Janata regime brought back the Congress regime under the leadership of Indira Gandhi once again to dominate the Indian State and polity. With a remarkable shift in development priorities, Indira Gandhi in her second political incarnation opted for dislodging the public sector to encourage private investment. And as part of her political strategy, she geared up the State machinery to destabilize oppositional consolidations, even at the cost of promotion of insurgent elements. But, soon she became a victim of her own political design and was assassinated. Continuing the Congress regime at the center, Rajiv Gandhi not only followed the economic programmes of his mother, but also revealed his commitment to accelerate the pace of economic liberalization.

The Indian polity in the 1980s, fraught with several regional and ethnic discourses often accompanied by secessionism posed a much greater political challenge than ever before not only for the Congress regime but also questioning the bourgeois-landlord State hegemony. While Rajiv Gandhi, through his politics of 'accord' was trying to bring back political stability, the nation started experiencing communal re-assertion in an environment of political instability and economic crisis. The Janata Dal that replaced the Congress regime for a short period provided the ground for communal mobilization.

Without giving a deeper historical and economic thinking to the politico-economic questions raised by the process of capitalist development, the Congress regime headed by Rajiv Gandhi sought to extend the political space of the Indian State to the grass roots gratuitously bypassing the state governments, many of which were either headed by the non-Congress political elites or the Left Front alliances. In the shadow of the recommendations made by several expert committees, the Constitutional (64th Amendment) Bill was introduced in the Parliament in May 1989. However, it was defeated, and subsequently modified by the National Front. The modified version though could be placed for discussion in the Parliament during the short tenure of the National Front in power.

The Congress regime again came to power but had failed to monopolize over the State and the entire polity. When the policy of economic liberalization led to a grave financial crisis for the Indian State and its autonomy, the union government once again expressed its willingness to share the burden of development by juxtaposing panchayats in the existing federal ethos and making them an integral part of the Constitution. The Seventy-third amendment was made and it generated much hope and expectations. Nevertheless, lack of serious thinking on the issue of devolution of powers and functions to the PRIs in the given federal set up once again tended to cripple the so-called institutions of self-government. The subsequent communal regime led by BJP ignored the pertinent issues related to unsatisfactory performance of the panchayat system in the country.

Certain steps have been initiated by the present government that witnesses a renewed concern for the panchayats of the Indian State under control of the present Congress regime. The newly created Ministry of Panchayati Raj, considering the anomalies of the state legislature, organized a series of round table conference in the second half of the year 2004. Covering a wide arena of issues, the conferences made several resolutions in order to strengthen the PRIs setting a sort of uniform code of conduct for all states to follow besides suggesting certain measures to be taken by the central government. Nevertheless, the conferences also ignored some of the vital issues, especially, a clear division of powers between the state government and the PRIs at different levels, a mechanism on which devolution of functions, functionaries and finances can take place.

The question, however, is whether or not the present generation PRIs can meet the constitutional direction and legislative mandate of economic development and social justice. If not, what are the factors that do not allow the panchayats to emerge as institutions of self-governance at the grassroots? Are the political elites at the state/regional level willing to share their limited powers granted by the existing federal structure? To what extent is the Indian State sincere to promote the process of democratic decentralization by substituting the bureaucracy driven development process with democratically elected institutions at the grassroots? All these fundamental issues demand a deeper probe with substantial empirical insights.

NOTES

1. The sponsors enlisted various items connected with the following broad categories to be undertaken by the projects. (1) Agriculture and related matters; (2) Communications; (3) Health; (4) Training; (5) Social Welfare; (6) Supplementary Employment; and (7) Housing.
2. Nirmal Mukherjee considering the success of Zila Parishad in West Bengal and Karnataka later developed the concept (Mukherjee, 1986).
3. This was marked by enforcement of legislations regarding distribution of ceiling surplus and tenancy reform, and preferential advantages to small farmers in distribution of agricultural inputs (Ghosh, 1981).

4. The states enjoyed exclusive powers to enact legislations on the subjects included in the List II-State List of the Constitution. Local government is included in Entry 5 of this list, which reads 'Local government, that is to say, the Constitution and powers of municipal corporations, improvement trusts, district boards, mining and settlement authorities and other local authorities for the purpose of local self-government or village administration'.
5. It was held in Kolkata on 24-25 July 2004.
6. Referred to the matters listed in the Eleventh Schedule to the Constitution.
7. It was held in Mysore on 28-29 August 2004.
8. It was held in Raipur on 23-24 September 2004.
9. It was held in Chandigarh on 7-8 October 2004.
10. It was held in Kashmir on 28-29 October 2004.
11. It was held in Guwahati on 27-28 November 2004.
12. It was held in Jaipur on 17-19 December 2004.

5

PANCHAYATI RAJ IN ASSAM: A BRIEF HISTORY

The ancient Assam witnessed a social formation marked by some sort of decentralized village administration. It is, however, difficult to ascertain the definite shape and the nature of the decentralized administration due to absence of enough historical evidence. A good number of historical research have pointed out that the kingdom of Pragjyotisha or Kamrup, that went through the process of sanskritization[1] was divided into smaller units such as *bhuktis, mandalas, visayas, puras, agraharas* etc. This information has been derived from the different grants made by various kings. From the contents of these grants, it is, however, not clear whether these were simply geographical divisions or administrative units. Nevertheless, the historians have tried to conclude that this region also witnessed, more or less, the same type of local administration as that of many other parts of the ancient India. The term *nayaka* or *Nayaka Sriksikunda* as referred to in the Nidhanpur Grant generally means a village headman. This division was perhaps continued till the twelfth or thirteenth century. It has been observed that there was no supreme power having an extensive domain during that period, which required administrative divisions and sub divisions for smooth and efficient management. After the disintegration of the Pala kingdom in the first half of twelfth century, there was practically no paramount power during the next few centuries resulting in the emergence of many petty Chiefs who styled themselves as kings or *Bhaumika.*

The Ahoms settled down in the Brahmaputra Valley as migrants from Upper Burma in the early thirteen century, and initiated their kingdom in Upper Assam. With their growing political and economic influence, the Ahoms established a strong state covering almost the entire Brahmaputra valley by the end of the seventeenth century. The social formation and the politico-administrative arrangement of Assam under the Ahom rule fostered certain local institutions such as *khels, mels* etc., which had some judicial functions.

In the areas under Ahom domination, the villages were the smallest administrative units, where the *khel* system was in vogue with regard to the administrative affairs including the judicial functions. The *khels* were essentially occupational groups constituted by the *paiks*, (the adult male manual workers) with regular gradation of officers within a specific territorial jurisdiction. The *khel* officers such as, Bora and Saikia had the powers to settle the criminal as well as civil disputes while, appeals were referred to the Phukans and Baruas, the higher officials of the concerning *khels.* The *mels* were, in fact, the estates conferred on the sons, brothers, wives, and other close relations of the reigning monarch, and the chief of a *mel* was empowered to settle the minor disputes. In this context one can also refer to the popular assemblies such as *barmel, raijmel* etc. that were organized to discuss the problems of the local people.

In addition to that, the neo-Vaisnavite movement, which secured a strong footing towards the last part of the fifteenth century under the leadership of Sankardeva, also fostered a rapid proliferation of the institution of *namghar* in almost every Assamese village and *satras* in different parts of Assam.

Such institutions were initially set up for the proselytizing functions of neo-Vaisnavism, but in course of time, these religious institutions, especially the *namghars,* began to emerge as the nerve center of the village community. Other than working for the spread of intellectual and cultural activities, the institution of *namghar* also began to play a significant role in the political and judicial spheres.

Therefore, the institutions of *mel, khel,* and *namghar* were some of the very important social institutions of local character that emerged during the period of Ahom rule in Assam. The political chaos in the mid-eighteenth century that culminated in the Civil War (1769-1806) and the Burmese invasion of Assam brought an end to the era of Ahom rule. Assam became a part of colonial India in 1826. Consequently, the *khel* system became irrelevant, but the institution of *mel* assumed the character of a broad social institute since the beginning of the colonial rule in Assam. The *mel* emerged as an assembly of the village elders, not only for settlement of disputes but also for arriving at important collective decisions, when required. For instance, the people of the erstwhile district of Kamrupa and central part of Assam, organized themselves into local *mels* and decided to oppose the enhancement of land revenue rates notified by the colonial authorities in 1892. There were many more such instances. Similarly, the institute of *namghar* also remained an intrinsic part of the rural Assamese life.

The secular institutions, that emerged towards the later part of Ahom rule were essentially the outcome of the pattern of class domination in medieval Assam. The ruling aristocracy of Ahom Assam composed of seven leading Ahom clans (Satghariya Ahom) along with the petty vassal kings, tribal chieftains and the *apkain chamua* who had hereditary landed estates or *khats* (farms). With royal patronage, also emerged a section of spiritual aristocracy constituted of *goswamis* and *mahantas* of approved *satras* as well as Brahmans, who were favoured with land grants. All these categories of people had their hereditary landed estates or *khats* mostly developed out of wasteland grants. The king was naturally the biggest *khat* holder and had a network of royal stores all over the country. Besides his own *khats*, there were *khats* to maintain the dowager queen, the queen, royal brothers, princes and princesses along with their respective establishments. Both the royal and spiritual aristocrats had a considerable number of *bandi-beti* (male and female household slaves) and *bohotia* (serfs) to work on their khats. When the khat holders were in office, the *paikes* were assigned for their private works (Guha, 1991).

The overwhelming majority, however, belonged to the class constituted by the paikes who were classified into two broad categories – *kanri paiks* and *chamua paiks* – both of which were organized into *khels*. The *kanri paiks* were liable to obligatory manual services of any kind to the State, while the *chamua paiks* such as those of goldsmiths, gold washers, braziers, fishermen, oil-pressers had the obligation to contribute periodically shares of their specialized products or their skilled services. At the bottom of the class hierarchy of the Ahom State were the *bahatia* and the *bandi-beti*. Along with this, debt-slavery was also widespread during the last days of the Ahom rule. Persons often mortgaged themselves for an indefinite period, and the mortgagers, called bandha were in course of time converted into slaves in most cases. Guha estimated that towards the end of the Ahom rule, the top aristocracy, i.e. the ruling Ahom families who had *khats* and monopolized the offices as well as the privileged Brahmans, perhaps constituted some one per cent of the total population, and along with this category, the chamua including both the paikan and apaikan constituted almost 25 per cent of the total population. The *kanri paiks* constituted about 65 per cent and the slaves constituted about 10 per cent of the population of Ahom State (Guha, 1991).

British colonialism annexed the Ahom State in 1826 in a situation of extreme chaos, lawlessness and unprecedented oppression caused by the Moamaria Civil War and Burmese invasion (1817-1824). During the following decade and a half, the kingdom of Jaintia and Cachar along with the dependencies, and all the petty, independent tribal states of the Khasi Hills were annexed. Further annexation of the remaining hills was subsequently completed. The North Cachar Hills were organised into a separate administrative unit, after their subjugation was completed by 1854. A part of Naga Hills was annexed in 1866; the country of Lhota Nagas, in 1875; of the Angami Nagas, in 1878-80; and the Ao Nagas, in 1889. The Garo Hills was brought under full control by 1873. The Lushais (Mizo) were brought under control during the years 1871-89 and formed the Lushai Hills district in 1898 (Guha, 1977). The move to consolidate colonial power in the hills was, of course, violently resisted by many tribes. Nevertheless, the British province that came to be known as Assam, took shape in the last quarter of the 19th century, and territorially, it included the entire present North East India except Manipur and Tripura.

Alongside territorial expansion, British colonialism also initiated drastic changes in the institutional arrangements of the semi-feudal Ahom State, to push the war-torn Assamese society to the trajectory of an exotic capitalism. The colonial project in the Brahmaputra valley was initiated with the monetization of the economy and building of the infrastructure with British capital to sustain the capitalist set up. The process of colonial transition exposed the closed Assamese society not only to new skills and vices, but also to large scale immigration of labour, Marwari traders cum money lenders who monopolised the internal trade, Bengali clerks, lawyers and doctors, who with their advantage of an early induction to the English education system and colonial administrative system, monopolized government jobs and professions.

The growing prospects of tea plantation in the Brahmaputra valley caught the imagination of the British enterprises and capital, and the colonial regime adopted a set of rules in 1838, known as the Wasteland Rules, to make the land available on attractive terms for the initiation and growth of tea plantations. Available wastelands were offered to an applicant on lease for forty-five years on the condition that a quarter of the area must be cleared within five years. One fourth of such a grant was to be held revenue-free in perpetuity. The remaining portion of the leased area could also be revenue free for the initial 5 to 20 years depending upon the nature of the wastelands concerned. However, no such grants for agricultural purpose could be made for less than 100 acres at a time and to one who did not possess capital or stock worth at least Rs. 3 per acre. To make such grants more attractive to the British capital, the rules were revised in 1854 extending the lease period to 99 years on more liberal terms, and at the same time, the minimum area of land for which one could apply was raised to 500 acres.

The wasteland settlement policy encouraged the European planters to grab much more land than what they could effectively use for growth of the tea industry. But at the same time, it boosted the plantation economy in the valley. About 0.7 million acres of land had been settled with the planters in Assam by 1870-71, and the area actually under tea was a little over 56,000 acres (Guha, 1977). Witnessing a tremendous expansion of the tea sector during the last quarter of the nineteenth century, the total land area in possession of the tea industry doubled and accounted for some one-seventh of the entire settled area in the Assam plain. The acreage, actually under tea increased to 338 thousand acres in 1901 (Guha, 1977).

The indigenous people remained the sole source of labour for the tea industry till the end of the 1850s, and in 1859, the total labour force was about 10,000. However, the rapid growth of the industry demanded a much stronger labour force than what could be managed locally. As a result, immigration of labour to the Brahmaputra Valley began since the mid-1860s. Of a total plantation labour force of 34,433 in Assam proper in 1867-68, 22,800 or two-thirds were imported labour. By the end of 1872, the total number of imported labour increased to approximately 24,000 (Guha, 1977). By 1905-06, the adult labour force on Assam plantations swelled to a total of 417,262, and the indigenous labour constituted a very small fraction of it (Guha, 1977).

Parallel to the rapid expansion of the tea industry mainly with European capital and imported labour, had been the process of colonial transformation of the land-abundant semi-feudal agrarian structure of Assam. Although the colonial regime did not disturb the old pattern of land distribution, immediately after the annexation of the Assam plains, the existing practice of personal service was done away with, and each *paik* was required to pay a lump sum of Rs. 3 for the land he possessed. In 1832, arrangements were made to introduce a system of annual settlement to replace the old practice of poll tax, and the responsibility of collection of land tax was given to certain commission agents called *chaudhuris, mauzadars and kakotis*. The system of annual settlement continued till 1835, when it was replaced by settlement for a short term, but the system of revenue collection remained the same. In 1854, the system of annual settlement was re-introduced as it proved to be more suitable for maximizing revenue collection.

In 1870, the colonial regime adopted a set of much more rigorous rules essentially to maximize land revenue. For introduction of the ryotwari system of land settlement, the five districts of Assam proper, viz. Kamrup, Darrang, Nowgong, Lakhimpur and Sibsagar, were divided into *mauzas* or circles, and each such unit covered an area of a few square miles to 200 square miles. Each *mauza* was placed under the control of a *mauzadar* for accurate assessment and collection of revenue. The *mauzadar* had to be an influential and well-to-do resident of the *mauza* itself, and was bound to pay the entire land revenue due from his *mauza*, by the end of April. The commission agent called *mauzadar* for his obligation, received a commission at ten per cent on the first Rs.10, 000 and five per cent on the balance of the revenue paid by him. Each *mauza* was further divided into revenue villages comprising not less than 200 households.

The new set of rules required each *mauzadar* to take personal responsibility to actually measure the land prior to settlement. It was the responsibility of the *mauzadar* to record correctly the result of the actual measurement in a field register (*chitha*) from which he had to prepare an abstract (*khatian*), and finally the revenue roll (*jamabandi*). For the purpose of settlement and revenue collection, the entire area under cultivation in the valley was divided into two broad categories, depending primarily upon the nature of cropping. The first category included the area under wet-paddy and homesteads held permanently by the farmers, while the second category covered the land used for fluctuating cultivation. In case of the land under wet-rice cultivation and homesteads, the settlement with each cultivator was completed by issuing him a lease or *patta* for a period not exceeding ten years, and taking from him a *kabuliyat* (acceptance) in a prescribed form. The holdings thus settled, were considered as heritable and transferable property subject to the condition that all transfers were dully registered in the office of the Deputy Commissioner. However, in case of the land under fluctuating cultivation, the Settlement Rules allowed only annual lease. Therefore, the colonial policy of settlement of agricultural land, for the first time in the history of Assam, recognized permanent heritable and transferable right over land of the cultivators who took periodic leases from the Government. The policy, however, did not confer the same rights in case of the annual leases or for land occupied by fluctuating cultivation.

The spiritual aristocracy favoured by land grants by the Ahom kings had to deal with the colonial policy, when the right to hold lands, free of assessment founded on grants, was cancelled in 1834. Initially, the colonial administration disregarded all claims to hold land revenue-free, and assessed at five annas a pura (four bighas). Later on, however, for the purpose of assessment, a broad distinction was made between debottar lands i.e. land grants made to the temples and *brahmottar/dharmottar* lands i.e. land devoted to some religious purposes, but not temple lands *per se*. The *debottar* grants were exempted from revenue while the *brahmottar* or *dharmottar* grants were assessed at half rate, and all such estates were also declared as heritable and transferable property of the holders. Therefore, regarding their status, such land-holders came to the same footing as decennial settlement holders at full rates having a permanent, heritable and transferable interest in their lands.

The settlement rules of 1870 remained in force until superseded by a set of more comprehensive regulations in 1886. The Assam Land and Revenue Regulations, 1886 basically retained all the features of the previous set of rules. Meanwhile, a cadastral survey was ordered and completed during the years 1882-93. Though the land revenue rates remained unchanged till 1893, the total revenue demand had substantially increased due to expansion of the settled areas and detection of concealed cultivation.

The capitalist set-up built upon the semi-feudal agrarian structure had several severe socio-economic implications. The rapidly growing modern sector comprising especially of tea industries along with coal mines, oil-fields and associated infrastructure, led to large-scale immigration of labour into the valley from the second half of the nineteenth century. This not only influenced the demographic and ethnic composition of the valley significantly but also led to a serious economic imbalance between the land-abundant peasant economy and the expanding capitalist sector. While the immigration of adult labour force particularly to the plantations swelled manifold, the land-abundant agricultural sector marked by considerably poor technology coupled with the widely prevalent practice of shifting cultivation failed to produce enough to feed the additional non-agricultural workforce. Consequently, annual import of food grains into the valley increased from 0.3 million *maunds* around 1872 to some 0.7 million *maunds* during the last five years of the century (Guha, 1977).

Despite the increasing demand of food grains, the agricultural sector remained more or less stagnant, neither registering a proportionate expansion of the gross cropped area nor witnessing a significant shift in the cropping pattern in the absence of any positive intervention of the colonial state. However, imposition of rent in cash and its frequent revisions, and the settlement policy for maximization of revenue had substantially restricted growth of the agricultural sector in the valley. Yet, the gross cropped area, exclusive of the area under tea had increased to an extent till 1892-93, but went on decreasing from year to year until 1900-1901. This decline was, however, primarily caused by black fever epidemic, a disaster that the valley witnessed before it could make up for the losses caused by the Civil War and the Burmese invasion in the first quarter of the century. The black fever epidemic first appeared in Goalpara in 1883, entered Assam proper in 1888, and gradually engulfed the entire valley. During the 1890s, the population of Kamrup decreased more than 7 per cent; that of the Mangaldai sub-division of Darrang, 9 per cent and of Nowgong, about 25 per cent. Being the non-tea districts, it was a loss of indigenous population, and the cumulative decline of indigenous population of the valley as a whole, was at least 7.7 per cent (Guha, 1977). At the same time, the immigrant population in the major tea districts had grown substantially as these districts were least affected. The population of Lakhimpur actually increased more than 46 per cent between 1891 and 1901 – an estimated 16 per cent through natural growth while the remaining 30 per cent due to immigration. Similarly, the population of Sibsagar increased more than 24 per cent, and half the increase could be attributed to immigration. The non-indigenous population of Assam proper increased from less than a lakh in a total population of 15 lakh in 1872 to an estimated five to six lakhs in a total population of about 22 lakhs in 1901 (Guha, 1977).

Since the beginning of the last century, adding a new chapter to the political history of Assam, the colonial regime encouraged immigration of land hungry peasants from East Bengal not only to enhance land revenue through new settlements but also to enhance agricultural production by bringing more wastelands under cultivation. The East Bengal peasants responded favourably because, apart from abundance of land in the valley, they found the ryotwari system in Assam proper less atrocious than the zamindari system in the place of their origin. As Guha observes:

> 'Immigration was no doubt a welcome phenomenon for labour short, land-abundant Assam from the economic point of view. Landless immigrants from over-populated East Bengal – of them some 85 per cent were Muslims – found land in Assam's water-logged, jungle-infested, riverine belt. Used to an amphibious mode of living and industrious, these immigrants came by rail, steamers up to the Brahmaputra to reclaim these malarial areas. All that they wanted was land. From their riverine base, they further pressed themselves forward in all directions in search of more of living space in the areas held by the autochthones. ...' (Guha, 1977, p.206).

The process of large-scale immigration of the land hungry Muslim peasants from East Bengal, that began in the first part of the last century continued throughout the colonial period and even after independence. This had undoubtedly resulted in substantial growth of population in all the districts of Assam proper. The table below indicates the growth of population in the districts of Assam proper during the colonial period since 1872.

DENSITY OF POPULATION IN THE DISTRICTS OF ASSAM PROPER

(per sq. mile)

District	1872	1881	1891	1901	1911	1921	1941
Kamrup	146	167	164	153	173	198	328
Darrang	69	80	90	99	110	170	263
Nowgong	68	82	90	68	79	108	299
Sibsagar	64	79	96	120	138	162	301
Lakhimpur	27	40	56	82	104	143	219

Source: Guha, 1977, p. 339

While the growth of population in the valley till the end of 19th century was mainly due to immigration of non-agricultural workforce, the same for the subsequent decades, was for immigration of the landless peasants from East Bengal. Consequently, adding land revenue to the colonial coffer, fully assessed area exclusive of tea plantation had substantially increased since the beginning of the last century. The table below shows the growth of such area in each of the districts of Assam proper during the last four decades of colonial rule.

FULLY ASSESSED AREA FOR ORDINARY CULTIVATION IN ASSAM PROPER (Area in acres)

District	1912-13	1917-18	1922-23	1927-28	1944-45
Kamrup	542,199	602,573	678,124	783,174	1,072,783
Darrang	309,935	363,235	412,281	485,348	645,644
Nowgong	261,700	295,581	374,938	463,677	628,868
Sibsagar	566,035	609,529	650,591	696,708	786,647
Lakhimpur	262,129	311,802	360,786	433,557	592,260
Total	1,940,998	2,182,720	2,476,720	2,862,464	3,726,202

Source: J.N. Das, *Assam Land Revenue Manual*, 8th edition, Govt. of Assam, Shillong, 1968

The fully assessed area for agriculture exclusive of tea plantation registered a growth of about 92 per cent in Assam proper during the last four decades of colonial rule. The district of Nowgong recorded the highest (more than 140 per cent) while in case of the major tea district of Sibsagar, it was the lowest, less than 40 per cent. The large-scale immigration of peasants from East Bengal, given their agricultural skills and ability to work, positively contributed and brought a qualitative breakthrough in the agricultural scenario of the valley. Nevertheless, settlement of agricultural land to the immigrants, who belonged to a different socio-cultural as well as religious identity, besides their hunger for more and more agricultural land, created enough space for conflict of interests with the indigenous people of the valley. Since 1920s, this issue has continuously been disturbing the political process of the valley.

British colonialism in Assam, therefore, demolished the entire edifice of the semi-feudal Ahom State. The upper echelon of the pre-colonial ruling landed aristocracy that benefited by royal grants and assigned *paiks*, slaves and other such categories of people who rendered their services, as well as the supporting institutional arrangements could not withstand the colonial interventions bringing about rapid changes in the agrarian structure. The introduction of land revenue in cash and formal abolition of the system of slavery in 1843 affected the landed aristocracy. In many cases, their large holdings were confiscated or they had to sell off, for land revenue that continuously increased. Dhekiyal Phukan noted that assessment on some of the poorest classes of *rupit* lands was found to be nearly equal in value to one-half of their gross produce (Mills, 1984). The total land revenue demand more than quadrupled between 1865-66 and 1897-98 from about Rs.1million to more than 4 million, while the growth of cultivated acreage under all crops other than tea remained as low as a little over 7 per cent with no visible increase in productivity (Guha, 1991).

The colonial regime, however, preferred to compromise with the religious aristocracy headed by the Brahman priests and Gossain Mahanta clerics of Vaishnavism allowing them to retain the revenue-free *debottar* grants and giving some concession to *brahmottar* or *dharmottar* estates. Besides such concessions, they could continue with some of their feudal privileges like the appropriation of labour of their followers. By offering such privileges, the colonial rulers tried to ensure loyalty of the masses through the powerful satras. In the Sibsagar district alone, the Gossains of Auniati Satra, Dakhinpat Satra and Kamalabari Satra respectively owned 21,000, 10,400 and 5,900 acres of revenue free land in addition to the large tracts of land on concessional land revenue (Gohain, 1978). Total number of surviving landlord estates ranged from 2000 to 3000 over the last quarter of the 19th century. Out of the 17,33,267 acres settled for cultivation by 1880, as much as 18 per cent was reportedly found settled with big landlords styled as *lakhirajdars, nisfkhirajdars, khatdars and chamuadars.* While the first two categories were holders of privileged tenants, the last two were full rate paying substantial ryots. Though family members and bondsmen cultivated a part of their holding, the remaining part was cultivated by their tenants (Guha, 1991).

At the same time, with the introduction of ryotwari system in the valley, which never witnessed strong feudalism, colonialism promoted a tiny section of *mauzadars* and revenue officials as landlords, who in turn remained loyal to the regime. When the ryot had failed to clear his revenue dues for two consecutive years, it was the duty of the *mauzadar* to put a *bakijai* or statement showing the arrears. In such cases, the district collector was to issue an attachment order. If the arrears were not cleared within 15 days, the attached properties were sold. The *mauzadar* instead of instituting a *bakijai* case, used to convert the arrears into loan by asking the cultivator to execute a bond, and in due course acquired the land.

The landowning section that survived and grew at the mercy of the colonial rule, though not quite big in number, became, socially as well as economically, an influential category of rural elite. Their relatively easy access to money helped them to maintain a form of tenancy, which involved leasing out of land on cash rent. Further, gradual expansion of the administrative towns and job facilities attached this section to the urban vicinity. This was both, historically and socially significant, because colonialism propelled a new class of absentee landlords hitherto absent in the pre-colonial social formation. The indigenous urban middle class that thus emerged maintained its linkage with the rural society as absentee landlords.

The section of rural elites constituted primarily of the *mauzadars* and other revenue collectors who also found tenancy convenient for getting their newly acquired lands cultivated. As a result, a new form of tenancy emerged and the area under tenancy had gradually increased. The cadastral survey operations completed during the period between 1883 to1893 ascertained that about 18 per cent of the settled area was leased out in Kamrup district, and in no other district was it more than six per cent. At the end of the century, the proportion of leased out land to total settled area was officially estimated at about 25 per cent for Kamrup, 9 per cent for Darrang, and 7 per cent for Sibsagar, although it remained below 6 per cent in two other districts of Assam proper. A remarkably higher percentage of the total leased out area in every individual district was based on cash rent arrangements (Guha, 1991). The privileged section of the big land holders [2] leasing out their lakhiraj and nisfkheraj lands promoted the new form of tenancy, involving land rent in cash.

The colonial land settlement and revenue policies embodied in the ryotwari system, and recognition of permanent heritable and transferable right over land, converted the vast majority of population to a broad class of small holders. They possessed the major portion of their cultivated land on long-term lease. Yet, annual leases were also widely prevalent. Therefore, it is difficult to estimate the average size of holding held by the small landholders. However, as Hunter pointed out, a holding of 15 bighas in Kamrup and Darrang, 12 to 15 bighas in Nowgong, and 12 bighas in Sibsagar and Lakhimpur districts would mean a small as well as average size of holding (Hunter, 1982). Though land was abundant, the considerably high rate of revenue restricted growth of the average size of holding in Assam proper.

The slaves, serfs, bondsmen and such categories of people who constituted about 10 per cent of the pre-colonial Assam were considered as slaves by the colonial state. With formal abolition of slavery in 1843, this broad category of manual labour became legally free, but they continued to depend upon their masters for a long time. Monetization of the economy compelled many of them to borrow cash by mortgaging themselves as bondsmen. The borrower as bonded under the system, tilled the owners' land besides working as a servant for all other daily work of the master. For the service he rendered, he used to get a monthly deduction of the principal he had borrowed. The common practice in the late 1880s was that if the borrower was fed but not clothed by his master, he had to work for 20 months towards settling an advance of Rs.20. In this case, a month's wage was deemed equivalent to the food, interest and a rupee in case. If the principal happened to be higher, his monthly wages used to be much less to adjust the higher amount of interest (Guha, 1991).

Paucity of capital rather than of land had been the major factor responsible for impoverishment of the peasants and the existing form of exploitation. Yet, the number of bonded and free agricultural labourers together was not very high. In the Census of 1891, those occupationally classed as farm servants and field labourers along with their dependents numbered only 4,498 and 632 persons respectively. Presumably, the first category included the bondsmen while the second category implied the free agricultural labourers. Therefore, colonization pauperized the vast majority of indigenous cultivators. Many of them preferred to be tenants, but could not be pushed to the labour market as wage earners. The agrarian structure, nevertheless, retained the practice of bondage to a certain extent.

The class of agricultural labourers as well as the marginal and small farmers gradually swelled up with the large-scale immigration of landless peasants from East Bengal and the ex-tea garden labourers settled for cultivation during the subsequent period. This resulted in a far more complex pattern of agrarian relations involving various forms of tenancy, land alienation and consequent conflicts of interests between the indigenous population and the immigrant community.

The exotic capitalism devised its own institutional arrangements with a highly centralized bureaucracy, supported by a tiny section of local commission agents. On the one hand, the colonial exploitation heavily taxed the peasants and on the other hand, the institutional arrangement estranged the overwhelming majority of the illiterate indigenous community. The old system of governance at the local level had died a silent death due to the colonial distortions. But, there was no sincere attempt on the part of the colonial State to create an alternative. The Commissioner of Assam Valley Division, W.E. Ward, was of the opinion in 1882 that the soil of the Brahmaputra Valley was not 'fertile enough for local government institutions to flourish' because, according to him, the Assamese were devoid of 'those business-like habits which are so needful to make a man a useful member of any committee to which he may be appointed' (cited in Guha, 1977).

A.J.Moffatt Mills expressed his desire 'to reconstitute village communities'. However, he wanted it to happen so that the village community would gradually promote 'an influential class of men as middlemen between the *Rayats* and the Government to do away with constant interference in village concerns which now overwhelm the Collectors.' This testifies the intention of the colonial policy of the day, towards the institutions of local government. Yet, till 1870 there was no institution of local rural government worth the name. After the enactment of the Bengal Village Chowkidari Act in 1870, it was introduced only in Goalpara, Cachar and Sylhet. The Act failed to leave any significant impact on the population, and there was no further attempt to introduce any other legislation. However, the enactment of the Assam Local Rate Regulation for levying the local rates for local purposes was an important event in this context.

In 1881, the Government of India proposed certain reforms for local boards. The Government of Assam opposed the proposals on the plea that the province was backward. Thereafter came the famous Ripon Resolution of 1882, on local self-government. Though it contained directives for extending and maintaining a wide network of local boards in every district, not much could be achieved on the front of the rural local Government, till the second decade of twentieth century.

The Assam Local Self-Government Act of 1915 was enacted following the recommendations of the Royal Commission on Decentralization, and the enactment provided for establishment of the village Panchayat system for the first time on a formal and legal basis. The Chief Commissioner of Assam accepted the major recommendations of the Royal Commission. And, he believed that some of the problems such as sanitation and water supply of the villages could be solved by giving responsibilities to the villagers to undertake these work themselves. The Chief Commissioner of Assam, therefore, proposed to include in the Local Self-Government Bill, provision for delegation by local boards to Village Authorities, of the powers and duties regarding sanitation, primary education and other such petty village work. Accordingly, the Assam Local Self-Government Act of 1915 was passed, and this Act empowered the Chief Commissioner to constitute a Village authority in each village. As per the provisions of the Act, the members of such a Village Authority could be wholly appointed or elected or, a combination of both for a period of three years. The Chief Commissioner was authorized to decide the number of elected or appointed members. In practice, most of the so-called village authorities were comprised of nominated members.

In the mean time, the Government of India Act, 1919 transferred the subject of local self-government to the provincial government. Thus in the ethos of diarchy, the Assam legislative council brought the Assam Rural Self-Government Bill, 1925 and subsequently passed the Rural

Self-Government Act 1926. The new Act provided that every village should have a Village Authority, consisting of not more than nine members elected on the basis of adult manhood franchise. As per the provision of this Act, the members of the Village Authority were to be elected for a term of three years. This Act was passed with the objective of creating a mechanism through which the villagers might undertake the management of their own affairs and develop capacity for self-help. The village authorities, however, failed to bring about any significant change mainly due to inadequate financial support from the colonial government. Therefore, the village authorities only had nominal existence.

Independence and inclusion of village panchayats in the Directive Principles of the Constitution of India inspired the government of Assam to establish panchayats in the state. With the stated objective of all-round development of the villages, the Chief Minister of Assam introduced the Assam Rural Panchayat Bill in the State Legislative Assembly as early as March 1948. The Bill was referred to a Select Committee, which submitted the report with certain modifications in the same month. Subsequently, the Act was passed, and it received assent of the Governor General in November 1948.

The Assam Rural Panchayat Act provided a two-tier structure of panchayat system comprising the Primary Panchayats at the village level and the Rural Panchayats at the mouza level. The members of the Primary Panchayats were elected directly. Each Primary Panchayat was provided with an Executive body consisting of not more than 15 members and a President. These local units were looked after by the Rural Development wing at the district level, which was under the control of the concerning Deputy Commissioners. The Act also empowered the government to declare any area to be a Rural Panchayat area, and in any such area, there might be as many Primary Panchayats (not exceeding fifteen) as deemed necessary by the Deputy Commissioner or the Sub-Divisional Officer. Covering almost all aspects of rural life, the Act included as many as 34 functions.

The Assam Rural Panchayat Act, 1948 was in operation in the state for a decade, and the number of Rural Panchayats gradually increased from 29 at the end of 1950-51 to 422 in 1959. In 1959, the Rural Panchayats covered a total of 2,657 Primary Panchayats scattered in all the plains districts of Assam. The system, thus evolving as a mere residue of the district administration, failed to realize its objectives. To make an in-depth study of the system, the State Government appointed a committee, which came up with several suggestions and recommendations. Following these recommendations, a fresh Act was drafted and introduced in 1955. But due to the constitution of the Mehta Committee by the Government of India to study the local self Government in the Country, the Bill remained pending without any action taken.

The State Government accepted the Mehta Committee recommendations and in tune with these the next Panchayat Act was enacted as the Assam Panchayat Act, 1959. The Act provided a three tier structure to the rural local government i.e. Gaon Panchayat at the village level, Anchalik Panchayats at the block level and Mahkuma Parishad at the apex level i.e. the Sub-Division. Under the system, a Gaon Panchayat, being at the bottom, consisted of all adults, whose names were included in the electoral roll of an area with a minimum 2500 persons. The Gaon Panchayat was the executive of the Gaon Sabha. The Gaon Panchayat would consist of eleven members including the President and the Vice-President, elected directly by the Gaon Sabha. The Act also made provisions for co-opting one woman, if no woman was elected, and one each from the Scheduled Castes and the Scheduled Tribes, if they constituted at least five per cent of the total population of the area. The term of the Gaon Panchayat was three years, and the Act empowered the Gaon Panchayat to appoint its own Secretary.

The Assam Panchayat Act, 1959 provided that every Gaon Sabha would elect one representative to the Anchalik Panchayat, and besides that, it made provision for co-option of two members, one each from Scheduled Castes and Scheduled Tribes, if such members were not elected. However, there was no such provision for co-option of any woman member. In addition to such elected and co-opted members, an Anchalik Panchayat would include one representative elected by the Chairman of the Co-operative Societies falling within the area and the member of the Legislative Assembly representing the area as an ex-officio member. The Act also empowered the State Government to appoint members to the Anchalik Panchayats without the right to vote. The President and the Vice-President of an Anchalik Panchayat were to be elected by the members from among themselves.

The Mahkuma Parishads at the apex would consist of the following four categories of members:

a. Presidents of all the Anchalik Panchayats falling within its jurisdiction;

b. All members of the Legislative assembly and the Parliament representing the area;

c. Chairman of the Municipalities, Town Committees and School Boards falling within the Sub-Division as ex-officio members; and,

d. Officers appointed by the Government as ex-officio members.

Further, the Act provided for co-option of one member each from the Scheduled Castes and Scheduled Tribes, if no member was elected from such categories, but denied a similar provision for woman. The President and the Vice-President were to be elected by the members from among themselves.

The efforts of the Assam State Legislative Assembly made through the Assam Panchayat Act, 1959 proved to be futile as the panchayats at different levels failed to emerge as democratic institutions to address the real socio-economic issues of the overwhelming majority. After four years of experimentation, the Government of Assam appointed another study team to suggest the modifications required for the satisfactory functioning of the panchayat system in the state. Following the recommendations of the study team, the Legislative Assembly enacted the Assam Panchayat (Amendment) Act, 1964, to accommodate a couple of changes in the previous provisions.

The important changes made at the Gaon Panchayat level included abolition of the provision of direct election of the President and the Vice-president. The amendment provided that, instead of direct election, the President and the Vice-president be elected by the elected members to the Gaon Panchayats. The provision for appointment of the Secretary by the Gaon Panchayat was removed by handing over this responsibility to the Government of Assam. Further, the amended Act extended the term of the Gaon Panchayat from three to four years, and brought the system of secret ballot instead of open voting in the elections, to the Gaon Panchayats. At the level of both the Anchalik Panchayat and Mahkuma Parishad, the amended Act made provision for co-option of two women members, if no one was elected, and one, if one woman member was elected. The Act also empowered the State Government to nominate some members to the Anchalik Panchayats from the forest villages and tea gardens falling within the area, which were excluded so far. The amended Act also further expanded the Mahkuma Parishad making provision for inclusion of the Chairman of the Co-Operative Central Bank, the Deputy Commissioner and the Sub-Divisional Officer as members.

Following the recommendations of the Estimate Committee of the Government of Assam, the state Legislative

Assembly enacted the Assam Panchayati Raj Act, 1972, which repealed the previous Act. The Act abolished the three-tier structure of the rural local bodies by eliminating the Anchalik Panchayats from the purview, and in its place re-introduced a two-tier system, i.e. only Gaon Panchayat at the base and Mahkuma Parishads at the sub-divisional level. The area coverage of the Gaon Panchayats was enlarged to cover a population of up to 20,000. Earlier the tea gardens were excluded from the system, but this Act also covered the tea gardens within the panchayat system. The Act came into force in 1974 and was in force till 1986.

The Act empowered the State Government to appoint any officer as an ex-officio member of the Gaon Panchayat. Besides, the Councilor of the Mahkuma Parishad representing the area of the Gaon Panchayat was an ex-officio member of the Gaon Panchayat. The Act provided for direct election of the President of the Gaon Panchayat, while its Secretary was to be appointed by the Mahkuma Parishad.

The Act also changed the composition of the Mahkuma Parishad, which was to include as members:

a. One Councilor elected by each of the Gaon Panchayats;

b. One representative each, not being a member of the State legislative Assembly or the Parliament, from the Municipality, Town Committee, Regional Board of Education and the Central Co-operative bank as ex-officio Councilors;

c. The other Government officer to be appointed as an ex-officio Councilor, by the Government from time to time; and

d. Two Councilors nominated by the State Government from the tea gardens.

The Chairman and the Chief Executive Councilor of the Mahkuma Parishad were elected by the non-official Councilors from amongst themselves. The term of the Panchayat bodies under this act was four years.

In the mean time, the Asom Gana Parishad, a regional party, formed the Government in the State in 1985, on its own. The Act of 1972 was repealed by the Assam Panchayati Raj Act, 1986, which was adopted with effect from September 1990. The Act again changed the basic structure of the Panchayat system. It re-introduced the three-tier system by bringing back the Anchalik Panchayat in the middle. Under the Act, the Mahkuma Parishad was entrusted with the role of a supervisory character.

The new Act under the new political regime provided for the constitution of a Gaon Panchayat for an area having a population of six to ten thousand, and the bottom level of the institution was to be constituted of ten elected members and a President directly elected by the people, for a period of five years. The Anchalik Panchayat was to be formed by the presidents of the Gaon Panchayats. The MLAs and the MPs were ex-officio members, and the Government could nominate such officers as deemed necessary.

The Mahkuma Parishad consisted of all the presidents of the Anchalik Panchayats of its jurisdiction, MLAs and MPs representing the area, and the district heads of different departments as nominees of the State Government. The Act, however, substantially enhanced direct control of the State Government through the bureaucracy. The power to appoint their own staff was taken away from the Panchayats. The Panchayats could retain only such stuff as was prescribed by the State Government and appointed by the Director of the Panchayat. The Act of 1986 was amended, and the enactment that followed was the Assam Panchayati Raj (Amendment) Act, 1992. The few amendments, however, made the structure of the Panchayati Raj in the state, more bureaucratic.

The year 1990 was, nevertheless, a significant year in the history of Panchayati Raj in Assam, because it was in this year that the state Government by an amendment, provided for a 30 percent reservation of seats for women in the panchayats. Thus, the reservation of the seats for women in Assam was not just a follow up action of the Constitutional provision, it was a statutory provision adopted prior to the 73rd amendment of the Constitution. Under the 1986 Act, the first election to the rural local bodies was held in the year 1992, which for the first time elected a huge number of women members in each tier of the system.

In terms of electoral politics, Assam witnessed almost an unimpeachable hegemony of the Congress till the late 1970s.[3] Despite the strong anti-Congress wave that blew off the Congress from power at the centre immediately after emergency, the electoral performance of the party in Assam was fairly satisfactory in the sixth Lok Sabha elections held in 1977. In the predominantly rural society of Assam, the support base of the Congress was constituted of both the indigenous and immigrant communities cutting across their ethnic and linguistic boundaries. For its political legitimacy, as pointed out earlier, the Congress regime also took the initiative to introduce the Panchayati Raj in the state immediately after independence. Nevertheless, the structure of Panchayati Raj that emerged in Assam had always been sandwiched between the bureaucracy from above and the section of landowning rural elite created by the colonial regime from below. When the bureaucratic stranglehold on the system estranged the people at large, the notion of power associated with the formal structure of Panchayati Raj helped the rural elites to continue with their domination in the agrarian society. The Congress regime in Assam, being dependent to a large extent on the rural elites for its electoral gains, avoided the vital agrarian questions and made no serious attempt to restructure the rural society to create an environment conducive to democratic decentralization.

At the time of independence, the overall agrarian scenario of Assam was not much different from the rest of the country.

The degree of land concentration in the state was perhaps not as high as it was in the zamindari areas of Uttar Pradesh and Bihar, and in some other parts of the ryotwari areas. Yet, the phenomenon of concentration of cultivated land in the hands of the small, though socially and economically quite influential, landed aristocracy created by the colonial design in Assam, cannot be overlooked. Some empirical studies conducted in 1950-54 revealed that, of the total households, the households having holdings of 50 bighas or more constituted 3.6 per cent in Lakhimpur and 4.2 per cent in Darrang and Sibsagar. The households with such large holdings had command over 22.4 per cent of the total agricultural land in Darrang, 20.1 per cent in Sibsagar and 16.9 per cent in Lakhimpur (Gowsami, 1950; Sharma, 1952 and 1954).

Instead of making any serious attempt to restructure the agrarian society, the Congress, which ruled the state uninterruptedly since independence till the late 1970s, created a myth of land reforms by enacting several legislations. And, as elsewhere in India, the salient features of all the major legislations enacted in Assam after independence apparently aimed at abolition of intermediaries in the permanently settled areas; ceiling on landholding; consolidation of small farms; and protection of the interests of the tenants.

For acquiring the rights of the proprietors (zamindars) and intermediary tenure holders (jotedars and mirashdars) in the permanently settled areas of Goalpara and Cachar districts, the Government of Assam enacted the Assam State Acquisition of Zamindaris Act, 1951, and it was brought into force from June 1954. According to the official sources, the rights of all proprietors in respect to 3,628 estates and those of tenure holders in respect to 4,533 tenures covering an area of 16.74 lakh acres had been acquired in the permanently settled areas (Govt. of Assam, 1993). This, however, did not lead to any qualitative breakthrough, because such a reform failed to ensure equitable redistribution of land among the tenants of the erstwhile zamindaris. Similarly, the Assam State Acquisition of Lands belonging to Religious or Charitable Institutions of Public Nature Act, 1959 was enacted and brought into force from March 1963 to do away with the intermediary interests held by the Satras, Maths, public temples etc. This enabled the government to acquire a total of 3,30,157 bighas of land belonging to 164 such institutions. Nevertheless, the total area yet to be acquired from about 200 such institutions is estimated at 3,71,197 bighas (Govt. of Assam, 1993).

The Assam Fixation of Ceiling on Land Holding Act, 1956 was brought into force in February 1958 in all plains districts of Assam. The level of rural ceiling was 150 bighas to start with. However, the lag of two years between the enactment of the Act and its implementation, provided ample opportunities to the big holders to explore the legal loopholes, and initiate adequate measures to escape through illegal transfers. In the specific context of rural Assam, a size of 150 bighas of cultivated land was also big enough property to continue with the tradition of economic and political influence over the overwhelming majority in a village.

Considerably, a high population growth rate has caused excessive pressure on the agricultural sector, which has been a significant factor responsible for rapid fragmentation of operational holdings in the state. In order to prevent further fragmentation and to make a situation conducive to mechanized farming by consolidating the small-holdings, the Government of Assam enacted the Assam Consolidation of Holdings Act, 1960, which was to be applied in all the plains districts. The Act was amended in 1966 to make consolidation compulsory, and the government launched a scheme for consolidation of 50,000 bighas identifying few pockets in the state. The government, however, utterly failed in this attempt.

Being inspired by the peasant movements in different

parts of the country, especially the 'Tebhaga' movement in Bengal, the left parties, both RCPI and CPI, sought to mobilize the peasantry in Assam against the prevailing feudal practice of *Adhi* (share cropping on 50:50 basis) system. The peasant discourses with leftist ideology that followed independence compelled the Congress government to address the issue of tenancy in Assam, primarily involving three sets of measures – regulation of rent, security of tenure and ownership rights for tenants. The Government of Assam enacted the Assam Adhiar Protection and Regulation Act, 1948, which prescribed only one-fourth of the principal crop as crop rent to be charged from the *Adhiar* by the landlord. The legislative measure had, however, failed to protect the interests of the tenants or the *adhiars*. The tenants, with their perpetuate dependency on the landlords, generally preferred to avoid any confrontation as they were afraid of being ejected forcefully from the land, consequent upon demanding the statutory rent. In some isolated cases when the tenants insisted on implementation of the Act, the landlords with the help of police seized the entire crop from the tenants followed by their eviction (Dutta, 1986).

The overall impact of the land reform programmes enacted and implemented with subsequent amendments since independence are indicated by the pattern of distribution of operational holdings in Assam, as shown in the table below. The marginal farmers who constituted a little more than 57 per cent of the total farmers in the state in 1971, has increased to more than 62 per cent in 1995-96. However, the agricultural land in their command has not increased proportionately. As a result, the average size of holding for this category of farmers has decreased from 0.45 hectare (3.35 bighas) to 0.37 hectare (2.75 bighas). Therefore, approximately two-thirds of the farmers of Assam have to depend on an operational holding of less than 3 bighas, which cannot be an economic size of holding by any standard. The numerical strength of the category of large farmers has substantially eroded over the period. Thus far, only 0.19 per cent of the farmers in the state have command over more than 10 per cent of the total agricultural land. At the same time, the average size of large holding in the state has increased from about 57 hectares (about 430 bighas) to more than 65 hectares (approximately 460 bighas).

The legislative measures that aimed at the protection of interests of the tenants in Assam have, however, utterly failed, and all sorts of feudal practices are still marking the agrarian structure of the state. Almost one-third of the farmers in Assam, mostly the marginal and small farmers, have to depend on different forms of share-cropping, and in most of the cases, the land rent is half of the crop produced. In other words, the *adhi* system is widely prevalent in the state, and the tenants under the prevailing conditions are hardly benefited by the existing legislative measures. Besides the feudal practice of *adhi*, another issue is the practice of mortgage (commonly known as *bandhaki*), which often leads to alienation of land, frequently pushing a large section of the marginal and small farmers to the category of landless agricultural labour. Nevertheless, there is no legislation to prevent the peasantry from the rampant feudal practice of *bandhaki*.

Failure of the Congress during its continuous rule to carry forward the required institutional reform to restructure the agrarian economy, necessarily led to economic retardation in a situation where other sectors of the economy did not witness any appreciable progress. At the same time, the growth of population had always been substantially high, partly due to the continuous immigration, which further augmented pressure on the nearly stagnant agrarian economy of the state. The Congress regime, too, did not show any interest in enlarging the space for the institutions of democratic decentralization in the true spirit. As a result, the electoral

DISTRIBUTION OF OPERATIONAL HOLDINGS IN ASSAM
(Area in Hectare)

Category of Holdings	Number and Area of Holdings in							
	1970-71		1980-81		1985-86		1995-96	
	Number	Area	Number	Area	Number	Area	Number	Area
Marginal	1120405	509297	1363340	582755	1450310	600365	1669252	621368
(< 1 Hect.)	(57.04)	(17.67)	(59.34)	(18.68)	(59.95)	(18.99)	(62.22)	(19.80)
Small	466691	661528	522974	748395	546456	761452	561078	769698
(1 – 2 Hect.)	(23.76)	(22.95)	(22.76)	(23.98)	(22.59)	(24.09)	(20.91)	(24.52)
Semi-Medium	275780	757209	313562	859986	324357	874113	351245	924258
(2 – 4 Hect.)	(14.04)	(26.27)	(13.65)	(27.56)	(13.40)	(27.65)	(13.09)	(29.45)
Medium	93924	540345	92019	487068	92238	480913	96418	494658
(4 – 10 Hect.)	(04.78)	(18.05)	(04.00)	(15.61)	(3.82)	(15.21)	(3.59)	(15.76)
Large	7576	435195	5693	442303	5695	444655	5004	328467
(10 & above)	(0.38)	(15.06)	(0.25)	(14.17)	(0.240)	(14.06)	(0.19)	(10.47)
Total	1964376	2882573	2297588	3120507	2419156	3161498	2682997	3138449
	(100.00)	(100.00)	(100.00)	(100.00)	(100.00)	(100.00)	(100.00)	(100.00)

N.B. Figures in bracket indicate percetage.

Source: *Agricultural Census* of the year 1970-71, 1980-81, 1985-86 and *Statistical Hand Book*, 2004, Government of Assam.

hegemony of the Congress started declining, especially among the indigenous communities. The poll verdicts in the sixth Assembly elections held in 1978 came as the first major setback for the Congress, reflecting a dramatic shift. The tradition of one-party domination had come to an end when the strength of the Congress in the state Assembly declined only to 26 seats in 1978 from 95 in the dissolved Assembly. At the same time, however, none of the parties could secure a working majority in the house of 126 members. The Janata Party, despite the advantage of being in power at the center, and all possible efforts to emerge as the alternative to the Congress in Assam, could win only 53 seats while its electoral partner, the Plain Tribal Council of Assam (PTCA) won another 4 seats. The unprecedented victory of the Left parties was also significant. The CPI (M) alone returned 11 candidates while the CPI, the RCPI and the SUCI returned another 11 candidates. Except for the PTCA, all other existing regional political formations remained insignificant in the changed electoral scenario of the state.

The period between 1971 and 1977 was an eventful one in the political history of Assam, since independence. The state leadership of the Congress had to confront with an adverse situation caused by certain factors specific to the regional society, besides the inevitable implications of the simultaneous organizational crisis faced by the party in the country as a whole. One of the most significant developments in Assam during the period had been the political consolidation of the 'Other Backward Classes' (OBC) with a demand for expansion of the constitutional provisions of positive discrimination for their socio-economic uplift. In another very important development, a popular ministry headed by Mahendra Mohan Choudhury was asked to resign by Mrs. Gandhi. It was widely propagated in the state that Chaudhury's resignation symbolized the end of upper caste rule in Assam, and subsequently, elevation of Sinha to Chief

Ministership opened up a new era – the beginning of 'self assertion' by the OBC and other downtrodden groups who were 'exploited throughout the ages by the upper caste' (Deka, 1979).

The Congress consciously maneuvered a backlash of caste politics in Assam camouflaging the real issues of socio-economic development. In the process of propagating the OBC cult in Assam, the Congress could definitely make its support base wider by appealing to the numerically stronger section of the lower caste people. But alongside, it antagonized the politically more influential and vocal section of the upper caste and middle class indigenous Assamese that provided leadership to the Congress during the period of the freedom movement till the 1960s. The strategy of caste politics followed by the Congress had severe political implications in the subsequent period. The re-alignment of the organizational structure in view of the caste factor, had not only alienated a sizeable section of the core of the Congress leadership, but also disillusioned a substantial part of its traditional support base.

Immediately after its formation, the Sinha Ministry had to grapple with a series of agitations. Owing to a steady price-hike of the essential commodities, the food agitations in Assam started gaining momentum towards the later part of 1972. Meanwhile, re-appearance of the language issue in the form of an intense movement over medium of instruction sprang up in late 1972. The rash steps taken by Sinha to pacify the issue resulted in large-scale violence and communal riots in different parts of the state. The violent movement over the issue of medium of instruction was followed by a severe students' strike in the entire state during 1973-74 based on a 21-point charter of demands under the leadership of the All Assam Students' Union (AASU). In addition to that, the Sinha Ministry was also seriously threatened by an agitation of the college teachers led by the All Assam College Teachers'

Association and supported by the Teachers Associations of both Gauhati and Dibrugarh University in 1975.

The internal emergency declared by the Prime Minister on 25 June 1975 was in fact a great relief for the Sinha Ministry. As elsewhere in the country, excesses were committed in Assam on one or the other pretext during the period of emergency. The Sinha Ministry tried to settle old scores including personal ones, by throttling all democratic rights of the people. There were indiscriminate arrests of teachers and students who had antagonized the Ministry earlier. Assam was definitely not beyond the nefarious design of the emergency and all the excesses were committed in the state, as elsewhere in the country.

Meanwhile, the Ministry headed by Sarat Chandra Sinha had also substantially antagonized the land holding interests in the state by enforcing certain land reform measures, however, with only administrative vigour. Mahendra Mohan Choudhury introduced two major land reform programmes in Assam just before his resignation. First, an amendment of the Assam Fixation of Land Holding Act, 1956, which brought down the ceiling on private holdings from 50 acres (150 bighas) to 25 acres (75 bighas), was passed in 1970. This Act was amended during Sinha's regime and the ceiling was brought down to 50 bighas plus 4 bighas for orchards. Under the provisions of this Act, an area of 6,10,369 acres was declared as surplus, covering both individual holders and tea gardens. Although, about 14 per cent of the land declared as ceiling surplus could not be distributed due to various reasons, the remaining part was distributed to benefit quite a good number of landless farmers in the state. Second, the Assam (Temporarily Settled Areas) Tenancy Act 1971 was enacted essentially to protect the interests of the share-croppers or tenants. This Act was extended in 1974 to the permanently settled areas of the Goalpara district and the Karimganj subdivision of the Cachar district. In case of this

Act also, the ceiling was reduced to 50 bighas. Consequently, the total land acquired under the previous ceiling Act was 2,70,136 bighas which finally rose to 17,61,180 bighas during the emergency (Chaube, 1985).

The attempt to implement the land reform programmes bypassing the panchayats was politically counterproductive for the Congress. The reform programmes attempted with only administrative vigour challenged the hitherto socio-political influences of the Asomiya landed gentry and rich farmers, and consequently, this influencing section of the Assamese society became apprehensive about the Congress leadership in the state. It is evident from the fact that six of the twenty subdivisions (Dhubri, Goalpara, Kokrajhar, Guwahati, Tezpur, and Mangaldoi) had 54 per cent of the share of the total individual lands acquired by the Government, and these subdivisions constituted the Janata belt in the sixth Lok Sabha election comprising the constituencies of Dhubri, Kokrajhar, Guwahati and Tezpur (Chaube, 1985).

The Janata Party mainly comprising of a large number of ex-Congressmen, members of Jan Sangh, Swatantra Party and Socialist Party sought to establish itself as an alternative platform to the Congress in Assam. But, it had failed to emerge as a widely accepted alternative in Assam through the sixth Lok Sabha election. The broad political platform, which was primarily based on some amount of anti-Congress sentiments shared in common by its constituent elements, was undoubtedly successful in mobilizing wider support in the subsequent Assembly election. It had, however, failed to establish itself as a viable alternative before the common people of Assam. As a result, the state Government headed by the Janata Party collapsed within 20 months in 1979.

The later part of the 1970s also witnessed an increasing influence of the Left parties, particularly the CPI (M) as it was reflected by its conspicuous victory in the Assembly election held in 1978. The CPI (M) was successful to a great extent in expanding its support base particularly during the emergency and immediately after it. The mass organizations of the party recorded a rapid growth in the Brahmaputra Valley, and the party was successful in consolidating its position among the indigenous people of Assam towards the later part of the 1970s. Beyond any doubt, the victory of the CPI (M) in West Bengal and Tripura in late 1970s encouraged its committed activists in Assam too.

In order to ensure its victory in the Assembly election, the Janata Party forged an alliance with two regional parties, (a) the Plain Tribal Council of Assam (PTCA), which came into being in 1967 with a demand for creation of a separate state of Udayachal for the plains tribes of Assam; and (b) the Ujoni Asom Rajya Parishad (UARP), which was formed in 1970 with a demand for a separate state consisting of the three upper Assam districts where the Ahoms were largely concentrated. The Peoples Democratic Party (PDP), a regional party with little political influence that existed in the state since 1967 merged with the Janata Party in 1977. Nevertheless, two more regional parties, Asom Jatiyatabadi Dal (AJD) and Purbanchaliya Lok Parishad (PLP) maintained their independent identity in the Sixth Assembly election, but all the candidates put by these two regional parties had lost their security deposits.

The issue of foreign nationals (initially *bohiragoto* or outsiders) in Assam and their increasing threat to the Asomiya national identity was one of the major components of the election manifesto of both the newly formed regional parties, i.e., the AJD and the PLP in the 1978 elections. They could not capitalize on this issue for their immediate electoral gain, nevertheless, the anti-*bohiragoto* campaign in Assam continued vigorously even after the defeat of the AJD and the PLP. This issue became more serious when the Chief Election Commissioner in a conference of the state electoral officers held on 24 October 1978 stated that 'the large scale inclusion of foreign nationals (in the electoral rolls) in some states especially in the North Eastern region was alarming and required drastic action' (*The Assam Tribune*, 25 October 1978). Further, the Janata Party Chief Minister, Golap Borbora announced in the Assembly on 16 March 1979 that influx of foreign nationals was assuming alarming proportions (*The Assam Tribune*, 17 March 1979). Subsequently, the anti-foreigners movement in Assam started from April 1979 when a bye-election to the Lok Sabha in the Mangaldoi constituency was ordered.

The bye-election to the Mangaldoi constituency made the issue of foreign nationals in Assam, politically much more significant than ever before. In the process of revision of the electoral rolls, the police officials on instruction from the government of Assam, as it was alleged, hurriedly challenged the authenticity of citizenship of about 70,000 voters of that constituency. Consequently, the arrangements made for the bye-election were cancelled on one hand, and inaugurated an era of political turmoil in the state on the other.

A large numbers of scholars have already analyzed the anti-foreigners movement in Assam from different perspectives, and therefore, a fresh attempt is not required in the present context. Yet, cognizance of some of the basic features of the movement may definitely help to objectively analyze the political turmoil in the state in its totality. Beyond any doubt, the All Assam Students Union (AASU) was instrumental in making the issue of foreign nationals widely acceptable to the common Asomiya people. The AASU was acceptable to the common Asomiya people as it provided leadership to a series of popular movements in the state. The All Assam Gana Sangram Parishad (AAGSP) was formed on 27 August 1979 under the aegis of the AASU to run the movement. The major constituents of the AAGSP besides the AASU, were PLP, All Asom Sahitya Sabha and Sadau Asom

Karmachari Parishad. This newly formed united front of regionalist forces spearheaded the movement, which was started by the Asomiya middle class with a specific political design and an ideology of aggressive cultural nationalism.

Although it was apparently against the foreigners, the leadership of the movement from the very beginning launched a violent campaign against all the national political parties except the Janata Party and the BJP. Political assault, even assassination of the activists of the Left parties and the Congress became a frequent phenomenon in the state during the entire course of the movement. Similarly, the movement aroused destructive anger particularly against the Bengali speaking Muslim Community (also known as the Na-Asomiya) as they were indiscriminately characterized as 'Bangladeshi'.

In the meantime, Assam went under President's rule with the end of the Janata fiasco in November 1979. The state assembly experienced unprecedented defections followed by the efforts made by the Congress (I) to form a government. The numerical strength of the Congress (I) in the Assembly increased to 45 MLAs in December 1980 from its 8 MLAs in 1978. Being influenced by the changes in the correlation of forces at the centre with the emergence of Mrs. Gandhi as a powerful leader once again in 1980, a large number of right wing MLAs moved across to the Congress (I). However, it failed to gain a majority to form a stable government in the state. The Congress (I) ministry headed by Mrs. Taimur was formed on 6 December 1980, but collapsed on 26 June 1981. Once again Assam came under President's rule. Another Congress (I) government headed by Mr. Gogoi was installed on 13 January 1982 but he had to resign on 19 March 1982 as he failed to seek a vote of confidence. Therefore, Assam came under President's rule for the third time since 1979. The dissolution of the state legislature required a fresh election, and accordingly, the Government of India initiated the process of holding elections in February 1983.

The leadership of the movement was determined not only to boycott the poll, but also to stop the process of holding the elections without eliminating the names of the foreigners from the electoral roles and their subsequent deportation. The Janata Party, the BJP and the Lok Dal also decided not to participate and oppose the elections while the Congress (I), the Congress (U), the PTCA and the Left parties decided to participate.

The government of India with a stern decision to hold the election had geared up the state machinery to ensure polling. The opponent camp intensified the movement, and even adopted violent means to disrupt the election process. Consequently, the Brahmaputra valley experienced an unprecedented impasse. According to the government sources, more than 4000 people died in Assam as a result of election related violence. However, the non-government reports put the number of deaths at more than 7000 (Das Gupta & Guha, 1985). More than 1600 bridges were burnt in order to block the roads to prevent the entry of the election personnel into various constituencies. Even a good number of schools, which were likely to be used for elections, were burnt down. The Congress (I) had came back to power with its 91 MLAs out of the 109 seats for which election were held. The elections could not be held in the remaining 17 assembly constituencies.

The anti-foreigners movement came to a dramatic end with the signing of the so-called 'Assam Accord' between the leadership of the movement and the Government of India on 15 August 1985. The state assembly was dissolved immediately on demand of the AASU, and the date for fresh election in Assam was announced. Obviously, the leader- ship of the movement became enthusiastic to form a new regional party capable of capturing the power to implement the accord. The Asom Gana Parishad (AGP) came into being on 14 October 1985 under the leadership of P .K. Mahanta, Bhrigu Phukan, etc. who led the AASU during the six years of the movement (see for details, Sarmah, 2002).

The newly formed AGP very enthusiastically participated in the election held in 1985 without revision of the electoral rolls. Its major electoral plank was obviously, the victory of the Assam Movement symbolized by the Assam Accord. The AGP candidates, as it was expected, won 64 out of 126 Assembly seats and received support from another 7 independents. The first AGP ministry headed by P .K. Mahanta, the most prominent student leader of the Assam movement, was formed in December 1985. Other such ex-leaders of the AASU became cabinet ministers.

The AGP came to the power in the guise of a saviour of the Asomiya national identity with a pre-commitment to implement the Assam Accord. With the emergence of the AGP, all the national political parties became almost irrelevant to the common Asomiya people. The Congress (I) could gain only 23 seats. The Janata party was totally wiped out, and so was the BJP. Among the Left parties, the CPI (M) could get only 2 seats in 1985. It is, however, worth noting that another newly formed regional party, the United Minorities Front (UMF) became the third largest party with 17 members in the house. It may also be mentioned in this context that when the leadership of the Assam movement formed the AGP, the political leaders of the religious and linguistic minorities of Assam formed the UMF mainly to politically counter the AGP. The religious and linguistic minorities of Assam were considered as a traditional vote bank of the Congress in the state. But, they felt let down by the Congress (I) government at the centre when Rajiv Gandhi agreed to 1966 instead of 1971 as the cut off year for detecting foreign nationals and to the disenfranchisement of the entrants of 1966-71 for 10 years. The support base of the UMF was confined mainly to the Na-Asomiya Muslims, and most of its leaders were ex-congressmen. The main electoral plank of the UMF was opposition to the Assam Accord, which they felt would ultimately go against the interest of the religious and linguistic minorities living in Assam.

Owing to the tremendous sacrifice of the common Asomiya people during the six consecutive years of the Assam Movement, and also due to its pre-commitments, the AGP government became primarily responsible for the implementation of the Assam Accord. Besides the issue of foreign nationals, the accord also spelt out a host of measures for socio-economic development of Assam and restoration of normalcy in the state. Implementation of the accord required substantial support of the government of India, although there was no alternative to a strong political will and initiative on the part of the state government.

In order to identify the foreign nationals and to subsequently deport them from Assam, the AGP government constituted the tribunals. About four lakh people were served notice to prove their citizenship in the court during the first three years of the AGP government. But, only 22,800 names could be sent to the tribunals after the initial police inquiries, and not more than 200 foreigners could be deported from the state. Similarly, the AGP government had also miserably failed to make any headway in implementation of the other provisions of the accord.

Most of the young and politically immature leaders of the AGP after capturing the power got involved in large-scale corruption instead of making any sincere effort to implement the accord. Apart from the media reports almost every day particularly in the last two years of the AGP government, the removal of a dozen of ministers from their offices mainly on the charges of corruption testified the fact. As a result, the regional platform composed of different political parties and groups with their own interests, failed to remain politically cohesive. The repeated failures of the state government and charges of corruption over time increasingly made the constituent elements of the AGP, conscious about their own political legitimacy. In the wake of mass disillusionment and discontentment, the AASU began to openly criticize the AGP government, and launched an agitation. In addition to, the charges of corruption against most of the top leaders, absence of a concrete political ideology as well as inner party democratic discipline to carry forward the tasks of a responsible government, gradually alienated the AGP government from the common Asomiya people.

The AGP government was also increasingly threatened by the very fast growth of the United Liberation Front of Assam (ULFA), a by-product of the Assam Movement, besides a violent recurrence of the ethnic discourse for autonomy, again backed by a separatist ideology. The ULFA emerged and grew as a small secessionist outfit amidst the political chaos created by the Assam movement. With support from certain extra-territorial forces, the extremist outfit had substantially developed its strength in the later part of the 1980s. The accumulated failure of the AGP in the office undoubtedly contributed to a spectacular growth of the ULFA, when a sizeable section of the disillusioned Asomiya youth began looking at it, as a radical alternative. According to the official sources, a total of 113 persons including 58 political workers and 19 government officials were killed by the ULFA since 1985 till it was outlawed on 28 November, 1990 (*The Times of India,* November 19, 1990). Further, the ULFA collected a huge amount of money at gunpoint, particularly from the non-indigenous traders, tea gardens etc., and spent the major chunk of it for purchasing sophisticated weapons. According to a rough estimate, the ULFA had amassed nearly Rs. 500 crore from various sources, and as many as 40 training camps were functioning in broad day light before it was outlawed (*The Times of India,* November 19, 1990.) The AGP government, nonetheless, remained more or less quiescent, and its overall attitude was benevolent towards the reign of terror let loose by the ULFA. The extremist outfit could successfully carry the sentiment and emotion of the middle class Asomiya youth as well as the students who were the backbone of the Assam movement.

Yet, another regional party emerged in 1984 commanding support of the tribal people of Assam. The United Tribal Nationalist Liberation Front (UTNLF), which was later known as the United Bodo Nationalist Liberation Front (UBNLF), violently intensified the prolonged movement for a separate 'Bodo land' covering the entire northern tract of the Brahmaputra valley. The other two major demands were, inclusion of the Bodo language in the Eighth Schedule of the Constitution of India, and formation of Autonomous Councils for the people of Bodo group living in the south bank of Brahmaputra. Owing to the lack of political vision, the AGP government remained indifferent towards the basic issues raised by the Bodo movement.

Failure of the first AGP government to grapple with the situation once again led to a political chaos in Assam. Consequently, President's rule was imposed over the state on 27 November 1990 for maintaining law and order. The AGP rule thus came to an end before it could complete five years in the office. The President's rule was accompanied by a rigorous army operation against the ULFA.

The internal conflicts among the top AGP leaders had finally culminated in division of the party into two hostile camps just two months before the Assembly elections held in 1991. The splinter group had formed a new regional party called Natun Asom Gana Parishad (NAGP), which emerged as a strong opponent of the AGP. In 1991, the Congress (I) once again came back to power by winning 65 seats while the AGP and the newly formed NAGP could get only 19 and 5 seats respectively. The Congress (I) formed the government with Hitesrwar Saikia as the Chief Minister.

The ULFA resurfaced in July 1991 after hibernating during the period of the rigorous army operation following the end of the AGP regime. As a part of his policy to address the question of militancy, Saikia offered general amnesty to all the suspected ULFA militants who were arrested during the period of army operation, and most of them were released. Saikia, however, became a hard-liner when the ULFA became aggressive. Its re-assertion led to a fresh spate of military operation which demoralized a large section of its cadres. The extremist outfit was on the verge of a split when a section of its top leaders including the Chairman, Vice-Chairman, and the General Secretary expressed eagerness to negotiate with the government and to arrive at a compromise. The hardcore group, however, refused to abandon their struggle for a '*Swadhin Asom*'. Under the leadership of the Commander-in-Chief, the extremist outfit expelled the dissidents from primary membership of the organization, and the action of the Chairman was denounced as an 'unacceptable sell out' (Hazarika, 1994).

Saikia immediately took full advantage of the confusion and rift among the top leaders of the outfit, and with his skilful maneuvering, succeeded in convincing a large number of the militants to return to the 'mainstream'. Having failed to resist the aggressive Indian army and lured by the incentives offered by the government, hundreds of militants surrendered. The surrendered militants, SULFA as they are called, thus constituted a force which was used by the state machinery in its ongoing war against the ULFA. In addition to that, in the name of their rehabilitation, the SULFA cadres were allowed to keep their weapons, and the government provided them with soft loans and vehicles. They were even given the opportunity to work as uncontested contractors and government suppliers, and to impose what was commonly known as *goonda*-tax on the wholesalers. Thus, the Saikia government carefully nurtured a destructive force, which could be used by the state police as well as the politician in power, as and when required. The common people, however, had to bear the brunt of the SULFA hooliganism at a time when the ULFA still remained a force to be reckoned with.

Yet, in another move, the Congress government sought

to fulfill the political aspirations of the leadership of the Bodo movement by providing them with Autonomy in lieu of a separate state. Accordingly, in February 1993, a Memorandum of Settlement between the leadership of the Bodo movement and the Government of India in the presence of the Government of Assam was hurriedly signed. The Bodo Autonomous Council (BAC) thus came into existence, covering an area of 5186 square kms. However, as the territorial jurisdiction of the BAC was not properly demarcated, it soon became a serious issue, resulting in ethnic cleansing in the districts of Bongaigaon and Kokrajhar in 1993 and the most gruesome massacre in Barpeta district in July 1994. The soft targets were mainly the immigrant Muslims. Over 200 people including women and children were butchered and nearly 70,000 rendered homeless in the ethnic violence in lower Assam in 1993-94 (Sarmah, 2001). Yet, the basic issue remained unresolved.

The regional platform made an attempt to rejuvenate before the 1996 election, and consequently, the NAGP merged with AGP. To capitalize on the growing resentment against the Congress regime among different communities, the reunited regionalist platform decided to go for an electoral understanding with two political enemies - the Left parties and the UMIF - besides the United Peoples Party of Assam (UPPA). The AGP leadership realized that without electoral support of the religious and linguistic minorities, which were the traditional vote bank of the Congress, it would be almost impossible to come back to the power. To construct the image of the AGP as a saviour of the religious minorities of Assam, the regionalist leadership carefully avoided the issue of foreign nationals and the controversial IM (DT) Act, 1983 in the 1996 election. In turn, the leadership of the Jamiat-Ulema-Hind launched an extensive campaign in the minority-dominated areas and appealed to the people to ensure peace by electing the AGP. While the AGP revealed its eagerness to compromise with the religious and linguistic minorities, the leadership of the Left parties found the logic to extend their support to the AGP, to politically isolate their enemies, i.e. BJP and Congress. The leadership of the Left parties believed that the main protagonist of the 'Asomiya chauvinist ethos', i.e. the AGP had undergone a qualitative change assuming a 'secular-democratic' character. Therefore, as they viewed, the situation demanded an unconditional support to the AGP to defeat their major rivals.

As a result, in the Assembly elections held in 1996, out of 122 seats for which initially elections were held, AGP won 59 seats while the Congress could get only 34 seats. Therefore, the alliance helped the AGP not only to regain its strength to a large extent but also to spread its influence among the religious and linguistic minorities of Assam. Consequently the AGP-led government was formed and P.K. Mahanta became the Chief Minister for the second time.

The death of Hiteswar Saikia on 20 April 1996 was followed by a spate of militant activities of the extremist outfits. Both ULFA and Bodo extremists were re-grouping on the eve of the 1996 election and arms were being smuggled in huge quantity.[5] As a result, just after the formation of the AGP led government, Mahanta had to confront with an extremely violent situation in the wake of ethnic conflicts, again in the Bodo dominated areas in Kokrajhar and Bongaigaon districts. Retrieval of the banned extremist outfits in the wake of the 1996 elections compelled Mahanta not only to seek help of the armed forces but also to compromise with the SULFA, like his predecessor did. The government failed to recover the clandestine arms from the SULFA although they were asked to return all their arms *(The Sentinel,* 29 May 1996). Consequently, SULFA with the patronage of a section of politicians continued to be a menace to the civil society[6]. There were a large number of instances of assault, kidnapping, extortion and even killings of the common people who raised their voice against the SULFA. Yet, no visible action was taken by the government against the culprits. Similarly, the situation in the Bodo dominated areas of the lower Assam districts continued to be explosive, as the government had failed to resolve the basic issues related to the Bodo movement. The Bodo militants remained a terror for the non-tribal people, particularly the religious minorities.

Besides all these problems, the issue of foreign nationals in Assam, particularly the demand for scrapping the controversial IM (DT) Act 1983, once again started gaining momentum after the formation of the AGP led government. The question of foreign nationals in Assam, as it argued, would be impossible to resolve without scrapping the IM (DT) Act, which was perceived by a section of the Asomiya intelligentsia as discriminatory, a bad piece of law enacted by the Congress in 1983 essentially to protect the interests of the immigrants. The political forces which grew up championing the cause of the religious minorities besides a vocal section of the Muslims in Assam, however, believed that the IM (DT) Act was not anti-Asomiya, and therefore, they were in favour of retaining it till a better alternative for protection of minority interest could be found out. In spite of certain shortcomings, they regarded this Act as a relatively effective mechanism to protect the minority interest in Assam.

Under such circumstances, the AGP, which first captured power with the pre-commitment to implement the Assam Accord and then projected itself as a saviour of the interest of the religious and linguistic minorities of Assam, had obviously been in a very difficult situation to take any concrete position on the issue of controversial IM (DT) Act 1983. Failure of the AGP to resolve the issue of foreign nationals in Assam and to suitably amend the IM (DT) Act 1983 had paved the way for the communal forces. These two interrelated issues were being increasingly communalized, and both Hindu and Muslim communal forces tried to fish in the disturbed water.

In the political process, which began since the late 1970s, marked by political instability, insurgency, ethnic cleansings, lawlessness to a great extent and similar other problems, the panchayats remained moribund institutions in isolation. While mobilizational politics sharpened the ethnic and communal divide, the civil society remained busy squabbling over several social issues, ignoring the historical realities. Owing to the controversy over an acceptable electoral roll, panchayat elections in the state had been stalled for a long time after the last elections held in 1979 under the Act of 1972. The first elections under the Act of 1986 were held in 1992. In 1993, the Chief Minister announced that a separate election commission for the panchayats would be established, and the panchayat laws would be suitably amended to prevent dissolution of elected bodies with every change of government.

Nevertheless, with the change of the government in 1996, the new government headed by the AGP dissolved all rural bodies on 4 April 1997. Accordingly, the elections to the panchayats should have been held within six months. But, the government headed by the regional party carefully avoided the panchayat elections in the state. The pretext was insurgency and the problem of law and order[7]. Apparently, the AGP government made some preparation for the panchayat elections in the year 2000, after being pressurized by different sections of the people including public litigations. Again the process was stopped when the issue of autonomy for the plains tribes was raised rather sharply. As a result, Assam had to wait till 2001 to get the first batch of panchayat functionaries elected in accordance with the provisions laid down by the seventy-third amendment of the Constitution.

SUMMING UP

Though the relics of a system of 'decentralized governance' can be traced in the ancient history of Assam, the emergence of a strong state covering almost the entire

Brahmaputra valley in the 17th century under the aegis of the Ahom kings fostered certain institutions of rural governance. The institutions, which grew essentially as an integral component of the medieval social formation, were instrumental in perpetuating class domination in a semi-feudal society. Nevertheless, such non-exclusivist institutions enjoyed some amount of autonomy to address many socio-cultural, religious as well as petty judicial issues in the predominantly rural society. Not being under a strong feudal structure of social domination, the village institutions of the medieval Assamese society were guided by the basic democratic norms of social participation to a large extent, and the relics of this tradition are still visible in rural Assam.

British colonialism, which appeared in the guise of a saviour in a situation of extreme political crisis, drastically changed the entire institutional arrangement of the semi-feudal Ahom state to put the war-torn closed economy on the trajectory of exotic capitalism. Colonization inevitably led to large-scale immigration that had changed the ethnic configuration of the Brahmaputra valley on the one hand, and pauperization of the peasantry on the other. The ruling Ahom aristocracy was virtually ruined and it lost its hegemony. In the process, however, emerged a tiny rural landed aristocratic class, mostly from the indigenous upper castes including the spiritual aristocracy of the Ahom state, and the indigenous Muslim community. This class with colonial patronage started dominating the agrarian society and all its social institutions, and being loyal to the colonial administration, monopolized all the benefits including education. A large section of it, nevertheless, became nationalist in the later period and constituted the top leadership of the Congress during the freedom movement.

Though the colonial regime initiated some sort of 'decentralized' administrative arrangements since the early part of the last century, the legislations being determined by the colonial political economy, had very little to do with both development and democratization. The existing social institutions were ruined in the process of colonial transformation, but the conscious attempt to bridge the resultant gap between the state and the rural society had always been essentially through promotion of a section of rural landed elite loyal to the regime, which could share some amount of responsibilities particularly in collection and augmentation of revenue. This had not only crippled the democratic tradition, however limited it was, but also subjected the rural society to a hitherto unknown form of exploitation and domination. The process was not much different from many other parts of colonial India. Yet at the same time, with all other pernicious implications, the large number of immigrant population had substantially influenced the ethnic configuration of the Brahmaputra valley, and sharpened socio-cultural as well as linguistic divisions in the rural society. This had perpetuated constant conflicts of interests between the indigenous community and the immigrants, and consequently, the entangled questions of nationality and ethnic identity continued to influence the political discourses in Assam.

With the ethos similar to most of the states in India after independence, Assam too initiated the process to promote institutions of democratic decentralization on one hand, and land reform on the other. Through the legislations, though some of them were quite radical in nature, the government had failed to alter the agrarian structure as well as establish democratic institutions in the rural society. The structure of Panchayati Raj that emerged in the state as an implementing agency of the rural development programmes was sandwiched between the bureaucratic apparatus and the rural landed gentry. In the absence of agrarian reforms, not only did the rural power structure remain exploitative as before and the processes of grassroots democracy not take off, the agrarian economy also began retarding. The unresolved agrarian question substantially contributed to economic stagnation. Coupled with the entangled questions of national and ethnic identity, it led to political chaos and instability in the later part of the 1970s. The indigenous communities being frustrated by the continuous rule of the Congress enthusiastically responded to the middle class-led political movements in an overwrought state. Such political mobilizations, which were often accompanied by large-scale violence, resulted in a wide acceptance of secessionist ideology with a serious threat to the federal structure as well as the democratic political process.

The regional political formation with a distinctly 'Asomiya national chauvinist' ideology that emerged as an alternative to nationalist political parties, and came to power, completely ignored the real issues, and failed to remain as a cohesive political platform. While in power, neither did it initiate any agrarian reforms nor did it make any attempt to revitalize the moribund panchayats. The elections to the panchayats were carefully avoided in some pretext or the other. The ethnic situation became worse leading to ethnic cleansing in the absence of any conscious attempt to address the genuine grievances and demand for democratization.

After coming back to the power once again, although the Congress revitalized the panchayats, it failed to promote them as democratic institutions at the grassroots. The panchayats still remained as mere implementing agencies of some of the centrally sponsored rural development programmes, fully controlled by the bureaucracy, beyond the reach of the common people. Failure of the Congress to bring about any positive change in the insurgency infested state once again brought back the regionalist political formation, which pretended to be democratic and secular for its electoral gains. In practice, nevertheless, it once again preferred to be indifferent to panchayats like all other vital issues. In the mean time, most of the states not only amended their panchayat legislations in conformity with the Seventy-third amendment but also elected the first batch of the panchayat functionaries with their redefined tasks. Though the necessary legislative measures were taken well in time, the state had to wait till 2001 for the panchayat elections and to begin with the new experiment.

NOTES

1. Suniti Kumar Chatterjee argues that the 'Aryanisation' of the ruling classes in the western part of assam, i.e. Kamrupa, was completed as early as circa A.D. 400. According to him, the Brahmaputra valley definitely appears to have become a part of Aryaspeaking India by A.D. 1200. (Chatterjee, 1955). Amalendu Guha argues that reference to the kingdom of Kamrupa in the epics and puranas, rock incriptions going as far as the fifth century, subsequent epigraphic and archiological ruins found in the region, and predominance of Sanskrit based languages in the plains – all clearly testify to an early beginning there of the process of Sanksritization. Howeve, even after becoming a part of Aryaspeaking India, many tribes in the valley continued to maintain their own speech, their modes of cultivation, housing and other socio-religious practices and beliefs. On the other hand, the Aryan way of life itself was permeated with non-Aryan ways of the Boro-kachari people referred to as the Kiratas (Guha, 1991).
2. According to the Census of 1891, the landlords constituted less than one per cent, and the tenants constituted about 7 per cent of the population of Assam proper.
3. In the Lok Shabha elections held in 1952, the Congress won 11 out of the total 12 seats of Assam, and polled almost 44 per cent of the total valid votes. In the second and the third Lok Shabha elections, the Congress won 9 out of the total 12 seats, and polled 48 per cent of the valid votes. In the fourth and the sixth Lok Shabha elections, the Congress won 10 seats out of total 14 seats, and polled almost 46 and 50 per cent of the total valid votes. Witnessing a remarkable success in the fifth Lok

Shabha elections, the Congress won all the 14 seats and polled more than 54 per cent of the valid votes. Similarly, in the first five assembly elections too, the Congress had absolute majority.

4. In 1972, the ASSU led a movement to make the Assamese as the medium of instruction together with English up to the graduation level. The ASSU also led a series of movements on different economic issues including industrialization, control of floods etc. till the mid 1970s.
5. For instance, it was reported that a ship carrying a large cache of highly sophisticated arms for ULFA was intercepted by Bangladesh Security personnel near Cox bazaar. Arms and ammunition shipped from Bangkok were smuggled to Mizoram and then to Assam. *The Statesman*, 2 July 1996.
6. In the conference of the Rural Development and Panchayat Ministers organized by the Eleventh Finance Commission at Delhi on 9 September 1998, the Minister of Panchayat and Rural Development, Assam reported that the panchayat elections in the state could not be held 'because of problems of insurgency and law and order'.

6

PANCHAYATI RAJ IN ASSAM AFTER THE SEVENTY-THIRD CONSTITUTIONAL AMENDMENT: THE PERSPECTIVE AND ISSUES

With the promise of good governance, the Congress came back to the power in Assam in 2001 and initiated the process of rejuvenating the moribund Panchayati Raj. By the end of the year, the rural masses of Assam elected their representatives to the PRIs to ensure an efficient and transparent system of rural self-governance based on the principles of democratic-decentralization. The first batch of panchayats elected after the Seventy-third amendment is now completing its term in December 2006. There are many achievements, but there are also some lessons to learn from the experiences. An attempt has been made in this chapter to understand and analyze functioning of the PRIs – the achievements as well as the limitations of the process of democratic decentralization that has been envisaged by the Constitution within its liberal democratic framework.

FULFILLING THE CONSTITUTIONAL MANDATE: AN OVERVIEW OF THE STRUCTURE OF PANCHAYATI RAJ IN ASSAM

The Assam State Legislative Assembly enacted the Assam

Panchayati Raj Act, 1994 broadly in conformity with the Seventy-third Amendment of the Constitution. Reinforcing the ethos of the constitutional amendment, a three-tier system of Panchayati Raj has been worked out to cover the rural areas of the entire state, except for the two hills districts i.e. Karbi Anglong and North Cachar covered by the Sixth Schedule of the Constitution. A five-year term was fixed for the panchayat bodies comprising the Gaon Panchayats (GP) at the bottom, Zila Parishad (ZP) at the top and the Anchalik Panchayats (AP) at the intermediate level. This has been followed by adoption of the Assam Panchayat (Constitution) Rules, 1995 specifying the code for panchayat elections, delimitation, and determination of constituencies for the different tiers, reservation of the constituencies for Scheduled Castes, Scheduled Tribes and women, and allied matters, and the Assam Panchayat (Financial) Rules, 2002 required for financial devolution through the Panchayati Raj.

The Act of 1994, in the spirit of the Seventy-third amendment of the Constitution, makes provision for GPs as the democratic base of the Panchayat Raj. Consisting of all the voters in a village or group of villages falling within the jurisdiction of a GP, the Gaon Sabha has become a permanent institution. The Act makes it mandatory for the Gaon Sabha to meet in every three months to make recommendations and suggestions to the GP on the development programmes to be undertaken. As most of the legislations enacted by the state assemblies after the Seventy-third constitutional amendment, in Assam too, the Gaon Sabha has been imagined as the democratic space to ensure participation of the common villagers in the discussion on the development issues, village planning as well as in implementation of the development programmes.

For each well-defined territorial jurisdiction of the Gaon Sabha with six to ten thousand populations, the Act of 1994 provides a GP consists of ten directly elected members besides one directly elected President. The Vice-President, however, is to be elected from amongst the members in the first meeting of the GP. The Act fulfills all the constitutional provisions regarding elections and reservation of seats for women, the Scheduled Castes and the Scheduled Tribes. Along with this, following the directives laid down in the Article 243G of the Constitution, the Act of 1994 endows the GPs with certain powers and authority "to enable them to function as institutions of self-government." The general functions of the GP include preparation of annual plans and budget, mobilization of relief at the time of natural calamity, removal of encroachments on public properties, organizing voluntary labour and contribution for community works, and maintenance of essential statistics of the villages. Besides these general functions, the Act has also envisaged the GPs to play a crucial role in respect of altogether 29 subjects supposedly transferred to the domain of the panchayats.

The Act of 1994 has also made it mandatory for the GP to constitute three Standing Committees – development committee, social justice committee and social welfare committee – by election amongst the elected members. The development committee is expected to address essentially the poverty issues through the poverty alleviation programmes and perform specifically the functions relating to agricultural production and animal husbandry. The social justice committee has been envisaged to address the issues relating to socio-economic, cultural, educational and other similar interests of the Scheduled Castes, the Scheduled Tribes and Backward Classes, and welfare of women and children. The social welfare committee has to perform functions in respect of education, public health, public works and other similar activities of the GP. Besides the elected members, the Act has authorized the GPs to co-opt to each standing committee the members of Field Management Committee, Mahila Samiti and other such civil society organizations, without the right to vote.

For all such functions, the Act empowers the GP to constitute a fund mainly with contribution and grant made by the State and the Central government, ZP, AP and any other local authority. The institution at the grass roots has also been given some amount taxation powers and levy duty to generate its own resources.

For each Development Block, the Act provides an AP to be constituted by the directly elected members from the territorial constituencies of the GPs, the Presidents of the GPs, and the MLAs and MPs representing constituencies, which comprise wholly or partly, the AP. Every such member has the right to vote, whether or not chosen by direct election. However, only the directly elected members of the AP are given the right to elect the President and the Vice-President from amongst themselves in the first meeting of the AP. The Act fulfills all the constitutional provisions regarding election, reservation of seats for women, the Scheduled Castes and the Scheduled Tribes in the APs.

The Act of 1994 has envisaged a crucial role for the APs in respect of all the 29 subjects supposedly transferred to the PRIs. Besides that, the regular activities of the APs are preparation of annual plan in respect to the schemes entrusted to them, consideration and consolidation of the annual plans of all GPs under the AP and submission of the consolidated plan to the ZP, and preparation of annual budget of the AP. For all its functions, in addition to the contribution and grants from the Central or State Government or ZP, the Act has empowered the AP to levy certain tolls, cess, and tax within the limit prescribed by the State Government.

It is also mandatory for the AP to constitute three standing committees – general standing committee; finance, audit and planning committee; and social justice committee – to be constituted by the members of the AP from amongst themselves. The general standing committee is responsible for the tasks relating to the establishment matters, communication, buildings, rural housing, relief etc. The functions of the second standing committee includes, apart from financial issues of the AP, training, planning and development and other similar activities, while the functions of the social justice committee are same with that of the GP.

The Act of 1994 provides a ZP to each district. Included in its jurisdiction is the entire district excluding those portions, which are included in the urban bodies such as Municipality, Municipal Corporation, Town Committee or Cantonment area etc. The ZP is constituted by the members directly elected from the territorial constituencies of the district, the President of the APs, and the MLAs, and the MPs representing a part or whole of the district, whose constituencies lie within the district. All the members have the right to vote. However, the President and the Vice-President of the ZP are to be elected by the directly elected members of the ZP from amongst themselves. The ZP has been entrusted with the responsibility of planning for economic development and social justice, and to ensure co-ordination among the PRIs in the implementation of the plans in respect to the transferred subjects, besides taking the responsibility of implementing its own plans. Further, the ZP has been entrusted with the power to examine and sanction the budget estimates of the APs in the district. Besides the amount transferred to the ZP from the consolidated fund of the State and other grants and contributions made by the government, the ZP has also been empowered to generate its own resources by levying tax, cess etc. on certain services to the limit prescribed by the State Government.

The ZP is provided with four standing committees. The general standing committee has been entrusted with the responsibilities such as establishment, communications, rural housing, and other development programmes. The finance and audit committee, besides preparation of budget for the

ZP and looking after the regular financial matters, is also responsible for constant monitoring and evaluation of the development programmes. The functions of the social justice committee are the same with that of the AP or GP. The planning and development committee has been entrusted with the responsibility of educational planning in the district. In addition to that, this standing committee has to plan for the promotion of rural health, agriculture and industry including cottage industries.

The Act of 1994 also made provision for constituting the District Planning Committee (DPC) for each district. The primary responsibility of the DPC is to prepare a draft development plan for the district consolidating the plans prepared by the PRIs and the other urban bodies such as the Town Committees, Municipalities and Municipal Corporation located in the district. Therefore, a DPC is to be consisted of the MLAs and the MPs representing the whole or part of the district, the President of the ZP, the Mayor or the Chairperson of the Municipal Corporation/Municipal Board/Town Committee as the case may be, and not less than two-third of the members of the ZP, councilors of Municipal Corporation or the Municipalities or the Town Committees on rotation and in proportion to the rural and the urban population of the district. The President of the ZP is the ex-officio Chairperson of the DPC. While preparing the development plan for the district, the DPC has to look into the common interests of the PRIs and the urban bodies of the district, sharing of the natural resources, and should be guided by an integrated approach of development. The Chairperson of every DPC is required to forward the district plan to the state government within a specified period.

The Act has also made provision for a State Election Commission to prepare the electoral roll as well as to conduct all elections to the PRIs. The Act has also made it mandatory for the state government to constitute a State Finance

Commission to look into the financial aspects of the PRIs and sharing of taxes, duties, tolls and fees, which may be assigned to and appropriated by the PRIs at different levels. The State Finance Commission is also required to look into the grants-in-aid to the PRIs from the consolidated fund of the state.

Although the constitutional mandate has been satisfied, for some of the obnoxious provisions it contains, the legislation has turned out to be repugnant to the ethos of the Seventy-third Amendment. The legislation has made the elected representatives of the panchayats subservient to the state bureaucracy. For instance, the Act requires the Secretary of the GP to consult the BDO even after receiving approval from the President of the GP for convening a meeting of the Gaon Sabha. The Secretary of the GP has also been authorized to convene a meeting of the Gaon Sabha in consultation with the BDO, if the President fails the convening of the Gaon Sabha. Similarly, the legislation has also provided opportunities of encroachment by the state political masters on the space earmarked for the elected representatives at the local level. For forging vertical linkages among all layers of elected representatives (panchayat representatives, MLAs and MPs) it may be desirable to make the MLAs and the MPs, members of the APs or the ZPs along with the directly elected members. However, conferring the right to vote also to the MLAs and the MPs on issues exclusively falling within the jurisdictions of an AP or a ZP is an over democratic provision, which makes some people more equal than others.

THE PEOPLES MANDATE: VERDICT OF THE PANCHAYAT ELECTIONS

As indicated earlier, one of the glaring failures of the AGP government had been its disinclination to conduct the panchayat elections in Assam due since 1997. Projecting this as a deliberate maneuver, the Congress in its election manifesto for the Assam assembly elections in 2001, committed itself to holding elections to the PRIs. Finally, panchayat polls were conducted in the last week of December in two phases[1] after a gap of four years, and the ruling Congress decisively eclipsed all its major opponents including the AGP. The failure of the AGP in all fronts paved the way for the Congress to come back consolidating its traditional support bases in the tea gardens, in the areas dominated by the religious minorities and also making inroads into many other areas believed to be strongholds of the AGP. Apart from the state assembly elections in May 2001, the Congress was successful in the elections to the autonomous district councils in the two hills districts of the state in November and in the elections to the PRIs in December.

Although preparation for the panchayat polls in all the 21 plain districts of Assam was made, the Congress had to succumb to political pressure of the Bodo leadership including the All Bodo Students' Union and excluded the area covered by the Bodo Land Autonomous Council from the panchayat elections. However, in the remaining parts, the Congress made a clean sweep. Of the 390 Zila Parishad seats, the Congress secured 311 while the AGP and the BJP secured only 14 and 19 seats respectively. Significantly enough, as many as 42 independent candidates won the elections, while the other parties were almost marginalized. The scenario of the APs and GPs was not much different. The Congress established its monopoly over almost all the ZPs and APs occupying about 80 per cent of the ZP seats and more than 67 per cent of the AP seats. Similarly, the overwhelming majority of the GPs had also come under direct control of the Congress when nearly 67 per cent of the elected GP Presidents and about 50 per cent of the GP members belonged to the Congress.

The elections to the PRIs held in 2001 after a long gap of more than four years witnessed a great amount of enthusiasm both on the part of the voters and the political parties. Quite a good number of candidates belonging to various political parties filed their nominations for elections to different tiers, while a sizeable number of candidates who were refused party tickets, especially by the Congress and the AGP, decided to contest independently. The top leaders of all the political parties were involved in the campaign, appealing to the people to vote for their candidates. It witnessed a considerably high level of political participation of the people in the democratic process with about 70 per cent of the rural voters exercising their franchise in the panchayat polls, and the pattern was more or less similar throughout the state. The people elected their representatives to the PRIs (the results are shown in Annexure – 2) in a peaceful environment, barring a few minor incidents related particularly to the snatching of ballot papers in some places.

GAON SABHA IN ASSAM: ABORTION THAT HAS WEAKENED THE SYSTEM

Most of the states in India, with a very few exceptions such as Kerela and Tamilnadu, attempted to institutionalize Gram Sabhas through their respective Panchayat Acts enacted much before the Seventy-third amendment of the Constitution. In such statutory provisions made in Bihar (Bihar Panchayati Raj Act, 1947) and Punjab (Punjab Gram Panchayat Act, 1952) the Gram Sabhas also had the power to 'recall' the Sarpanch. Analysis of the Panchayat Acts of various states as they were prevailing before the Seventy-third Amendment reveals that the functions of the Gram Sabhas generally included consideration and power to make recommendations with regard to matters such as the annual statements of the accounts, administrative report of the preceding financial year, the last audit report and replies, report of the development programmes proposed to be undertaken during the current year, mobilization of voluntary labour and contributions in cash and kind for community welfare programmes, and identification of beneficiaries for the implementation of development schemes pertaining to the village. (Bhargava and Venkatakrishnan, 1995).

The statutory institutions at the grassroots, nevertheless, did not function and remained dormant in most of the states due to several factors. Besides a lack of clear direction, it remained under the control of the dominant rural elites to serve their vested interests, and the common citizens, with the little space provided to them, remained apathetic towards its functions. Even when the common citizens showed genuine interest, they found that the gram sabha's opinion was not binding on the gram panchayats, nor was the latter ready to respect the opinions of the former (Jain, 1997)

The Seventy-third Constitutional Amendment Act has formally recognized the Gram Sabha. It has been defined by the Constitution (article 243) as 'a body consisting of persons registered in the electoral rolls relating to a village comprised within the area of Panchayat at the village level'. And according to the Constitution (article 243A), it 'may exercise such powers and perform such functions at the village level as the Legislative of a State may by law, provide'. The Constitution, therefore, makes it mandatory to re-institutionalize Gram Sabha in a new form decreed by legislation by the states. Considering the Seventy-third amendment in its totality and also taking cognizance of the context of the amendment, the Indian State apparently aimed at providing opportunity for active participation of the mass of the rural people in self governance including local level planning, and to institutionalize the political space at the grassroots to ensure some amount of transparency and accountability of the elected functionaries of the panchayats, the instrumentality of 'good governance' below the states.

Such being the constitutional mandate, all the states ostensibly attempted to re-institutionalize Gram Sabhas through their respective Panchayat Acts. The scope and functions of the Gram Sabhas were also outlined. The constitutional mandate has also inspired enormous hope and several euphoric theoretical constructions, often without much deeper probe into the rural context. It was hoped that the constitution of the Gram Sabhas consisting of all adult members of a village Panchayat would give 'voice' to the 'voiceless' people living in 6,00,000 villages of India (Gangrade, 1995). The Gram Sabhas were viewed as the gateway to grassroots democracy (Jain, 1997) and it was expected that it would lead to participatory democracy as distinct from representative democracy (Aram and Ravichandram, 1995). Similarly, it was viewed as one of the three basic institutions of new direct democracy at the village level (Narayanasamy, 1998). The re-institutionalized Gram Sabhas were also perceived as a mechanism to bridge the gaps between the civil society and its political wing – the state (Jaamdar, 1995). These are only few instances.

Nevertheless, owning to the lack of a clear constitutional mandate towards operationalization of the grassroots institution, there have been considerable variations across the states regarding structure and jurisdiction of the Gram Sabha, as well as its powers and functions. In most of the states, the jurisdiction of the Gram Sabha has been mechanically determined to cover the entire GP irrespective of the number of villages as well as population it covers (for details see Manoj Rai et.al. 2001; R.C. Choudhury and S.P Jain, 1999). Considering the small size of villages in India, there is a justification in constituting a GP covering a group of villages with clearly demarcated constituencies. But, in some of the major states such as Uttar Pradesh, Madhya Pradesh, Andhra Pradesh etc., besides having a considerably high density of rural population, the territorial jurisdiction of the Gram Sabhas is coterminous with the GPs. Therefore, for all practical purposes, a Gram Sabha in such states would mean an assembly of considerably large numbers of extremely heterogeneous population, where the caste and class domination is bound to marginalize the voice of the socially and economically oppressed sections of the rural society. Experiencing such difficulties, some of the states have, however, attempted to ensure meaningful deliberations and wider participation at the grassroots by replacing the Gram Sabhas with Ward Sabhas. Rajasthan happens to be the first state to have taken a step in this direction. Kerala and Orissa have also adopted a similar policy, while West Bengal has introduced the system of Gram Sansad, which is equivalent to Gram Sabha at the ward level, to guide and advice the GP.

The frequency of meetings of the Gram Sabhas and the prescribed number of members to form its quorum are not merely a matter of technicality. These are two important aspects in order to ensure wider participation of people in local governance ensuring transparency and accountability, and also to make the Gram Sabhas the base of Panchayati Raj. The majority of the state legislations have made a mandatory provision to convene at least two meetings of the Gram Sabhas in a year, either by the President or the Secretary of the respective GP. Only in case of very few states, the minimum number of meetings in a year is three or four. In many of the states such as Gujarat, Madhya Pradesh, Rajasthan, Haryana, Tamil Nadu etc. the meetings of the Gram Sabhas are to be convened on the dates specified by the respective state. Yet in practice, the minimum number becomes the maximum in all states completely ignoring the question of actual requirement of such meetings. A similar adhocism and narrow technical consideration of the quorum for a meeting of the Gram Sabha has also been a stumbling block. Though some of the state legislations have not specified any such quorum, it is no less than one-tenth of the total members of the Gram Sabha in a majority of the states. In some of the states such as Himachal Pradesh and Uttar Pradesh, the quorum is even one-fifth of the total members of the Gram Sabha. However, except for Kerala, a mandatory provision for participation of women in the meetings of the Gram Sabhas has completely been ignored. Though the quorum is specified in most of the states, usually attendance of the minimum specified number of members is not required for a meeting of the Gram Sabha that has been adjourned for lack of quorum. Such abortive practices reduce the spirit of participation to a question of mere formality or technicality often providing opportunities to abuse the statutory provision.

Many of the state Acts have not clearly defined the powers and functions except for making some vague reference to certain responsibilities such as consideration of administrative and financial reports of the GPs, mobilization of voluntary labour and contribution in kind or cash, and promotion of unity and harmony among all section of people in the village. Even in case of the Acts, which listed certain functions of the Gram Sabhas, the procedural details in a proper perspective are conspicuously missing. Consequently, identification of beneficiaries for the development schemes sponsored by the Centre has often been the major item in the agenda of the Gram Sabhas. Based on the observation of actual Gram Sabhas, it is seen that the agenda of the meeting in most cases is limited either to selection of beneficiaries for various poverty alleviation programmes. As a result, attendance in such meetings is limited to potential beneficiaries or persons interested in taking various works on contract (Manoj Rai, 2001). Being guided by a very limited approach, the Acts enacted by most of the states have mechanically made the provision of Gram Sabhas, more or less similar to the provision that existed in different states prior to the Seventy-third Amendment.

Coming back to the specific context of Assam, Gram Sabha (Gaon Sabha) is not a new addition to the Panchayati Raj system in the state. The Assam Rural Panchayat Act, 1948 made the provision of Primary Panchayats composed of all adults having permanent residence within its area, who formed the electorate for the Rural Panchayats. Every Primary Panchayat was required to elect one representative for every two hundred of its members or a fraction thereof to the Rural Panchayat. The Assam Panchayat Act, 1959 also made provision for Gaon Sabha consisting of all persons of a specified area whose names were included in the electoral roll of the Assam Legislative Assembly. However, the institution of Gaon Sabha, in both cases, did not have much to contribute to the functioning of the panchayat system, except for electing their representatives to the Rural or Gaon Panchayats.

Re-institutionalizing the Gaon Sabhas following the constitutional mandate, the Assam Panchayat Act, 1994 made the provision of Gaon Sabha consisting of persons registered in the electoral rolls relating to a village or a group of villages comprised within the area of Gaon Panchayat. The latter may, however, include a revenue village or a group of revenue village or a forest village or a Tea Garden area or hamlets forming part of such administrative units with a population not less than six thousand and not more than ten thousand. The sole criterion for demarcating the territorial jurisdiction of a Gaon Sabha or the Gaon Panchayat, therefore, is the size of population, which is not less than six thousand. Considering the average size of population of such administrative units, a Gaon Sabha means an assembly of the total electorates of not less than four villages covering a geographical area of about six square kilometers on an average.

The Gaon Sabha is required to consider the report regarding the development programmes of the Gaon Panchayat relating to the preceding year, and such activities proposed to be undertaken during the current year, and may make necessary recommendations and suggestions to the Gaon Panchayats. The functions of the Gaon Sabhas are mobilization of voluntary labour and contribution in cash and kinds for community welfare programmes, and identification of beneficiaries for implementation of development schemes pertaining to the village. The other responsibility prescribed for the Gaon Sabha is promotion of unity and harmony among all sections of society in the village.

The Congress, which came back to power in 2001 with the mandate to revive the Panchayati Raj in the state, announced a new concept 'Raijor Pudulit Raijor Sarkar' (Redressal of Public Grievances at People's Door). While it was projected as an initiative to ensure accountable and transparent administration through community participation at the grassroots, as well as preparation for the panchayat polls, the 'people-centric development programme' of the government was generally welcomed by a large section of the rural people.

The procedural details are clearly laid down. Raijor Padulit Raijor Sarkar (RPRS) is to be convened at every quarter of a year, i.e. October, January, April and July. Gaon Sabhas are the basic unit for each round of RPRS focusing on a special theme[2]. During each round, called as the RPRS Week, Gaon Sabhas are to be held in all the GPs in the state. A Nodal Team, consisting of the Block/village officials of all the line departments including the Sub-Inspector of police, headed by a Nodal Officer deputed by the Deputy Commissioner of the concerned district is responsible for conducting each round of RPRS, organizing a Gaon Sabha meeting in a GP in the specified week. It is the Nodal Officer's prerogative to decide the programme for meeting of the Gaon Sabha, as well as its time and venue.

However, each Gaon Sabha meeting is required to follow more or less an agenda specified by the state government, and the agenda of such one-day meeting normally includes a discussion on the 'theme' of the RPRS Week (two hours), lectures to generate awareness on the government sponsored development programmes (one hour), selection of beneficiaries (one hour), grievance petitions and discussion on problems (two hours) and distribution of individual/ community benefits (one hour). Since the first round of RPRS held (between 8th and 14th October, 2001) in the entire state about four months before the panchayat polls, it has been the convention that the meeting of the Gram Sabha always starts with a long 'message' from the Chief Minister to the people of the concerned district to be read before the people by the Nodal Officer. The message always contains a long list of 'achievements' in different spheres made by the government in the district[3].

In each round of RPRS, the Nodal Officer is required to accept the petitions, categorize the grievances either as Individual Family Need (IFN) or Community Need (CN) in a prescribed format. This is to be handed over to the Redressing Department with a copy to the Zonal RPRS team constituted for each Development Block headed by a Zonal Officer (usually a senior officer such as the Additional Deputy Commissioner or the Sub-Divisional Officer), and the Deputy Commissioner of the concerned district within three days after the completion of the RPRS Week. The Deputy Commissioner has to compile the information for the whole district and apprise the government. The basic objective, however, is to ensure monitoring by the zonal Officer and also to be reviewed by the Deputy Commissioner whether or not the concerned department takes steps for redressal. The Deputy Commissioner is also responsible for convening fortnightly review meeting with the Redressal Departments to ensure that the necessary actions have been taken.

The Congress after coming back to the power in May 2001 had geared up the entire state machinery to launch RPRS in all the plains districts, making provision for disciplinary actions against the officials showing reluctance to it. A good number of officers, for the first time in life, took the pain to visit the remote villages under compulsion[4]. The programme was successfully launched in October with the initiatives taken by the officers in mobilization of a large section of rural mass, a difference that generated hope and expectation. The first round of RPRS held about four months prior to the panchayat polls provided a platform for the people to express not only their grievances but also expectations from the newly formed government in the state. And politically, it helped the Congress immensely to articulate the expectations of the people when its major opponents remained silent just four months after the defeat they experienced in the Assembly polls.

The initial efforts made by the government to re-institutionalize Gaon Sabhas through RPRS, involving the bureaucracy in the absence of elected panchayats, were laudable, and rural people in the state enthusiastically availed the opportunity to interact with the officials. Nevertheless, when the government decided to continue with the RPRS, a well-designed political strategy of bureaucratic domination even after the panchayat polls, it led to confusion and chaos jeopardizing the spirit of participation. As it has been designed, the elected GP President has a very little role to play in the affairs of the camouflaged Gaon Sabhas dominated by the officials and panchayat secretaries. The RPRS rounds in each GP have gradually become a ritual alienated from the people at large. In most of the cases, only the potential beneficiaries attend the meetings, which often end with quarrels on the issues relating to identification of beneficiaries and distribution of the benefits, hardly arriving at any concrete decision.

It is interesting enough to note that the elected panchayat functionaries including the Presidents are guided by the notion that a Gaon Sabha is to be called only when the instruction for holding the RPRS round in the concerned GP, comes from the Deputy Commissioner of the respective district [5]. Presence of the Nodal Officer and his team in the meetings is compulsory, and the first item in the agenda should always be the 'message' from the Chief Minister followed by lectures by the officials on the theme of the RPRS Week. The people neither find the mere political propaganda attractive in the absence of any follow up actions of their ventilated grievances, nor do the officials find it interesting or meaningful to deliver a lecture to the inattentive and disinterested audience. Yet, it is responsibility of the concerned GP to bear the entire cost of the political idiosyncrasy, both in terms of money and working hours of the rural poor. When the poorer section comes with the expectation of being identified as a beneficiary, the additional financial burden of holding the so-called RPRS has to be 'managed from the limited fund received by the GP for implementation of development schemes'[6]. To be precise, there exists a big gap between the statutory provisions and the ground realities, not to speak of the constitutional ethos. The precarious gap is one of the key issues to be addressed politically, if the political parties in Assam want to make the PRIs an effective instrument of democratic decentralization.

PANCHAYATS IN ASSAM: INSTITUTIONS OF LOCAL GOVERNANCE OR APPENDAGE OF DRDA?

The Seventy-third Amendment has endorsed afresh the role that the PRIs can play in promoting economic development with social justice. In this context, economic development, as distinct from mere economic growth, has to be seen as a process of social transformation covering the needs of the most needy and empowerment of the citizens, especially the socially oppressed and economically deprived section. Though social as well as economic equality has always been a part of India's primary goal[7], since independence the country has been following the policy of 'growth with social justice', which has nether led to any conspicuous economic growth nor promoted social justice. While the Seventy-third

Amendment came alongside the economic reform programmes, which necessitated a major shift in India's development strategy seeking to redefine the role of the State, some of the scholars preferred to put the panchayats in what is called the 'people's sector' together with other institutions such as voluntary agencies, Self Help Groups etc. Though panchayats were a constitutionally established tier of the government, considering their intended participatory character with representation of the poor and the burden of responsibility placed on them for poverty eradication, such scholars found it reasonable to include them in the people's sector. (Rao, 1998) In such a theoretical formulation, panchayats are implicitly denied the constitutional status as the institution of local self-governance.

The counter formulations, however, reinforce panchayats as the 'state' at the local level or institutions of self-governance, political institutions, which are subject to the vagaries of electoral fortunes. Therefore, the PRIs cannot be equated to NGOs or classified in some omnibus called a 'people's sector'. In the given context of economic reform and redefined role of the state, the panchayats are instrumental in getting state intervention right, to 'unbundle the country' the state (Vyasalu, 2003).

The constitutional mandate followed by the state legislations to re-institutionalize panchayats, the elections and party political initiatives in revitalizing them, an explicit legitimacy of political mobilization through the grassroots institutions etc. have clearly differentiated the system from the civil society initiatives. Nevertheless, the synergy of panchayats and the civil society organizations (specifically the NGOs and the SHGs, which largely depend on the state for their existence) is imagined in the context of the redefined role of the state. The fundamental issue pertinent to the present mode of state intervention is, however, effectiveness of the panchayats – the instrumentality of rural self-governance – in promoting economic development with social justice independently and also by bringing about the synergy. The limitations set by the 'area managers' of the state i.e. the power hungry political elites and the bureaucracy, cannot be addressed in the subjective domain isolating them from the redesigned mode of state intervention.

The Act of 1994, reintroducing the three-tier system of Panchayati Raj in Assam, brought together all the 29 subjects to the functional domain of the PRIs, which are responsible for the preparation of the annual plan for development of the area that comes under their respective jurisdiction. The practices of the PRIs in the state have, however, reduced the notion of annual 'development plan' to a mere budget, the country the country enlisting certain scheme to be implemented in their respective areas. Following the Assam Panchayat (Financial) Rules 2002, before end of February each year, the State Government or the Central Government or the ZP/AP, as the case may be, is required to intimate each GP, the amount of contribution, grant or loan, if granted any. Accordingly, the GP is required to prepare the estimate of revenue and expenditure including other receipts for the ensuing Panchayat financial year (1st July to 30 June). This constitutes budget of the GP, and this has to be submitted to the concerned AP for approval. The AP may approve the budget or return it to the GP for reconsideration. In case of any modification, the GP has to re-submit the budget to the AP concerned for its approval, and if the concerned AP fails to convey its approval within 30 days from the date of re-submission, the budget shall be deemed to have been approved by the AP. The same is the laid down procedure for the AP vis-à-vis the ZP.

In case of the ZPs, the budget has to be submitted to the government, the Department of Panchayat and Rural Development through the Directorate of Panchayat and Rural Development of the state for its approval. The Director of

Panchayat and Rural Development is required to forward the budget to the government latest by the 15th of August with his comment. The state government may either approve the budget or return it to the concerned ZP for the required modifications. On such modifications being made, the concerned ZP may resubmit the budget directly to the state government for approval. If the state government fails to convey its approval within 30 days from the date of re-submission, the budget shall be deemed to have been approved by the state government.

In such a set pattern of 'annual planning', the Director, a senior IAS officer accountable to the Minister of Panchayat and Rural Development of the state, has obviously become the de facto guardian of the PRIs, which are accustomed with only enlisting the schemes in their respective budget to be implemented mainly under the SGRY with the fund allocated to them by the concerned DRDA. Even with this limited approach, on the route that the PRIs in Assam have to follow to reach the state or the central government through the Directorate of Panchayat and Rural Development via B.D.O/ Project Director, DRDA, the people's representatives have to grapple with the bureaucratic stranglehold at every walk.

At the district level, to converge the DRDA with the ZP, provision has recently been made that the Governing Body of each DRDA in the districts having PRIs is to be chaired by the Presidents of the ZP, and the Project Director is required to act as the Secretary. All MLAs and MPs representing the constituencies or their part in the district are members of the Governing Body of the DRDA, which also includes representatives of political parties and the heads of all the line departments of the concerned district. The Governing Body is required to examine the pattern of allocations made by the DRDA. However, it is only a recommendatory body. Neither are its recommendations binding upon the DRDA nor does the DRDA need its approval for implementation of any programme. The ZPs in the state overwhelmingly depend upon the DRDAs both for approval of the schemes to be implemented and allocation of fund.

The bureaucratic stranglehold on the PRIs has not been weakened even in the states where the DRDAs are no more independent entities. In the states such as Karnataka, Kerala, Madhya Pradesh and Maharastra where the DRDAs are merged with the ZPs, as it has been observed, the bureaucratic system remains overwhelming as before. "What used to be called the DRDA is now the ZP. An officer called a Chief Executive Officer has been brought in as head of the ZP administration. In theory, all the district offices come under him. In reality, he is indeed the administrative head, but in all technical matters, things get referred to the departmental bosses, who have the power of "approval" – an important bureaucratic power. The CEO is supposed to listen to the President of the ZP. May do, as they recognize political authority. Yet, they have the power to refer decisions of the ZP to the state government, and thus not implement them. The CEO's bosses are in the bureaucracy in the state capital. Thus, we have a local government which does not have a bureaucracy under its control" (Vyasalu, 2003).

For the APs and the GPs, the B.D.O is both de facto and de jure guardians[8]. The BDO is the Secretary of the AP and also the Executive Officer to 'supervise and control the execution of all work of the AP'. The BDO, as directed by the Project Director DRDA, informs the AP and GPs under its jurisdiction about the probable budget allocation for the ensuing year usually by the end of February. Accordingly, The AP and the GPs prepare their budgets (the Action Plan) enlisting the schemes specifying the amount required for that.

In the process of preparation as well as implementation of the schemes, both the AP and the GPs under its jurisdiction have to depend heavily on the technical persons, normally the Junior Engineers (JE), of the Block Development Office.

The technical staff of the BDO is not accountable to the PRIs, though each JE has been assigned the responsibility of looking after, on an average, four to five GPs, sometimes even more than that. The JE has to assist the GP in preparation of the Action Plan. After implementation of every scheme enlisted in the Action Plan, the concerned JE has to verify the completed work and report to the BDO It has been observed that the President of the GPs has to constantly pursue the JE to do the verification required for making the payment for the completed work. Such persuasion, more often than not, amounts to bribery. In some cases, as it has been found, the BDO has also been exercising almost complete control of the limited financial powers given to the PRIs through this process. On completion of a particular scheme and verification of the work by the concerned JE, the Secretary of the GP through the GP President has to officially request the BDO to advice the concerned bank to make payment against the cheque issued by the GP. It is the prerogative of the B.D.O. to issue the necessary 'Advice of Payment of Cheque' to the concerned bank[9].

The statutory provision of constituting different standing committees by the PRIs at various levels has been mechanically fulfilled. The so-called standing committees constituted immediately after assuming the offices by the elected PRIs are now defunct, especially in case of an overwhelming majority of the APs and the GPs. In some cases, even the elected functionaries are not aware of the existence of such standing committees in their respective panchayats. Lack of proper understanding on the part of many of the elected representatives about the structure and functioning of the Panchayati Raj has been, undoubtedly one of the major factors responsible for this ridiculous state of affairs. Yet, no conscious attempt has been made so far by the state government to ensure functioning of the standing committees as an integral part of the process of democratic decentralization.

The uprooted GPs, which are hardly guided by the elementary considerations of economic planning, are now busy, primarily with enlisting the small schemes for the SGRY and their implementation, which was earlier done by the Block Development Offices through the petty contractors. Besides the SGRY, involvement of the GPs is also necessary for construction of houses for the rural poor under the IAY. But the mechanism that has evolved in Assam provides a very limited scope for the GPs. The GP is required to constitute a construction committee involving the beneficiaries identified by the GP for the houses to be constructed under the IYA. The Secretary of the GP is also the Secretary of such a construction committee while one of the beneficiaries is its Chairman. The amount required for construction of the houses is disbursed by the concerned BDO to the account jointly handled by the Secretary and the President of the construction committee. The GP has no role to play after constitution of the construction committee. As far as the IAY is concerned, the role of the GP is, therefore confined primarily to identification of the beneficiaries.

The ground reality is that the set patterns of functioning followed by the PRIs in Assam have made a mockery of all notions such as democracy at the grassroots, transparency, accountability etc., when every decision is taken by the political-bureaucratic nexus at the local level. Identification of beneficiaries for different development programmes, in practice, is the basic responsibility of the GP. This has, however, been done by the elected representatives often on political consideration alone when the Gaon Sabha has merely been of token existence. Accountability is not a factor to be reckoned with. In many cases, the elected representatives at different levels are now the contractors[10] who are implementing the schemes in the name of the panchayat concerned.

THE MYTH OF DEVOLUTION

The Indian State, in the wake of economic liberalism envisaged a new variant of fiscal federalism through the Seventy-third constitutional amendment. Emphasis has been more on involvement of people in determining local priorities in development programmes and enabling them to satisfy the local needs than achieving merely allocative efficiency in the provision of public needs. The effort, at the same time, has also been to create a countervailing force for the demand for more state autonomy from the central government. The state governments have to concede more autonomy for the PRIs while demanding the same for themselves. (Thimmaiah, 1998) With the legal status, the panchayats, therefore, are expected to become the third level of government similar to that of the state government itself. The units of local government are supposed to be the federating unit of the state through a process of true devolution of funds, functions and functionaries to the appropriate level. Such a process of devolution has been emphasized upon by the plethora of literature on panchayats generated particularly by the Seventy-third amendment of the Constitution.

The powers, authority and responsibilities, which may be endowed with the panchayats by the state legislations are enlisted by the Article 243G of the Constitution. The goal is to promote the panchayats as the institution of self-government. Alongside the devolution of responsibilities upon panchayats at the appropriate level, the Constitution makes the provision that state legislations may authorize the panchayats to levy, collect and appropriate certain taxes, duties, tolls and fees. To ensure the desired pattern of financial devolution, the Constitution makes it mandatory for the states to constitute the State Finance Commission to review financial position of the panchayats and to make recommendations. The principles, which should govern the State Finance Commissions, are also laid by the Constitution.

The State Finance Commissions are expected to ensure distribution of the net proceeds of the taxes, duties, tolls and fees levied by the state, between the state and the panchayats, and to ensure allocation between the panchayats at all levels, of their respective shares of such proceeds; determination of the taxes, duties, tolls and fees which may be assigned to or appropriated by the panchayats; and recommend grants-in-aid to the panchayats from the Consolidated Fund of the state. Correspondingly, in Article 280 (deals with the Central Finance Commission) in clause (3), after sub-clause (b), the following sub-clause (bb) has been added: 'the measures needed to augment the Consolidated Fund of a State to supplement the resources of the Panchayats in the State on the basis of the recommendations made by the Finance Commission of the State.'

Therefore, it is absolutely clear that the Central Finance Commission can recommend the measures for augmentation of the Consolidated Fund of the states only when the State Finance Commissions ascertain the need for such augmentation. The measures recommended by the Central Finance Commission may not necessarily ensure transfer of resources from the Centre to the states. The transfer of duties and functions listed in the Eleventh Schedule of the Constitution necessarily implies concomitant transfer of staff and resources to the PRIs, and logically, such transfer should not entail any extra financial burden upon the states.

The Seventy-third amendment made it mandatory for the states to constitute the State Finance Commissions 'as soon as may be within one year from the commencement of the Constitution (Seventy-third Amendment) Act, 1992, and thereafter at the expiration of every fifth year' (Article 243I). As a result, there is no synchronization of the periods covered by the State Finance Commissions with that of the Central Finance Commission, and this has been a major problem for the latter to play whatever the role assigned to it by the

Constitution. The Eleventh Finance Commission, constituted in July 1998 for recommending on specified aspects of Centre-State fiscal relations during 2000-05 was required to make recommendations following the new addition to the Article 280 for the first time. It has, however, been found that only in case of very few states, the period covered by their respective State Finance Commission synchronized with that of the Eleventh Finance Commission. As a result, though most of the State Finance Commissions could make available their reports to the Eleventh Finance Commission, they were for different periods of time, and related to only the first or at best the second year of the period to be covered by the latter. At the same time, most of the reports have neither addressed the specific terms listed in Article 243I nor provided any clear idea of the powers, authority and responsibilities actually entrusted to the PRIs in their respective states. Nor have the reports clearly indicated the principles formulated for sharing or assignment of taxes, duties, tolls, fees and the grants-in-aid between state and the panchayats.

With the notion of devolution of resources from the Centre to the states and thence to the PRIs, most of the states expected that the Central Finance Commission would recommend a higher level of devolution of funds to the states to augment their Consolidated Funds for meeting the development and other requirements of the panchayats. Accordingly, the financial requirements of the panchayats were posed with the expectation that the funds transferred by the states to the panchayats would be provided by the Central Finance Commission[11]. In other words, the common expectation was that, after re-institutionalization of the PRIs following the constitutional amendment, the Central Finance Commission would be instrumental in greater devolution of fund to the states, and accordingly, the demands were placed before the Eleventh and the Twelve Finance Commission. The Eleventh Finance Commission, however, did not find any legal justification for such demands. Yet, "sympathetically" considering the demands of the states, and also keeping in view the availability of resources and the overall limits set for the flow of resources from the center to the states, recommended a grant of Rs. 1,600 crore for the panchayats for each of the five years starting from the financial year 2000-01 i.e. a total Rs. 8000 crore for five years.

With a similar approach, the Twelfth Finance Commission recommended Rs. 20,000 crore for the PRIs of the country for the next five years i.e. 2000-01 to 2005-06. Though it is a substantial increase over the levels recommended by the previous commission, the Central Finance Commission wants the grants to be utilized to improve the service delivery by the panchayats in respect of water supply and sanitation, specifically to maintain the schemes implemented by the states under the *Swajaldhara* programme launched by the Government of India. The commission also noted that the grant is not sufficient even for this specific purpose, and therefore, the PRIs should mobilize at least 50 per cent of the recurring costs of the schemes in the form of user charges.

Therefore, in the scenario that has emerged, to be precise, the state is solely responsible for appropriate devolution of funds to the PRIs along with the functions and functionaries following the recommendations of the State Finance Commission. However, to augment the Consolidated Fund, the states are expected to follow the recommendations made by the Central Finance Commission along with certain conditions[12]. Re-institutionalization of the PRIs does not necessarily imply reconstruction of the pattern of financial relations between the Centre and the states; it essentially implies devolution of functions, functionaries and the required funds from the state governments to the PRIs. However, the primary objective of true devolution has not been to strengthen the states at the cost of the Centre, nor does to strengthen the PRIs at the cost of the states. The objective is to strengthen the Indian State, which includes both tiers of government i.e. the states and the PRIs, so that the State can become more accountable to the people and sensitive to their demands. Therefore, devolution in the true sense implies greater devolution of resources from the Centre to the states and thence to the PRIs and decentralized planning. It cannot be merely seen as decentralization of decision-making to the level below the states.

Coming back to the specific context of Assam, the Assam Panchayat Act, 1994 has supposedly transferred altogether 29 subjects to the PRIs following broadly the Article 243G of the Constitution. The fundamental issues relating to the functional domain of the PRIs in the state have already been pointed out earlier, and therefore, further discussion in this regard is not required in the present context. Nevertheless, it will be pertinent to point out a glaring gap between the Eleventh Schedule of the Constitution and the statutory provisions regarding functions of the PRIs in Assam. While pointing out the powers, authority and responsibilities of the panchayats, the Constitution wants the states to entrust with the panchayats the responsibility of implementation of the land reform programmes[13] to ensure economic development and social justice. However, this vital issue has been ignored by the Act of 1994. The Act makes the panchayats responsible for identification and implementation of various agricultural schemes with technical assistance from the concerned departments, development of wastelands, and maintenance of grazing land. Though more or less the same provision has been made in almost all the Panchayat Acts enacted by the states after the Seventy-third Amendment, in practice the PRIs have been playing a decisive role in implementation of land reform programmes, particularly in the states ruled by the left parties. In Assam, however, land reform neither figures in the list of statutory functions of the PRIs, nor has it been considered in the political agenda of the present ruling party. As a result, the attempts that have been made to improve the agrarian scenario of the state have utterly failed.

Deliberately avoiding even the narrow constitutional approach, the restriction imposed on the functional domain of the PRIs by the ruling Congress Government in the state has also been substantiated by the pattern of devolution of functionaries to the PRIs. The present size of non-elected functionaries in each tier of panchayats is extremely small to discharge the responsibilities. The average situation in the state is as follows. In each of the 20 ZPs, there are one Chief Executive Officer, one Deputy Chief Executive Officer and three other office staff only. In each of the 196 APs, there are one Executive Officer (who is the BDO of the respective Development Block) and three other office staff. The situation is even worse at the GP level. In each of the 2151 GPs, there are one Secretary and only one Grade IV staff (SIRD, 2004).

This skewed pattern of devolution of functionaries clearly reveals the attitude of the state government towards the PRIs. The subjects enlisted in the Eleventh Schedule of the Constitution have been transferred to the PRIs in Assam through the Act of 1994. However, the legislation has merely enumerated the subjects without specifying the schemes that can be implemented by the PRIs as contemplated by the Article 243G. Consequently, both funds and functionaries relating to these schemes have remained in the exclusive domain of the state government. However, it is mandatory for the state to transfer the functions and the schemes to the PRIs through the legislation. Similarily, the Act of 1994 has contemplated a hierarchical structure of the PRIs with the APs supervising the GPs and the ZPs supervising, advising and coordinating the activities of the GPs and the APs. However, the legislation has not clearly delineated the role of the three tiers of the PRIs, which has led to a high degree of uncertainty as well as confusion.

Functional control over village level functionaries by panchayats is an indicator of the self-government status of the PRIs. Karnataka has placed the village level functionaries such as VLW, ANM, Patwari, Anganwadi Sebika and Primary school teachers under the control and supervision of the Taluk Panchayat. Madhya Pradesh has ensured functional control by the GP over all village level functionaries except the Patwaris. Similarly, the GP in Rajasthan has control over VLW and Primary School teachers, and in West Bengal too, the similar control over the village level functionaries has been followed. However, no such effort has so far been made in Assam to ensure self-government status for the PRIs.

Mechanically following the Article 243 I, the Government of Assam constituted the First State Finance Commission in September 1995. The commission was asked to make the report available to the government by 31st December 1995, covering a period of five years[14], 1996-97 to 2000-01. Though the PRIs in Assam had no existence from 1997 to 2002, the Assam State Finance Commission had made some recommendations in order to strengthen the Panchayati Raj in the state. It recommended devolution of 2 per cent of the state's taxes and 10 per cent of motor vehicle tax to the PRIs. The Commission observed, "the current tax domain of the local bodies is very narrow and relatively inelastic. Taxes levied and collected by the local bodies do not yield substantial revenue and therefore, they depend on higher transfer from Government level. Considering the wide range of responsibility like social, economic and administrative and the resource position of the Government as well as the state, the possibility of transfer of fund of any higher magnitude appears to be bleak and therefore, *it is expected that the local bodies will have to generate their own resources by exploring the untapped areas to match with the additional responsibility they are vested with for ensuring basic services and amenities to the people*" (emphasis added).

The above observation made by the Assam State Finance Commission reflects its perception about the role of PRIs, and understanding on the issue of financial devolution. In this context the recommendations made by some of the other State Finance Commissions are worth considering. Despite the status quo of financial relations between the Centre and the states, the respective State Finance Commission has recommended significantly high financial devolution in those states where the panchayats are expected to play an active role. For example, the Kerela State Finance Commission recommends 25 per cent of surcharge on Stamp Duty, 25 per cent of motor vehicle tax, and 25 per cent of court fee stamps to the panchayats. The West Bengal State Finance Commission recommends 16 per cent of the net proceeds of the state taxes, while the Karnataka State Finance Commission recommends 36 per cent of the total non-loan gross revenue receipts. The Madhya Pradesh State Finance Commission recommends 3.24 per cent of the net total revenue of the preceding year and 40 per cent of Plan funds. In Punjab, the State Finance Commission recommends 20 per cent of the stamp Duty, motor vehicle tax, electricity duty, and, entertainment tax. In Tamilnadu, the State Finance Commission recommended 15 per cent of the state's tax revenue every year during the period 1998 to 2001. The Tripura State Finance Commission recommends 20 per cent of the state's share of central taxes, 50 per cent of the revenue from sales tax, purchase tax and luxury tax, 35 per cent of professional tax, 32 per cent of agricultural income tax and land revenue and 15 per cent of forest revenue. As against the above, the Assam State Finance Commission recommends merely 2 per cent of the State's taxes and 10 per cent of motor vehicle tax. In the perception of the Assam State Finance Commission, panchayats are local bodies performing activities of a peripheral nature.

Notwithstanding the fact that, the constitutional

mandates are ostensibly fulfilled, the Congress regime in the state, has totally failed to address the question of financial devolution to the PRIs. With an adhoc attitude towards the PRIs, the state government has not taken any initiative even to follow the recommendations made by the Assam State Finance Commission. As a result, the main sources of fund for the PRIs in the state are: (a) amount received as the award of the Eleventh Finance Commission; (b) amount transferred by the DRDA for implementation of the SGRY schemes; and (c) fund generated from own resources.

As awarded by the Eleventh Finance Commission, according to the official sources, the state had received Rs.23,34,00,000/- in the financial year 2003-04 and Rs.45,02,93,000/- in the financial year 2004-05. The entire amount was released to the GPs against their proposed schemes through the CEO of the respective ZP. Therefore, on an average, a GP in Assam was supposed to receive Rs.1,08,406/- in the financial year 2003-04 and another installment of Rs. 2,09,146/- in the financial year 2004-05 as award of the Eleventh Financial Commission.

However, the ground realities substantially differ from the above average scenario. A couple of instances may substantiate it. The Dimoria Anchalik Panchayat/ Development Block has the jurisdiction covering 144 villages scattered in 12 GPs. The total population of the AP is about 1.20 lakh, of which more than 14 per cent and 13 per cent belong to the SCs and the STs respectively. For its physical proximity to the city of Guwahati as well as ethnic composition, the Development Block/AP is treated as the showcase of rural development programmes in Assam. Of the total amount received by the state as awarded by the Eleventh Finance Commission, the total amount received by the 12 GPs together till the end of the financial year 2004-05 was only Rs.10.03 lakh. Similarly, the Bezera AP, which is also located near Guwahati, covers 57 villages under the jurisdiction of seven GPs. The total population of the AP is little more than 80 thousand, of which nearly 16 per cent and 9 per cent belong to the SCs and the STs respectively. The total amount received by the seven GPs together against the award of the Eleventh Finance Commission till the end of 2004-05 was only Rs. 6.56 lakh. In case of the GPs under both Dimoria and Bezera, the fund was approved in 2003-04, but it was made available to the GPs for implementation of their schemes in 2004-05. This suggests that the larger part of the total amount awarded to the PRIs by the Eleventh Finance Commission was not made available to the GPs at least till the end of 2005.

The details of the fund utilized (as claimed by the government of Assam) for various rural development programmes in the state for the period of 2001-02 to 2004-05 are shown in Annexure – 3 clearly differentiating the fund received by the state from the Centre during last four years under the SGRY and matching grant of the state in each year vis-à-vis other rural development programmes. The central share for SGRY, together with the state share constituted the total fund to be transferred to the PRIs for implementation of various schemes. The details of the fund received by the state and the possible allocations to the PRIs are shown in Annexure – 4 and 5. The total fund available for implementation of the schemes by the PRIs under SGRY constituted 48.63 per cent of the total fund available for various rural development programmes for the year 2001-02. In the year 2002-03, the Central as well as the state share under SGRY had increased substantially compared to the total fund available under other rural development programmes. As a result, the fund, which was to be released to the PRIs had also increased to more than 70 per cent. However, as funds for some other rural development programmes started flowing to the state, the ratio between the fund available for SGRY and the total fund available for other rural development programmes declined to 49.65 per cent in 2003-04 and then to 48.45 per cent in 2004-05. Therefore, the overall pattern of fund to be released to the PRIs and the fund that could be utilized by the DRDAs through the Development Blocks bypassing the panchayats has not gone under any noticeable change in the state since 2001-02. But at the same time, the share of the food grains component as required specifically by SGRY has also substantially increased.

As mentioned earlier, the fund available under SGRY has to be released by the DRDA to the PRIs against the schemes they propose. Of the total fund available in a year, 20 per cent is to be released to the ZP. And, 30 per cent and 50 per cent has to be released to APs and GPs respectively through the concerned Block Development Office. As the total amount under SGRY had increased substantially during the period, the fund that was to be released to the PRIs had increased significantly. Even if only the cash component is considered, on an average, the fund that was to be released to each ZP had increased from Rs. 310.35 lakh in 2001-02 to Rs. 470.56 lakh in 2004-05. Correspondingly, the average amount that was to be released to each AP had increased from Rs. 50.88 lakh to Rs. 77.14 lakh, while the average amount to be released to each GP had increased from Rs. 7.20 lakh to 10.93 lakh.

In the context of devolution of SGRY fund to the PRIs also, the ground realities significantly differs from the average scenario that can be drawn on the basis official information. One can hardly find an AP or a GP, which can be matched with the average scenario in terms of the fund received under the SGRY, including both cash and food grains component. The amount deducted by the DRDAs and the Block Development Offices as contingency from the share of the PRIs, however, partially explains the gap between the amount due to the PRIs and the amount they actually receive. The

DRDAs, while disbursing the cash component deducts 10 per cent to 15 per cent from the amount allocated to the APs as contingency, and in turn, the Block Offices deduct another 10 per cent to 15 per cent from the fund allocated to the GPs on the similar ground. It has been observed that, the food grains component of SGRY has always been a contentious issue. Apart from the problem of space for preservation and quality, usually a large amount of food grains are being sold in the open market. Instances of such corrupt practices of the panchayat functionaries are many, and often reported by the print media.

As pointed out earlier, the Assam State Finance Commission strongly recommends that the PRIs in the state have to generate their own resources to match with the additional responsibility they are vested with for ensuring basic services and amenities to the people. The Commission believes that taxes on the immovable property such as building/houses, non-agricultural land, and non-motorized vehicles would be a rich source of revenue for the PRIs in Assam.

Mainly exercising the power given by the Act of 1994 to levy tolls and taxes on various things such as non-motorized vehicles, animals, markets, etc., the PRIs in Assam are trying to mobilize some additional amount from their available resources. However, the experiences of the last four years have clearly shown that the PRIs in Assam, on the basis of their present sources of earning can hardly generate an amount, which is worth considering for any development initiative. An analysis of the resource base of four APs[15] and the additional revenue they have generated during the last three years reveals that, on an average, an AP from its own resources can generate an amount of Rs. 8.25 lakh in a year. The example of Sarupathar AP, which is coterminous with the Golaghat South Development Block, is worth noting, because it is one of the largest APs in Assam. The AP has a total population of about two lakh inhabiting in more than 400 villages scattered in altogether 21 GPs. The total revenue that has been annually generated by such a large AP, on an average, is only about Rs11.05 lakh.

In a similar exercise done for six GPs[16] revels that, on an average, a GP from its own resources can generate only about Rs. 30,000/- in a year. Therefore, the additional amount generated by a GP is not even enough to pay the small amount as honorarium to the President, Vice-President and the members[17].

There are several constraints before the PRIs in mobilization of revenue from their own sources. To cite some of the major constraints, first of all, the resource base that has been brought under the control of the PRIs, especially the GPs, is extremely narrow. The power given to the PRIs to levy tax on the non-motorized vehicles such as Bicycle, Rickshaw, Bullock cart, Handcart etc. sounds good. But in practice, the cost of collection of such tax is often found to be much more than the amount that has been actually collected in a year. Yet, the PRIs, especially the GPs, have taken the exercise of collection such tax in the spirit of the right given to them. Secondly, the common property resources such as Beels, Fish ponds etc. brought under the control of the PRIs along with the weekly markets constitute a relatively viable source of revenue for the APs. Such sources are supposed to be leased out by the AP to the highest bidder. It has, however, been observed that usually this does not happen due to political interference. The local MLAs who are ex-officio members of APs often exercise their political influence at the time of bidding for the resources. Besides political consideration, concern for personal gain of the local level political leadership, particularly of the party in power, overwhelmingly influences the bidding process. The biddings often become a mockery to jeopardize interests of the panchayats. The third, and perhaps the most important hindering factor is the considerably high incidence of rural poverty in Assam. More than 80 per cent of the rural population depends on agriculture for livelihood, but more than 25 per cent of the rural households do not have any cultivable land. Nor has the agricultural sector been adequately developed to provide a sustainable labour market. Consequently, more than 40 per cent of the rural people in the state still live below the poverty line.

PANCHAYATI RAJ AND WOMEN: THE NOTION OF GENDER JUSTICE AND ATROCIOUS MANEUVERING OF THE STATUTORY PROVISIONS

Within the liberal democratic framework of the Constitution, the Seventy-third amendment advocates a process of decentralization in decision-making, which is expected to provide greater efficiency, transparency, accountability and opportunity for wider participation of people at the grassroots. Constructing the notion of gender and social justice, the State through this amendment attempted to accommodate the demand for representation and participation of women in politics (see for details Mazumdar, 1997) making the constitutional provision of reservation of women in the PRIs, notwithstanding that the same provision has yet to be extended to the state Assemblies and the Parliament.

The demand for political representation of women has undoubtedly been a contentious issue, and evidently, it has significantly influenced the political discourses sharply focusing on redistribution of power and resources articulating the basic interests of the women. Political representation of women, therefore, is not seen as a goal in itself, and reservation in this context has been justified not only as a means to address the issue of gender imbalance but also as an instrument for redistribution of power and resources challenging the patriarchal hegemony. Therefore, the fundamental questions of participation and representation of women in politics are to be addressed in a much wider context of the political processes, power equations determined by patriarchy as well as class and caste combination and, ideology of the State.

Although it is a narrow political space ensured by the Constitution, the provision of reservation of seats for women in the PRIs, has undoubtedly warranted a new political force in the rural political terrain. The provision has not only encouraged a section of women who volunteered to contest the elections but also provided a platform for the civil society institutions to address the issues of political participation and representation of women through the process of election. The political parties, irrespective of their understanding and ideology, are mandated to nominate only the women candidates in the reserved constituencies. Consequently, now there are about ten lakh rural women representatives who have access to at least some amount of power given by the Constitution.

The new women leadership that has been ushered in is, however, extremely heterogeneous in its composition, and obviously devoid of a cohesive political ideology. As observed in an empirical study, the women panchayat leaders are of different categories. They are educated, uneducated, highly sophisticated, rich, poor, wage earners, dalits among others. There are leaders with political orientation and party background who look at the issues only from their party perspective. There are leaders without any political background but under the clutches of their husbands or the males of their families. There are leaders who have commitments and values but no awareness and information. There are leaders with high political aspirations (Palnithurai and Ragupathy, 2003). The fundamental issue therefore, is to build the capacity of the women representatives enabling them to challenge the patriarchal influences with a wider perspective of political change.

Most of the empirical studies on the role of the elected women functionaries of PRIs have pointed out various structural constraints faced by the women representatives due to their illiteracy, lack of information and knowledge as well as dependency on their male counterparts. The common concern is to consciously highlight the constructive role played by the women representatives despite the resistance from the dominating patriarchal politico-bureaucratic structures in the traditional rural environment. For instance, an empirical analysis of the experiences of women representatives in panchayats in Madhya Pradesh, Rajasthan and Uttar Pradesh highlighted that the provision of reservation for women led to certain myths about their likely performance. The myths such as women's passivity and disinterest in politics would affect their performance, only the well-to-do and upper caste women would come through reservation, women are proxy and they do not participate in the panchayats etc. are empirically explored (Buch, 1999). A similar study for Haryana has pointed out the potential of the provision of reservation for women in providing them social recognition and respect (Teckchandani, 1998). A report from Orissa has also pointed out a positive pattern of women's leadership in a predominantly traditional setting with all patriarchal domination. (Panda, 1996) While documenting the experiences of women representatives in different states, alongside several success stories, PRIA has also focused on the structural problems faced by the women representatives (Rai, 2001). A recent analysis of the women representatives in PRIs of Assam, Gujarat, Haryana, Kerala, Madhya Pradesh and Orissa has pointed out that reservation for women has provided a window of opportunity for women to enter the public sphere and definitely set a positive trend overall. Despite many constraints and limitations, women have proved that given an opportunity they are capable of becoming equal partners in the development process. To an extent, women have managed to overcome the limitations set by illiteracy and lack of access to information (Prasad, 2005).

Being preoccupied with the apparently narrow structural problems, most of such studies have emphasized on institutional training as an effective means of empowerment. Such assertion undoubtedly amounts to de-radicalization of the gender issue. Yet, they constitute a rich source of empirical insights required for an objective understanding of the gender issue and to articulate the basic interests of women.

Though the statutory provision of one-third reservation for women was made in Assam prior to the seventy-third amendment, the women representatives constituted less than 30 per cent of the total members elected to the PRIs in 1992. With a positive response to the Seventy-third amendment, the proportionate strength of women representatives had increased to more than 38 per cent in PRIs constituted after the elections held in 2001. In all the three tiers of PRIs in Assam, the proportionate strength of women representatives crossed the mandated limit of 33 per cent (see Annexure – 2). A sample survey has projected quite a satisfactory socio-economic and political profile of the women representatives of Assam compared to many other states. Illiteracy is not a factor, more than 25 per cent per cent of the elected women representatives have primary education while about 44 per cent have studied up to the high school level. Alongside the satisfactory educational profile, it is evident that the provision of reservation has pushed to the rural political arena considerably a large section of the women engaged in household maintenance. More than 80 per cent of the elected women representatives belong to this category. Yet at the same time, as the study has pointed out, only about 27 per cent of the elected women representatives in Assam have political affiliation, the same ratio is, however, much higher in some of the states such as Kerala, Orissa, Haryana, Gujarat etc. (Prasad, 2005).

During discussions with 68 active women representatives[18] of Assam it has, however, been observed that, more than 23 per cent of them are quite influential local level political leaders, with an overwhelming majority belonging to the Congress. They have high political aspirations, and feel that the panchayat is a stepping-stone to reach the state Assembly, ultimately. They are keen to prove their efficiency. Being a part of the party structure, they are ready to adjust with the "party commands" – Block President to the local MLA. About 64 per cent of the women representatives decided to be panchayat members being inspired by the husbands or other male members of the family when the political parties approached them. They perceived the panchayat as an instrument of service to the community. Except for a few, the majority of them have not found any significant problems in discharging their assigned responsibilities. The remaining members, who were reluctant to reveal their party affiliation, were also guided by the ethos of service to the community. As they revealed, they were encouraged by the community to become panchayat members, and therefore, they strongly feel that they have some obligations to the community. They felt that, although the problems relating to the bureaucratic and political interference are common, they have to adjust with such problems to discharge their responsibilities.

The first category of women leaders with their distinct party political identity and keenness to prove their efficiency are found to be in conformity with the party structure rather than making any conscious effort to influence and change the institution, which institutionalizes patriarchy. The level of their efficiency is intrinsically linked with their ability to adjust and create a political space within the process. Individualism overrides all other considerations including the gender issue. For the second and the third category of women representatives, who apparently disapprove political considerations, the assigned responsibilities are sacrosanct.

Being a part of the formal process, the ethos is to "do something good for the community" by discharging the assigned responsibilities rather than influencing and changing the political process of gender discrimination. They believe that the provision of reservation has provided them an opportunity to work for the people, and seemingly they are not very despondent with the political process. Nevertheless, there exists a difference between the women representatives and their male counterparts. The initiatives taken by the women representatives are usually influenced by the day to day problems faced by the common women while the initiatives of the male representatives are often guided by other considerations, especially material benefits. This qualitative element is crucial for its gender dimension.

Being guided by the notion of "doing something good for the community" a good number of women representatives have demonstrated considerable courage, initiatives and also ability to assert themselves politically. For instance, the President of Namsungi GP (Jorhat) has been successful in drawing attention for her ability to organize and involve people in various development programmes (*Asam Bani*, 15 July, 2005). The President of Harmoti GP (Lakhimpur) has been successful in mobilizing people against trafficking of women, besides initiating several developmental programmes. The President of Rajabari GP (Golaghat) has proved her efficiency primarily in resource mobilization, rehabilitation of people displaced by floods, and also by arranging training for women weavers. There are many more such women representatives throughout the state who have made similar contributions and proved their ability, sometimes going beyond the assigned responsibilities. Such initiatives are worth noticing.

Nevertheless, the essence of the notion of "doing something good for the community" (which has significantly influenced the performance of the women representatives often projected as dynamic), has blurred the gender issue to a large extent. It has propelled a conformist ideology legitimizing adjustment and compromise rather than confrontation with the social and political practices determined by patriarchy. Even in a state like Kerala, which provides a model of decentralization of powers, function and resources, the women representatives have not been able to significantly change the style and practice of the wider political arena (Sharma, 2004).

When the Congress was instrumental in passing the Seventy-third amendment, most of the political parties welcomed the constitutional mandate of reservation for women. However, most of the political parties including the Congress have failed to demonstrate any appreciable degree of change in their perspectives. In practice, the women representatives are always expected to adjust and cooperate with the existing form of patriarchal domination. The non-conformists are often denied any political space, and are constantly reminded that they are weak and dependent. For this, the most common and effective means throughout the country has been the provision of no confidence motion (which is apparently gender neutral) adopted by the state legislations with a pre-commitment to gender justice. There is no reason for Assam to be an exception. Therefore, the profile of initiative and achievement coexists with a pathetic political scenario of not only deprivation and humiliation but also violation of the basic rights of the women representatives. In most of the cases, the local Congress leaders maneuver the statutory provision to push back the non-conformist women representatives. During the last four years, a large number of women representatives in Assam have been thrown out of their office by bringing a no confidence motion against them, mostly on the charges of corruption. Although the process to initiate any legal recourse is quite complicated and expensive, many of the victims have sought judicial remedy and are still awaiting justice.

The experiences of Ms. Minu Brahma Pathak, a local leader of the Congress with higher education, can be cited as an example. The narration is as follows. She was elected as a member of the Matia AP (Goalpara) with other 10 members. Of the total 11 elected representatives of the AP, five are women. Some of the members got elected as independent candidate, but they all joined the Congress after the election. Minu was elected as the President of the AP as the post was reserved for women. After four months in her office, Minu was asked by the ZP member elected from the same constituency to pay him Rs. one lakh or to lease out all the weekly markets, fisheries etc. of the AP to some contractors following his recommendations. Minu boldly refused him. Consequently, she had to face the first no confidence motion. The motion was, however, defeated.

The male Congress lobby became much stronger with the joining of the local MLA. And once again prepared the ground for a no confidence motion on the charges of corruption. When it was moved, the Deputy Commissioner of Goalpara after the necessary enquiry found that the allegations brought against Minu were baseless. While the Congress lobby was preparing ground for the third no confidence motion, the local MLA asked Minu to meet him personally in the Goalpara Circuit House. She became quite apprehensive about the motive behind it, and informed all the people concerned including the Chief Minister of Assam. However, no one came forward to intervene.

The third no confidence motion against Minu primarily on the charges of certain irregularities and procedural lapses was initiated by three AP members guided by the local MLA and the ZP member. Five other AP members signed the notification of the no confidence motion. But, four of them immediately wrote to the President of the AP that they signed the notification under pressure and "it is a conspiracy". They were not a part of the conspiracy, and therefore, decided to withdraw their signature. Suddenly all the AP members were not seen in the locality, kidnapped by the local MLA as it was alleged. In the mean time, the formalities were completed for moving a no confidence motion, and the members were brought to the office of the Deputy Commissioner accompanied by the local MLA. The no confidence motion was passed, and the local MLA demanded its immediate effect while the Deputy Commissioner insisted on the official procedures relating to approval of the minutes of the meeting.

To expedite the process, one of the AP members immediately approached the High Court and got the necessary order for immediate execution of the no confidence motion. Following the court order, the Deputy Commissioner asked Minu to vacate her office by handing over the charge to the Vice President, a male member of the AP. Minu vacated the office on 18 September 2004 and immediately filed a writ petition, but lost the case. As it has been alleged, the Advocate she engaged was bribed by the local MLA not to plead her case. Subsequently, she appealed before the Divisional Bench and is still waiting for the verdict.

Yet, another narrative in the *Asam Bani* (27 June, 2003) has clearly exposed the worst form of patriarchal influences on the political process. A young, educated, enthusiastic and popular AGP worker, Rita wanted to contest for the post of President of Bongaon GP (Nalbari), a stronghold of the AGP. The local unit of AGP was, however, reluctant to nominate her. Under pressure from the people, the party unit ultimately accepted her candidature, but unofficially sponsored another woman worker of the party as an independent candidate to part with Rita's vote. Yet, due to her tremendous popularity, Rita was elected with a margin of about 800 votes. With all her sincerity and dedication she began working for the panchayat and became more popular. But at the same time, she also emerged as a potential political threat to her male counterpart in the AGP. A grievous allegation was brought against Rita, portraying her character in a negative light. It was alleged that Rita and twelve other girls of the village, were engaged in a pornographic movie and there were allegedly some eyewitnesses too. Soon it became a publicity stunt, a hot story for the local media. Life naturally became difficult for the young "perverted" girls and some of them left the village. The administration could not remain indifferent to the crime. Rita and one of her friends were immediately arrested and Rita was compelled to undergo a virginity test.

With her courage and confidence, Rita approached various civil society organizations, individuals, the State Human Right Commission as well as the media. The government asked the state intelligence to conduct the necessary enquiry. The enquiry report submitted to the State Human Right Commission revealed that the allegations brought against Rita and her friends were baseless.

The instances of Minu and Rita are self-explanatory. Such experiences are to be seen along with the "success stories" of the women representatives. The totality that emerges suggests that 'institutionalized inequalities' demand institutionalized counter measures (Mazumdar, 1997). Nevertheless, the contentious issue of political participation and representation of women cannot be addressed only through the statutory provisions and appeal. The democratically elected women representatives, being a part of the institutionalized counter measure, are also expected to influence the institutional arrangement, political processes and structures, which are still decisively dominated by patriarchy, and yet, instrumental in determining the political aspirations, ambition as well as ability of the women representatives.

SUMMING UP

Following the constitutional mandate, like all other states, the Assam State Legislative Assembly too has envisaged a qualitative breakthrough in the scenario of rural governance by re-institutionalizing the moribund Panchayati Raj in the state. All the constitutional mandates are accommodated in the Assam Panchayat Act, 1994. Though the elections to the PRIs were carefully avoided, the Act was amended several times during the AGP regime. The legislation, in its totality, however, has made the elected representatives subservient to the state bureaucracy, and carefully avoided the contentious issue of land reform. The essence is decentralization of the decision-making process and the wider participation of people in the development programmes. With the so-called bottom up approach, the statutory provisions are made to ensure social and gender justice and the policy of reservation.

The elections to the panchayats were held in December 2001 after a lapse of more than four years. The people welcomed the move and enthusiastically participated in the elections with a lot of hope and expectations. The Congress, which came back to power in May 2001, alongside the procedural formalities, prepared for the panchayat elections launching the RPRS programme involving the state bureaucracy just four months before the polls. The conscious and meticulously calculated political move really worked. In the absence of elected panchayats, on the one hand it generated hope among the mass of the rural people and it helped the Congress to extend its political influences, on the other. But at the same time, it has also set a dangerous pattern of rural local self-governance to be followed.

The Congress monopolized the PRIs elected in 2001, and yet, decided to continue with the mechanism of RPRS. The political strategy of domination of the state bureaucracy has not only led to confusion and chaos in the rural political arena but also jeopardized the Gaon Sabhas, the constitutionally recognized institution for ensuring accountability and transparency at the grassroots. Therefore, the pyramidal structure of panchayats has grown in Assam on a considerably feeble edifice with little democratic content in it.

Although the Constitution has sanctioned a fresh role to the panchayat in the process of its re-institutionalization, the PRIs in Assam can be characterized as the mere appendage of the DRDA. Following the constitutional mandate, 29 subjects have ostensibly been transferred to the PRIs without establishing the linkage between the line departments and the elected bodies. In practice, for their existence, the panchayats are overwhelmingly dependent on the DRDA and the Block Development Offices. The ground reality is that the set pattern of functioning of the PRIs in Assam has made a mockery of all notions such as democracy at the grassroots, transparency, accountability etc.

The ethos of the Seventy-third amendment has been the wider participation of people in determining local priorities and accordingly planning for satisfying the local needs. This perspective of decentralized planning requires greater financial devolution not only from the state to the PRIs but also from the Centre to the states to facilitate the process of devolution of functions and functionaries to the level below the state. Therefore, the envisaged process of democratic decentralization logically demands reformulation of the existing fiscal federalism, the task that has remained incomplete. Consequently, since the Centre is not willing for a greater financial devolution, the state with its limited resources has been found to be extremely reluctant to initiate financial devolution to the PRIs to any appreciable extent. The PRIs are expected to generate their own resources to match with the additional responsibilities they are vested with. However, depending on the extremely poor resource base, the PRIs in the state can hardly generate an amount worth considering for any development activity, and therefore, are surviving primarily on a particular rural development programme sponsored by the Centre.

Despite several limitations both in the spirit and the structure inherited from the ideology of a liberal democratic State, like in many other states, re-institutionalization of panchayats in Assam too warranted a new political force in the rural arena, ushering in a considerably large force of women leadership than ever before. It has brought to light, a remarkable success of the women's movements for political representation and participation. The panchayats have not only provided a platform to reconstruct the identity of the women leadership but also opportunities for political assertion articulating the basic interests of the women through the initiatives distinctly different from that of the usual concerns of men. The newly elected women leadership provides a rich profile of enthusiasm, courage and initiatives to carry forward the movement against all patriarchal forms of domination.

NOTES

1. First phase of the poll was on 27 December and the second phase was on 31 December 2001.
2. The special themes in the first year were Women Empowerment; Rural Credit; Health and Hygiene; and Strengthening of PRIs. The special themes in the second year were Environment and Forestry; Empowerment of SHG; Elementary Education and SSA; and Sericulture, Veterinary and Dairy.
3. Such messages sent by the Chief Minister to the people of every district before each round of RPRS are preserved by majority of the GPs.
4. Revealed by some retired senior ACS officers involved in the initial rounds of RPRS.
5. The common practice is that following instructions from the Government of Assam, the Office of the Deputy Commissioner of each district sends circular to the concerned officials of the district to organize each round of RPRS with the specific theme. Such circular also specifies the agenda for the

meetings, asking the Nodal Officer to finalize the date and venue in consultation with the Sr. B.D.O./B.D.O., G.P. President, A.P. Member, Z.P. Member, G.P. Secretary and Zonal Officer, RPRS. After finalization of the dates and venue by the Nodal Officer, the Sr. B.D.O./B.D.O. sends a circular to each GP requiring to held the meeting on the specific date and time.

6. Discussion with several elected functionaries of the districts of Kamrup, Golaghat, Dibrugarh and Goalpara on functioning of Gaon Sabhas in their respective GP.

7. It is clearly specified in the Article 38 of the Constitution [Directives Principles of State Policy, Part IV] that the State shall strive to promote the welfare of the people by securing and protecting as effectively as it may a social order with social, economic and political justice; and the State shall in particular, strive to minimize the inequalities in income, and endeavour to eliminate inequalities in status, facilities and opportunities, not only amongst individuals but also amongst group of people residing in different areas or engaged in different vocations.

8. Often addressed as 'Sir' by the elected representatives of the APs including the Presidents, observed in the offices of the B.D.Os and also in discussions with them outside the offices.

9. Such letter to the bank, as it has been observed, normally does not have any official issue number. The BDO writes to the Branch Manager of the concerned bank branch 'please pay the following cheque to the President/Secretary... Gaon Panchayat' specifying name of the scheme, cheque number and the amount. Such letters are verified in some of the GP offices of Golaghat district.

10. In some cases, as it has been found, they were also contractors often engaged by the B.D.Os for implementation of various development programmes before they were elected as panchayat members.

11. It is evident from the demands placed by the states before the Eleventh as well as the Twelve Finance Commission.

For details, see the reports of the Eleventh and Twelve Finance Commission.

12. Like the condition of using the grants awarded to the PRIs by the Twelfth Finance Commission, the Eleventh Finance Commission laid down the condition of "power sector reforms" to be undertaken by the states to the satisfaction of the Centre to receive what was constitutionally their due.
13. Serial number 2 of the Eleventh Schedule to the Constitution.
14. The commission however, failed to submit the report on the specified date. Ridiculously, the pretext was non-availability of the information in respect of population of GPs as per 1971 census. Therefore, the Commission requested the government to extend the time till 29th Feburary, 1996.
15. Dimoria and Bezera in Kamrup district, Sarupathar in Golaghat district and Balijana in Goalpara district.
16. Nartap and Sonapur in Kamrup distric, and Rajabari, Tengani, Tenga Hola and Pub Sarupathar in Golaghat district.
17. The normal practice is that a GP has to pay Rs. 1000/- to the President, Rs. 600/- to the Vice-President and Rs.300/- to each member per month as honorarium. Therefore, the total amount required for this purpose is Rs.55, 700/- in a year.
18. Informal discussion during field study with 26 women representatives in Kamrup, 22 in Golaghat and 19 in Goalpara.

7

CONCLUSION

Gandhi constructed the notion of swaraj unequivocally disapproving what he called 'modern civilization' much before his appearance in the Indian political scene in the early twentieth century. The notion was developed essentially as a fundamental critique of bourgeois society and its entire political edifice to idealize a moral, non-competitive, just and peaceful pre-capitalist society. With his notion of swaraj, Gandhi attempted to influence the theme of Indian nationalism to reconstruct its political goal on a much wider ideological plane than the contemporary nationalist discourses. The ultimate goal before the nationalist movement in India, for Gandhi, was not a centralized capitalist State. He made a plea for return to a simple self-sufficient traditional village life, and idealized a pre-capitalist form of social formation. The utopian 'state of enlightened anarchy' projected by Gandhi as an alternative to a bourgeois State, was legitimized by glorifying the ancient Indian civilization.

The 'self-sufficient village republic' was imagined as the political base of the 'state of enlightened anarchy' and its legitimacy was drawn primarily from the ancient Indian village system. In the Gandhian scheme of decentralization with its ultimate goal of 'purna swaraj', a village was imagined as a republic for itself, capable of managing all its affairs. Such a 'self-sufficient village republic' would be non exploitative and also free from exploitation by others. Thus the egalitarian structure, capable of protecting all its interests, would be governed by a panchayat constituted by five elected members. Therefore, Gandhi's emphasis on panchayat as an institution of self-government cannot be comprehended in isolation for its intrinsic link with his utopia of 'purna swaraj'.

Nevertheless, with the help of his utopian construction of swaraj, Gandhi was successful to make the Congress a broad nationalist platform in the 1920s. Gandhi's contribution to the Congress, especially in the 1920s, was undoubtedly unparallel. The 'left intelligentsia' within the Congress, however, started contesting the utopianism when the political movement reached a more mature stage in the 1930s. At the crucial historical juncture after the Civil Disobedience Movement, the challenge before Nehru was to redefine the primary objective of Indian nationalism and to reconstruct the nationalist ideology to legitimize a sovereign nation state rejecting Gandhian utopianism. The imagination of a nation state was to be legitimized as a neutral autonomous political entity, an instrument of socio-economic development and post-colonial reconstruction.

The Congress leadership that led the nationalist movement with the nation state ideology consolidated in the late 1930s consistently demanded a Constituent Assembly to frame a Constitution for independent India. Finally, the Constituent Assembly came into being and started functioning under the exclusive ideological and numerical domination of the Congress Working Committee. Following the Euro-American constitutional traditions, the Constituent Assembly collectively envisaged a centralized parliamentary system for India after independence. The Draft Constitution, totally ignoring the Gandhian notion of decentralization, provided no space for panchayats. In the subsequent debates, some of the members including the prominent Gandhians argued strongly in favour of panchayats. Their arguments, nevertheless, did not reflect any sense of rejection of the basic principles of the Draft Constitution in support of the Gandhian notion of decentralization. Essentially, they emphasized on panchayat as a mechanism of decentralized administration of a centralized parliamentary system with a liberal democratic ethos. Finally, the compromise was reached by making the provision of a narrow space for the panchayats in the Directive Principles of the Constitution of independent India.

The primary challenge before the Indian State immediately after independence was to legitimize itself as an autonomous political institution with a welfare and development ideology. While the development interventions were directed essentially to promote a modern capitalist sector, the welfare initiative of the State apparently sought to address the issues of socio-economic inequalities caused primarily by the semi-feudal agrarian relations. At the same time, the Congress, which monopolized over the State apparatus, however, had to compromise with the rural propertied classes for its own political benefits in an electoral democracy. As a result, the legislative battle launched against landlordism by the Congress leadership in different states had failed to alter the structure of domination in rural India.

Yet, with a positive response to the Directive Policy, some of the states took initiative to institutionalize panchayats through their respective legislative enactment. The initiatives to institutionalize panchayats were, nevertheless, preceded by the Community Development Programmes funded by the USA, and implemented by an elaborate centralized administrative structure inherited from the colonial past. In the process, the incipient panchayats were either totally ignored or became mere appendage to the bureaucratic structure. Consequently, the State dispensation instead of initiating a process of transformation of the social and economic life of the villages again benefited the rural propertied classes. Remedy was sought from the expert committee under the chairmanship of Balvantray Mehta. The committee in its report, in 1957 recommended a strong system of Panchayati Raj elected and accountable to the people as a driving force for the rural development initiatives. At the same time, the committee had, however, expressed its concern about the democratic potential of the panchayats in the given scenario of rural India.

The recommendations of the Balvantray Mehta committee generated some amount of enthusiasm. Notwithstanding the fact that rural structure of class as well as caste domination remained unchanged, many of the states had made a fresh attempt to institutionalize panchayats. Consequently, the rural landowning class hijacked Panchayati Raj that came into being in the 1960s. The pattern of domination continued as before, and Panchayati Raj had almost entirely failed to become an effective instrument of democracy and development at the grassroots. When Indira Gandhi regime initiated the progressive agenda including land reform programmes, panchayats were again bypassed and left in hibernation. The development programmes were once again launched through the centralized bureaucratic structure.

In the changed political milieu after the collapse of the Indira Gandhi regime in the late 1970s, the heterogeneous political formation that emerged as an alternative to the Congress constituted a couple of expert committees in its attempt to revive the democratic institutions after the internal Emergency. The committee headed by Ashok Mehta was one of them to reassert importance of Panchayati Raj two decades after the Balvantray Mehta committee. Considering the pattern of oligarchic domination in rural India, the Ashok Mehta committee was also apprehensive about efficacy of Panchayati Raj as an instrument of democratization. Nevertheless, to ensure meaningful participation of the people at the grassroots, the committee recommended open participation of the political parties in the elections to panchayats, a policy of positive discrimination in favour of women and socially oppressed sections besides many other crucial measures required for strengthening Panchayati Raj.

The Ashok Mehta Commtiiee, once again inspired many of the states to revive Panchayati Raj. Broadly, in conformity with the recommendations of the committee, most of the states had either amended the existing legislations or decreed fresh steps. Notable among them were West Bengal and Karnataka. However, except West Bengal, the rejuvenated Panchayati Raj in most of the states had failed to survive. The success of West Bengal under the CPI (M) led Left Front government has been a landmark in the history of Panchayati Raj in India. Panchayats in the state have been developed as political institution with a class perspective, capable of addressing development issues including agrarian reforms. The success in West Bengal has proved the potential of panchayats as instrument of democratic decentralization to bring about the desired pattern of change in the rural society.

The Janata fiasco once again brought back the Congress regime. The challenges before the Congress regime were intensified by the regional and ethnic discourses often accompanied by secessionism questioning the bourgeois-landlord state hegemony. Without giving much serious historical and economic thinking to the political and economic crisis of the State, the Congress regime headed by Rajiv Gandhi sought to revive Panchayati Raj bypassing the state governments. The move was defeated in the parliament. The modified version of the Sixty-fourth amendment was moved when the policy of economic liberalization led to a grave financial crisis for the Indian State and its political autonomy.

Subsequently, with certain modifications in the previous Bill, the Seventy-third constitutional amendment was passed to make substantive space for panchayats in the Constitution, what was denied by the Constituent Assembly fifty years back. The historic move to rejuvenate panchayats by making them a mandatory constitutional provision has been occupying considerable intellectual and political space since the early 1990s. The factors, which hindered growth and development of panchayats in the past and still influential in determining the future, have been highlighted by several studies.

In the light of the previous experiments with panchayats in the context of changing politico-economic milieu in the country, the renewed concern followed by the Seventy-third amendment can be seen as mechanism of decentralization adopted by the Indian State with the neo-liberal ethos. The Seventy-third amendment was brought alongside the policy of economic liberalization, which essentially demanded more space for the market economy, reducing role of the State. Though the amendment envisages a new variant of fiscal federalism for greater financial devolution, it essentially emphasizes a pattern of devolution of fund, functions and functionaries from the states to the PRIs ignoring the crucial aspect of reorganization of the center-state financial relations to meet the challenges.

The brief analysis on the experiments with panchayats in Assam since independence clearly reveals that the state has also followed the path, which is not much different from its many other counterparts. Though some of the legislations were quite radical in nature, panchayats in the state had failed to become instrument of democratic decentralization in absence of agrarian reforms. Consequently, the panchayats that emerged under domination of the rural landed gentry remained as mere implementing agency of the centrally sponsored rural development programmes. However, the unresolved agrarian question coupled with the tangle questions of national and ethnic identity had led to an unprecedented political chaos and instability in the state since the late 1970s. The indigenous communities enthusiastically responded to the middle class led political movements for an alternative to the continuous rule of the Congress on the one hand, and secessionism that contested hegemony of the Indian State drew political legitimacy on the other. The AGP with unparallel mass support came to the power in 1985. Nevertheless, the regional political formation neither seriously attempted to address the fundamental political and economic issues nor could provide a viable alternative to the Congress. The government headed by the regional political forces left the panchayats in hibernation for long.

Failure of the first AGP regime almost in every front brought back the Congress to power in 1991. A fresh attempt was made to revive Panchayati Raj. But, it remained as mere implementing agency of the centrally sponsored rural development programmes fully controlled by the bureaucracy. The AGP came back to power for the second time in 1996, and the newly formed government dissolved all rural bodies in April 1997.

Finally, following the constitutional mandate, when the Congress government prepared for the panchayat elections in 2001, the common people enthusiastically responded to the move. However, alongside the procedural formalities for the elections to be held after a lapse of four years, the Congress government launched the RPRS programme involving the state bureaucracy just four months before the polls. The calculated political move undoubtedly benefited the Congress for further expansion of its political influences, but it had, at the same time legitimized bureaucratic stranglehold on the process of decentralization. The Congress monopolized the PRIs elected in December, 2001, and yet the government headed by the Congress decided to continue with the RPRS. The practices jeopardized the constitutional ethos of accountability and transparency at the grassroots that was to be ensured through reinstitutionalization of the Gaon Sabha.

The experiences with PRIs that came into being in Assam in 2002 apparently with the ethos of the Seventy-third amendment have clearly revealed that many of the concepts, such as democratic decentralization, transparency, accountability and devolution, have very little practical relevance. In practice, the PRIs in the state have been surviving at the mercy of the DRDAs, without witnessing any qualitative breakthrough from the past. With a mechanical approach, the subjects enlisted in the Eleventh Schedule of the Constitution have been transferred to the PRIs to fulfill the condition of devolution. But, in absence of any clearly demarcated functional domain of the PRIs, every decision is heavily influenced by the political-bureaucratic nexus at the local level deliberately keeping the people away from the process of decision-making. The Assam Panchayati Raj Act, 1994 was amended to ensure enough space for the MLAs and MPs to exercise their influence over the PRIs from the village to the district level.

Nevertheless, the present generation of panchayats in Assam, like many other parts of the country, has undoubtedly ushered in a new political force constituted by the women representatives. A significantly large number of the rural women representatives, despite the structural limits, have come forward to address the issues of the day to day life of women with the help of whatever limited political space they have been provided with. Some of the initiatives are quite conspicuous, but such initiatives coexist with political oppression caused by the persisting patriarchal influences on the structure of most of the political parties.

To be precise, the experiences of Assam too clearly demonstrate that the reinstitutionalized PRIs in the state have, to a large extent, failed to usher in the practice of democratic decentralization in its true meaning. The factors that hindered the process in the past are still influential. Panchayati Raj, that epitomizes all the attributes of 'good governance' and pious policy hopes will remain as a romantic notion unless the socio-economic conditions are radically changed. Decentralization does not imply withdrawal of the State from its autonomous role in the social sphere, and the panchayats are essentially institutions of the State. The fundamental issue, therefore, is to develop the panchayats as an effective mechanism to ensure greater accountability of the State rather than making them instrumental in creating an environment conducive for the market economy.

ANNEXURE – 1

A PROFILE OF THE INNER CIRCLE OF THE CONSTITUENT ASSEMBLY

Name	*Position in the Constituent Assembly*	*Position in the Govt. before independence*	*Important position in the Congress*
Jawaharlal Nehru Nehru	Chairman States Committee, Union Subjects Committee and Union Constitution Committee	Prime Minister	President and member of the Working Committee
Rajendra Prasad	Assembly President 1946-50, Chairman Rules Committee and Steering Committee	Minister of Food and Agriculture	President and member of the Working Committee
Maulana Abul Kalam Azad	Member Steering Committee, Advisory Committee, States Committee and Union Constitution Committee	Minister of Education	President, and member Working
Vallabhbhai Patel	Chairman Provincial Constitution Committee, Advisory Committee and member Steering Committee and States Committee	Deputy Prime Minister and Minister of Home, Information and Broadcasting	President and member of the Working Committee
Govind Ballabh Pant	Member Advisory Committee, Union Subjects Committee and Union Constitution Committee	Prime Minister of U.P.	Member of the Working Committee

(Contd...)

Name	*Position in the Constituent Assembly*	*Position in the Govt. before independence*	*Important position in the Congress*
B. Pattabhi Sitaramayya	Chairman Committee on Chief Commissioners Provinces, member Rules Committee, States Committee, Union Subjects Committee and Provincial Constitution Committee	–	President and member of the Working Committee
Alladi Krishnaswami Ayyar	Member Rules Committee, Drafting Committee, Advisory Committee, C.A. Functions Committee, Union Power Committee, Union Constitution Committee and ad hoc Committee on the Supreme Court	–	–
N. Gopalaswami Ayyangar	Member Rules Committee, Drafting Committee, C.A. Functions Committee, Union Constitution Committee, Business Committee, Union Subjects Committee, States Committee, and Committee on Chief Commissioners Provinces.	Prime Minister of Kashmir, Minister without portfolio in the Government of India	–
K.M. Munshi	Member Rules Committee, Steering Committee, Advisory Committee, Union Subjects Committee, Union Constitution Committee, ad hoc Committee on the Supreme Court and Drafting Committee	Home Minister Govt. of Bombay	Member of the Working Committee
Satyanarayan Sinha	Chief Whip and member Steering Committee and Provisional Constitution Committee	Member Central Legislative assembly	Member AICC
Bhimrao Ambedkar	Chairman Drafting Committee, Member Advisory Committee, C.A.Committee on Functions and Union Constitution Committee	–	–

Source: G. Austin, *The Indian Constitution: Cornerstone of a Nation,* Oxford University Press, New Delhi,1966

ANNEXURE – 2

Results of the Panchayat Election, 2001
Elected members of Z.P., A.P. and G.P. District-wise Male and Female

Name of District	Z.P.		A.P.		G.P.		Total	
	Male	Female	Male	Female	Male	Female	Male	Female
Karimganj	13	7	65	31	720	336	798	374
Hailakandi	8	3	39	23	459	218	506	244
Cachar	18	9	102	60	1164	629	1284	698
Dhubri	10	9	95	55	1086	564	1191	628
Goalpara	11	5	51	30	574	291	636	326
Bongaigaon	5	1	39	16	356	248	400	265
Kamrup	18	11	102	57	1110	618	1230	686
Nalbari	8	4	41	21	448	210	497	235
Barpeta	17	8	81	40	817	492	915	540
Darrang	5	3	39	22	404	267	448	292
Sonitpur	22	10	98	60	967	745	1087	815

(Contd...)

Name of District	Z.P.		A.P.		G.P.		Total	
	Male	Female	Male	Female	Male	Female	Male	Female
Nagaon	27	14	145	93	1619	1005	1791	1112
Morigaon	8	5	50	35	551	372	609	412
Jorhat	14	9	69	41	692	519	775	569
Golaghat	11	6	62	39	664	443	737	488
Sivasagar	16	8	75	43	748	549	839	600
Lakhimpur	11	6	53	28	601	289	665	323
Dhemaji	5	2	40	25	379	319	424	346
Dibrugarh	14	9	56	36	544	467	614	512
Tinsukia	14	6	53	35	584	370	651	411
Kokrajhar	0	0	2	1	21	12	23	13
Grand Total	**255**	**135**	**1357**	**791**	**14508**	**8963**	**16120**	**9889**

District with highest Women Representation – Nagaon (1112)
District with lowest Women Representation – Nalbari (235)
Last Panchayat Election held on 27/12/2001 and 31/12/2001

Source: State Election Commission, Assam.

Elected Anchalik Panchayat Members and Seats Reserved for SC, ST and Women

Name of District	Elected members	Reserved for					General	Vacant Constituency	Deferred BAC area Constituency	Remarks
		SC	ST	Women						
				Gen.	SC	ST				
1	2	3	4	5	6	7	8	9	10	11
Karimganj	96	10	-	24	4	-	58	-	-	
Hailakandi	62	4	-	16	3	-	39	-	-	
Cachar	162	14	1	43	10	1	93	1	-	
Dhubri	150	-	-	52	5	6	87	-	22	
Goalpara	81	3	10	22	-	3	43	-	-	
Bongaigaon	55	2	-	16	3	-	34	-	39	
Kamrup	159	10	10	46	4	4	85	-	19	
Nalbari	62	3	-	19	1	-	39	-	48	
Barpeta	121	-	-	21	5	-	95	-	28	
Darrang	61	2	-	14	1	2	42	-	94	
Sonitpur	158	2	4	35	8	7	102	-	-	
Nagaon	238	9	4	58	17	8	142	1	-	

(Contd...)

1	2	3	4	5	6	7	8	9	10	11
Morigaon	85	8	8	20	5	3	41	-	-	
Jorhat	110	6	10	30	3	3	58	1	-	
Golaghat	101	1	5	25	4	6	60	1	-	
Sivasagar	118	1	2	31	3	2	79	-	-	
Lakhimpur	81	2	11	18	-	4	46	-	-	
Dhemaji	65	1	13	11	1	5	34	-	-	
Dibrugarh	92	2	4	29	1	3	53	1	-	
Tinsukia	88	-	4	28	1	1	54	-	-	
Kokrajhar	3	-	-	1	-	-	2	-	85	
Grand Total	**2148**	**80**	**86**	**559**	**79**	**58**	**1286**	**5**	**335**	

Source: State Election Commission, Assam.

Elected Gaon Panchayats Members and Seats Reserved for SC, ST and Women

Name of District	Elected members	Reserved for					General	Vacant Constituency	Deferred BAC area Constituency	Remarks
		SC	ST	Women						
				Gen.	SC	ST				
1	2	3	4	5	6	7	8	9	10	11
Karimganj	960	86	-	252	34	-	588	-	-	
Hailakandi	615	48	-	172	20	-	375	5	-	
Cachar	1630	133	15	440	71	7	964	-	-	
Dhubri	1500	7	4	560	37	-	892	-	220	
Goalpara	784	26	77	92	-	32	557	26	-	
Bongaigaon	549	22	-	173	39	8	307	1	390	
Kamrup	1569	59	90	409	30	40	940	21	190	
Nalbari	596	16	18	179	4	5	374	24	480	
Barpeta	1188	16	1	335	29	8	799	22	280	
Darrang	610	4	-	218	19	2	367	-	940	
Sonitpur	1554	21	29	407	41	38	1018	26	-	
Nagaon	2384	106	32	741	106	47	1352	16	-	

(Contd...)

1	2	3	4	5	6	7	8	9	10	11
Morigaon	838	53	59	217	58	54	397	12	-	
Jorhat	1100	21	6	364	16	7	686	10	-	
Golaghat	1006	9	47	302	30	36	582	14	-	
Sivasagar	1179	8	11	425	16	18	701	1	-	
Lakhimpur	809	23	113	169	12	51	441	1	-	
Dhemaji	633	10	120	105	1	73	324	12	-	
Dibrugarh	918	2	33	305	15	52	511	17	-	
Tinsukia	866	-	10	286	11	25	534	14	-	
Kokrajhar	30	1	-	9	-	-	20	-	850	
Grand Total	**21318**	**671**	**665**	**6160**	**590**	**503**	**12729**	**222**	**3350**	

Source: State Election Commission, Assam.

Elected Zilla Parishad Members and Seats Reserved for SC, ST and Women

Name of District	Elected members	Reserved for					General	Vacant Constituency	Deferred BAC area Constituency	Remarks
		SC	ST	Women						
				Gen.	SC	ST				
1	2	3	4	5	6	7	8	9	10	11
Karimganj	20	2	-	6	1	-	11	-	-	
Hailakandi	11	1	-	3	-	-	7	-	-	
Cachar	27	3	-	7	2	-	15	-	-	
Dhubri	19	-	-	7	1	-	11	-	9	
Goalpara	16	1	2	4	-	1	8	-	-	
Bongaigaon	6	-	-	1	-	-	5	-	10	
Kamrup	29	2	2	9	1	1	14	1	5	
Nalbari	12	1	-	4	-	-	7	-	11	
Barpeta	25	-	-	7	1	-	17	-	8	
Darrang	8	-	-	3	-	-	5	-	20	
Sonitpur	32	1	2	9	2	-	18	-	-	
Nagaon	41	2	1	8	2	1	27	-	-	

(Contd...)

1	2	3	4	5	6	7	8	9	10	11
Morigaon	13	1	1	3	1	1	6	-	-	
Jorhat	23	1	-	-	-	-	22	-	-	
Golaghat	17	-	1	4	1	1	10	-	-	
Sivasagar	24	-	-	6	1	-	17	-	-	
Lakhimpur	17	2	2	4	-	1	8	-	-	
Dhemaji	7	-	2	1	-	1	3	-	-	
Dibrugarh	23	-	1	6	1	1	14	-	-	
Tinsukia	20	2	4	2	3	-	9	-	-	
Kokrajhar	-	-	-	-	-	-	-	-	16	
Grand Total	**390**	**19**	**18**	**93**	**17**	**8**	**235**	**1**	**79**	

Source: State Election Commission, Assam.

ANNEXURE – 3

FINANCIAL ACHIEVEMENT UNDER RURAL DEVELOPMENT PROGRAMMES IN ASSAM

Fund Received from Govt. of India and State Matching Share (Rs. in lakh)

Programme	2001-02	2002-03	2003–04	2004–05
Central Share				
1. SGRY-II (Cash)	13495.28	11026.94	14880.28	-
2. Value of Rice*	957.72	10074.54	10356.84	-
3. SGRY-I (Cash)	13490.96	11470.02	14800.73	32124.06
Value of Rice*	955.08	10536.60	11932.20	27099.04
4. Spl. SGRY	-	-	3000.00	8000.00
5. IAY	8621.13	9987.32	14702.75	22080.95
6. PMGY	2011.00	2500.00	3889.00	5789.00
7. SGSY	3328.48	2802.61	5313.00	6595.62
8. PMGSY	15492.00	-	19972.00	-
9. NSAP	-	-	3837.30	7307.00
10. Annapurna	-	-	253.36	134.45
11. IWDP	1619.93	1440.19	1729.91	2588.12
12. DRDA Admn.	1030.79	849.22	1012.26	1206.89
13. NFFWP	-	-	-	16645.79
Value of Rice*	-	-	-	8718.72
14. PURA	-	-	-	150.00
Sub-Total (A)	**61002.37**	**60687.44**	**105679.63**	**138439.64**

(Contd...)

Programme	2001 - 02	2002 - 03	2003 – 04	2004 – 05
State Matching Share				
1. SGRY-II (Cash)	2250.00	2884.13	3034.94	6931.64
2. SGRY-I (Cash)	1798.80	4833.25	1688.27	-
3. IAY	2081.52	1433.18	2688.12	4900.92
4. SGSY	492.20	1292.83	769.07	2305.50
5. IWDP	-	145.67	156.66	143.52
6. DRDA Admn.	128.88	340.64	157.16	337.42
Sub-Total (B)	**6751.40**	**10929.70**	**8494.22**	**14619.00**
Total (A) + (B)	**67753.77**	**71617.14**	**114173.85**	**153058.64**

*The value of food grains component of wage has been calculated at the issue rate i.e. Rs.6/- per kg. up to 2003-04 and Rs.8/- per kg. from 2004-05.

Source: Directorate of Panchayat and Rural Development, Government of Assam.

ANNEXURE – 4

FUND RECEIVED BY ASSAM UNDER SGRY

(Rs. in lakh)

Fund under SGRY	2001-02	2002-03	2003-04	2004-05
Total fund received under SGRY (including the value of food grains)	32,947.84	50,825.48	56,693.26	74,154.74
SGRY component as percentage of total fund received under the rural development programmes	48.63	70.97	49.65	48.45
Value of food grains as percentage of the total fund allocation under SGRY	5.80	40.55	39.36	36.54

ANNEXURE – 5

FUND AVAILABLE FOR ALLOCATION TO THE PRIs UNDER SGRY

(Rs. in lakh)

Amount available		2001-02	2002-03	2003-04	2004-05
Cash Component	ZPs	6207.00	6042.86	6880.84	9411.14
	APs	9310.51	9064.30	10321.27	14116.71
	GPs	15517.52	15107.17	17202.11	23527.85
Average amount of cash available for allocation	ZPs	310.35	302.14	344.04	470.56
	APs	50.88	49.53	56.40	77.14
	GPs	7.20	7.01	7.99	10.93
Value of food grains	ZPs	382.56	4122.23	4457.80	5419.80
	APs	573.84	6183.34	6686.71	8129.71
	GPs	956.40	10305.57	11144.52	13549.52
Average Value of food grains available for allocation	ZPs	19.12	206.11	222.89	270.99
	APs	3.13	33.79	36.54	44.42
	GPs	0.45	4.79	5.18	6.29

BIBLIOGRAPHY

Acharya, P. (1993), 'Panchayat and Left Politics in West Bengal', *Economic and Political Weekly,* 29 May.

Aiyar, M.S. (2002), 'Panchayati Raj: The Way Forward' *Economic and Political Weekly,* 3 August.

Aram, M. and Ravichandram, (1995), 'Panchayati Raj: a giant step towards participatory democracy', *Kurukshetra,* April.

Austin, G. (1966), *The Indian Constitution: Cornerstone of a Nation,* Oxford University Press, New Delhi.

Austine, G. (1999), *Working a Democratic Constitution: The Indian Experience,* Oxford University Press, New Delhi.

Bandyopadhyay, D. (1993), 'Fourth General Elections of Panchayats in West Bengal', *Mainstream,* June 26.

Bandyopadhyay, D. and Mukherjee, A. (eds.) (2004), *New Issues in Panchayati Raj,* Concept Publishing Company, New Delhi.

Bandyopadhyaya, N. (1988), 'The Story of land Reforms in Indian Planning', in A.K.

Bagchi (ed.) *Economy, Society and Polity,* Oxford University Press, Calcutta.

Bergmann, T. (1984), *Agrarian Reforms in India: With Special Reference to Kerala, Karnataka, Andhra Pradesh and West Bengal,* Agricole, New Delhi.

Bhargava, B.S. and Venkatakrishnan, V (1995),

'Constitutionalization of Panchayati Raj: the case of Tamil Nadu', *Kurukshetra*, April.

Bhattacharya, M. (1978), 'Administrative and Organisational Issues in Rural Development' *Indian Journal of Public Administration*, Vol.XXIV, No. 4.

Bose, S. (1993), *Peasant Labour and Colonial Capital: Rural Bengal Since 1770, The New Cambridge History of India,* III:2, Cambridge University Press.

Buch, N. (1999), *From Oppression to Assertion: A Study of Panchayats and Women in Madhya Pradesh, Rajasthan and Uttar Pradesh,* Centre for Women's Development Studies, New Delhi.

Chatterjee, P. (1999), 'The Moment of Manoeuvre: Gandhi and the Critique of Civil Society' in *Partha Chatterjee Omnibus*, Oxford University Press.

Chatterjee, S.K. (1955), *The Place of Assam in the History and Civilization of India*, Gauhati University, Guwahati.

Chaube, S.K. (1985), *Electoral Politics in India*, Universal Press (India) Pvt. Ltd.,Madras.

Choudhury, R.C. and Jain, S.P. (eds.) (1999), *Strengthening Village Democracy*, NIRD, Hyderabad.

Das Gupta & Guha, (1985), '1983 Assembly Poll in Assam: An Analysis of its background and implications, *Economic and Political Weekly*, 11 May.

Das, J.N. (1968), *Assam Land Revenue Mannual*, 8th Edition, Government of Assam, Shillong.

Datta, P. (1998), *Major Issues in the Development Debate: Lessons In Empowerment From India*, Kanishka Publishers, Distributors, New Delhi.

Deka, K.M. (1979), 'Shaking of Congress Monopoly in 1977 Lok Sabha Election: The Case of Assam', *Political Science Review.*

Dreze, J. (1990), 'Poverty in India and the IRDP Delusion' *Economic and Political Weekly*, September 29.

Dutta, D. (1986), 'Land, Land Relation and Reforms in N.E. Region of India (Assam)' in Atul Goswami (ed.) *Land Reforms and Peasant Movement,* Omsons Publications, New Delhi, Guwahati.

Frankel, Francine R. (2005), *India's Political Economy 1947-2004,* Oxford University Press, New Delhi.

Gangrade, K.D. (1995), 'Power to the Powerless – dawn of Participatory democracy, *Kurukshetra,* April.

Ghosh, B. and Kumar, G. (2003), *State Politics and Panchayats in India,* Manohar, New Dehi.

Ghosh, R. (1981), 'Agrarian Programme of Left Front Government', *Economic and Political WeeklyPW,* June.

Gohain, H. (1978), *Sahitya Aru Chetana,* Guwahati Book Stall, Guwahati.

Goswami, A. (ed.) *Land Reforms and Peasant Movement,* Omsons Publications, New Delhi, Guwahati.

Goswami, M.N. (1950), *A Survey of Rural Economic Conditions in Darrang,* Govt. of Assam, Shillong.

Goswami, S.(1997), *Language Politics in Assam,* Ajanta Publications.

Govt. of Assam, (1993), *Annual Report,* 1992-93, Revenue, Registration and Relief Department.

Govt. of India, (1989), *Collected Works of Mahatma Gandhi,* (Vols. 10; 13;20;23;35; 39; 42; 45; 48; 58; 59; 63; 67; 68; 71; 75; 76; 80; 84; 85; 87; and 90), Publication Division, New Delhi,

Guha, A. (1977), *Planter-Raj to Swaraj, Freedom Struggle and Electoral Politics in Assam: 1826 – 1947,* Peoples Publishing House, New Delhi.

————— (1991), *Medieval and Early Colonial Assam: Society, Polity, Economy,* K.P.bagchi & Company, Calcutta.

Harriss, J. (1993), 'What is Happening in Rural West Bengal? Agrarian Reform, Growth and Distribution' *Economic and Political weekly* June 12.

Hazarika, S. (1994), *Strangers of the Mist: Tales War and Peace from India's North East,* Penguine Books India (P) Ltd.

Hemalatha Prasad, C. (2005), *Empowerment of Women In PRIs: A Study of Six Select States,* NIRD, Hyderabad.

Hunter, W.W. (1982), *A Statistical Account of Assam*, Vol.I, Trubner & Co. London, 1879, (reprint) D.R. Publishing Crop. Delhi.

Jaamdar, S. (1995), 'Gram sabha in the new Panchayat system: concept and issues' *Kurukshetra,* December.

Jain, L.C. (1995), 'Panchayat from Gandhi to Present Day' paper presented at the national seminar on '*Rejuvinating Grass Roots Democracy and Federation'*. Satya Murti Centre for Democratic Studies, Madras, October 7.

Jain, L.C. (eds.) (1985), *Grass without roots,* Sage Publications, New Delhi.

Jain, S.P. (1997), The Gram Sabha : 'Gateway to Grassroots Democracy', *Journal of Rural Development,* Vol. 16 (4).

Jana and Sarmah (eds.) *Class, Ideology and Political Parties in India,* South Asian Publishers Pvt Ltd. New Delhi.

Joshi, P.C. (1969), 'Land reforms in India', in A.R. Desai (ed.) *Rural Sociology in India,* (fourth revised edition) Popular Prakashan, Bombay.

Kohli, A.(1987), *The State And Poverty In India, The Politics of Reform*, Orient Longman, Bombay.

Kothari, R. (1964), 'The Congress "System" in India, *Asian Survey,* December.

———— (1998), 'The Democratic Experiment', in Partha Chatterjee (edited) *Wages of Freedom: Fifty Years of the Indian nation-State,* Oxford University Press.

———— (1988), *State Against Democracy: In Search of Humane Governance,* Ajanta Publications, Delhi.

Kripalani, J.B.(1970), *Gandhi: His Life and Thought*, Publication Division, Government of India, New Delhi.

Lieten, G.K. (1992), *Community and Change in Rural West Bengal*, Sage Publications, New Delhi.

——————— (1996), *Development, Devolution and Democracy: Village Discourse in West Bengal*, Sage Publications, New Delhi.

——————— (2003), *Power, Politics and Rural Development: Essays on India*, Manohar, New Delhi.

Lok Sabha Secretariat, India, (1999), *Constituent Assembly Debates*, Vol. I to V, New Delhi.

Maddick, H. (1970), *Panchayati Raj, A Study of Rural Local Government in India*, Longman, London.

Mallick, R. (1993), *Development Policy of a Communist Government: West Bengal Since 1977*, Cambridge University Press, Cambridge.

Mathew, G. (2000), *Status of Panchayati Raj in the States and Union Terrirories of India*, Concept Publishing Company, New Delhi.

Mazumdar, V. (1997), 'Historical soundings' *Seminar*, September.

Mehta, U. (1969), 'The Impact of Panchayati Raj on Rural India' in A.R. Desai, (ed.) *Rural Sociology in India*, (fourth revised edition) Popular Prakashan, Bombay.

Moffatt Mills, A.J. (1984), *Report on the Province of Assam*, (Second Edition) Publication Board, Assam.

Mukherjee, N. (1986), 'The Alternative District Government?', in M.L. Dantwala et al. (eds), *Rural Development. The Indian Experience*, Oxford, New Delhi.

Narayanasamy, S. (1998),'The Role of Gram Sabha in the New Panchayati Raj System', *Kurukshetra*, April.

Nehru, J. (1936), 'Presidential Address' at the Faizpur Congress, December 27-28.

———— (2004), *An Auto Biography*, Penguin Books, New Delhi.

———— (2004), *Discovery of India*, Penguin Books, New Delhi.

Palnithurai, G. and Ragupathy, V. (2003), *Building Alliances and Capabilities among the Elected Women Representatives of Grassroots Institutions*, Gandhigram Rural Institute, Gandhigram.

Panda, S. (1996), 'Emerging Pattern of Leadership among Rural Women in Orissa' in *Indian Journal of Public Administration*, October-December.

Pyarelal, (1958), *Mahatma Gandhi: The Last Phase*, Vol. II, Navajivan Publishing House, Ahmedabad.

Raghavalu, C.V and Narayana, E.A. (1991), 'Reforms in Panchayati Raj: A Comparative Analysis of Andhra Pradesh, Karnataka and West Bengal', *Indian Journal of Public Administration*, 37(1).

Rai. M. (eds.) (2001), *The State of Panchayats: A Participatory perspective*, Samskriti, New Delhi.

Rajaraman, I., Bohra, O.P. and Renganathan,V.S. (1996), 'Augmentation of Panchayat Resources' *Economic and Political Weekly*, May 4.

Rao, V.M. (1998), 'Economic Reform and the Poor – Emerging Scenario', *Economic and Political Weekly*, July 18.

Rogaly, B. (et al.) (1999), *Sonar Bangla? Agricultural Growth and Agrarian Change in West Bengal and Bangladesh*, Sage Publications, New Delhi.

S.I.R.D. Assam, (2004), *Brief Profile on Panchayati Raj in Assam*. SIRD, Guwahati.

Sarmah, B. (2001), Self-Governance and Autonomy: Experience of the Bodoland Autonomous Council, *The Radical Humanist*, Vol. 64, No.11.

———— (2002), 'Asom Gana Parishad: Emergence and its

Performance', in Jana, Sarmah (eds.) *Class, Ideology and Political Parties in India*, South Asian Publishers Pvt Ltd. New Delhi.

Sengupta, S. (1981), 'West Bengal Land Reforms and the Agrarian Scene', *Economic and Political WeeklyPW,* June.

Sengupta, S. and Gazdar, H. (1996), 'Agrarian Politics and Rural Development in West Bengal' in Jean Dreze & Amartya Sen (eds.) *Indian Development: Selected Regional Perspectives,* Oxford University Press, Delhi.

Sethi, J.D. (ed.) (1986), *Trusteeship: The Gandhian Alternative*, Gandhian Peace Foundation, New Delhi.

Sharma, K. (2004), 'From Representation to Presence' in D. Bandyopadhyay and Amitava Mukherjee (eds.) *New Issues in Panchayati Raj*, Concept Publishing Company, New Delhi.

Sharma, M. (1990), *Social and Economic Change in Assam: Middle Class Hegemony,* Ajanta Publications, Delhi.

Sharma, S.C. (1954), *A Survey of Rural Economic Conditions in Lakhimpur,* Govt. of Assam, Shillong.

——————— (1952), *A Survey of Rural Economic Conditions in Sibsagar,* Govt. of Assam, Shillong.

Srivastava, T.N. (2002), 'Local 'Self' government and the Constitution' *Economic and Political Weekly,* July 27.

Swaminathan, M. (1990), 'Village Level Implementation of IRDP – Comparison of West Bengal and Tamil Nadu', *Economic and Political Weekly*, March 31.

Teckchandani, Bharati, Jyoti Kiran and Priti Sharma (eds.) (1998), *They Call Me Member Saab: Women in Haryana Panchayati Raj*, MARG, New Delhi.

The World Bank, (2002), *Building Institutions for Markets*, Oxford University Press.

Thimmaiah, G. (1998), '*Local Government Finances: Some Issues' in Local Government Finances in India*, Konrad Adenauer Foundation, Manohar.

Thorner, A. (1981), 'Nehru, Albert Mayer, and origins of Community Projects', *Economic and Political weekly,* January 24.

Thorner, D.(1969), 'Land Reform' in A.R. Desai, (ed.) *Rural Sociology in India,* (fourth revised edition) Popular Prakashan, Bombay.

Varshney, A.(1995), *Democracy, Development, and the Countryside: Urban Rural Struggles in India,* Cambridge University Press, New York.

Vyasalu, V. (2003), *Panchayats, Democracy and Development,* Rawat Publications, Jaipur and New Delhi.

————— (2004), 'Transformation in Governance since 1990s: Some Reflections, *Economic and Political Weekly,* June 5.

Index